CHICANA
CRITICAL
ISSUES

CHICANA CRITICAL ISSUES

Edited by

Norma Alarcón
Rafaela Castro
Emma Pérez
Beatriz Pesquera
Adaljiza Sosa Riddell
Patricia Zavella

Series in Chicana/Latina Studies

Third Woman Press
Berkeley

Cover Art: *Puntos Cardenales*, by Juana Alicia.

"The Sardonic Powers of the Erotic in the Work of Ana Castillo" by
Norma Alarcón. Copyright © 1989 by Norma Alarcón. Reprinted from
Breaking Boundaries: Latina Writing and Critical Readings, published by The
University of Massachusetts Press, by permission of the author.
"Presidarias y Pobladoras: The Journey North and Life in Frontier
California" by Antonia I. Castañeda. Copyright © 1992 by Antonia I.
Castañeda. Reprinted from *Renato Rosaldo Lecture Series*, Latin American
Studies, University of Arizona, by permission of the author.
"Sexuality and Discourse: Notes From a Chicana Survivor" by Emma
Pérez. Copyright © 1991 by Emma Pérez. Reprinted from *Chicana
Lesbians: The Girls Our Mothers Warned Us About*, published by Third
Woman Press, by permission of the author.
"Chicana Lesbians: Fear and Loathing in the Chicano Community"
by Carla Trujillo. Copyright © 1991 by Carla Trujillo. Reprinted from
Chicana Lesbians: The Girls Our Mothers Warned Us About, published by Third
Woman Press, by permission of the author.
"The Politics of Race and Gender: Organizing Chicana Cannery
Workers in Northern California" by Patricia Zavella. Copyright © 1988
by Patricia Zavella. Reprinted from *Women and the Politics of Empowerment*,
published by Temple University Press, by permission of the author.

First printing 1993
93 94 95 96 97 10 9 8 7 6 5 4 3 2 1

Library of Congress Cataloging-in-Publication Data

Chicana critical issues / edited by Norma Alarcón. . .[et al.].
     p.   cm. — (Series in Chicana/Latina studies)
    Includes bibliographical references.
    ISBN 0-943219-09-4 (pbk.) : $14.95
    1. American literature—Mexican American authors—History and
criticism.   2. American literature—Women authors—History and
criticism.   3. Mexican American women—Intellectual life.
4. Mexican American women in literature.   5. Mexican Americans in
literature. I. Alarcón, Norma. II. Series.
PS153.M4C45 1993   93-3097
810.9'86872—dc20   CIP

This book would not have been possible without the financial support and assistance of the Chicana/Latina Research Project at the University of California, Davis, Mujeres Activas en Letras y Cambio Social (MALCS), and the Chicano Studies Department at the University of California, Berkeley.

Special thanks to former MALCS Editorial Board members:

Margarita Melville
Tey Diana Rebolledo
Christine Sierra
Deena Gonzalez

Also thanks to:

Francisca Gonzalez
Anita Rocha
Suzanne Jacquez

Declaración de MALCS

Somos hijas de familias Chicanas de clase trabajadora que logramos recibir una educación universitaria. Crecimos en campamentos agrícolas y barrios proletarios en donde sólo se logra sobrevivir compartiendo los escasos recursos. De ello se derivan nuestra fuerza y valores. Compartimos la historia de la clase trabajadora —sus luchas, resistencias, y responsabilidades—así como los problemas que ha confrontado. Nos proponemos documentar, analizar, e interpretar la experiencia Chicana/Mexicana en los Estados Unidos. Nos interesan particularmente las condiciones bajo las cuales la mujer trabaja, dentro y fuera del hogar. Continuamos la lucha de nuestras madres por la justicia económica y social.

La escasa presencia de la Chicana en las universidades exige que nos unamos para definir problemas comunes, apoyarnos mutuamente, y buscar soluciones colectivas. Nuestro propósito es luchar contra la opresión que sufrimos en las universidades por nuestra clase, raza, y género. Rechazamos ademas cualquiera separación entre la actividad académica y la participación en la vida comunitaria. Nuestro trabajo académico se propone suprimir la separación entre la actividad intelectual y el compromiso activo en la comunidad. Nos inspiramos en nuestra tradición de la lucha política. Participamos en el desarrollo de estrategias para el cambio social—un cambio que proceda de nuestras comunidades. Reiteramos nuestra decisión de luchar por el cambio político, económico, y social a través del trabajo y la acción colectiva. Instamos a las Chicanas que comparten estos problemas y metas a sumarse a nuestro movimiento. Serán bien recibidas.

Universidad de California, Davis
Junio de 1983

MALCS Declaration

We are the daughters of Chicano working class families involved in higher education. We were raised in labor camps and barrios, where sharing our resources was the basis of survival. Our values, our strength, derive from where we came. Our history is the story of working people—their struggles, commitments, strengths, and the problems they face. We document, analyze, and interpret the Chicana/Mexicana experience in the United States. We are particularly concerned with the conditions women face at work, in and out of the home. We continue our mothers' struggle for social and economic justice.

The scarcity of Chicanas in institutions of higher education requires that we join together to identify our common problems, to support each other and to define collective solutions. Our purpose is to fight the race, class, and gender oppression we have experienced in the universities. Further we reject the separation of academic scholarship and community involvement. Our research strives to bridge the gap between intellectual work and active commitment to our communities. We draw upon a tradition of political struggle. We see ourselves developing strategies for social change—a change emanating from our communities. We declare our commitment to seek social, economic, and political change through our work and collective action. We welcome Chicanas who share these goals and invite them to join us.

University of California, Davis
June 1983

Contents

Introduction

It is with extreme pleasure that as past Chair of Mujeres Activas en Letras y Cambio Social (MALCS) and a member of the editorial committee, I introduce our readers to this premier edition of Chicana scholarship presented as the fruits of a labor of commitment. It follows the philosophy of MALCS that enjoins Chicanas in academia to strengthen their roots in the working class community of people of Mexican origin. We are scholars because of our own efforts, but the struggle of many sisters and brothers has facilitated our incorporation as academics. Our research capabilities should continue to serve our *comunidades*.

Let me offer you an image of who we are: as a solid and nurturing tree, our community of workers and scholars sinks its roots of pride deep into the heritage of our forebears. Our branches reach out in all directions to yield shelter, nurture and solace. Sometimes pruning has been painful, but even that has produced new growth.

This volume is a promise. It is the first fruits. We expect and hope for new harvests. But only if our readers feel the inspiration to offer the fruits of their own efforts. It has been possible with the unstinting support and cooperation of many more individuals than those whose names appear here in print. To all the *raza* of many hues who made this possible, congratulations!

Margarita B. Melville
Chicana Studies
University of California, Berkeley

Representations of
Identity and Difference

Survivor
Juana Alicia

Espejismo: Mujer Poesía

Elba Sánchez

ésta no viene engalanada
vestida de encajes
ni tampoco viene
con pelos en la lengua
no
ésta no llega
adornada de florecitas
a rosa olorosa
no señor

ésta viene
vientre puño
piedra hueso
velo espuma
raices tallos
manos brazos
espinas le curten
la lengua

a veces ofrece
hilos de miel
flor de naranjo
a veces
arroja veneno

ésta
ésta viene
a dar testimonio
expresar su dolor
abriendo la puerta
a su realidad

gritando verdades
abrazando fuertemente
su pasión

I kiss you then
our kiss
gurgles laughter
you shake your head
pull back
I smile and
tell you:
>I see the ancient one in you
>la anciana
>the one whose breath
>bore ours
>who passes down
>water and awakening
>agua y despertar
>kernels in flower
>maiz a flor
>I see her in you
>I feel your hands
>hers ours
>I see her in you
>ancient one

The Sardonic Powers of the Erotic in the Work of Ana Castillo

Norma Alarcón

Ana Castillo, a native of Chicago, first made an impact on the Chicano writer's community with the publication of her chapbook, *Otro Canto* (1977). Written mostly in English (as is almost all of Castillo's work), it ensured her reputation as a "social protest" poet at a time when it was difficult to be anything else. As a result, some of the ironic tones already present in the early work have been easily over-looked in favor of the protest message, which in fact is re-doubled by irony. It can be argued that irony is one of Castillo's trademarks. Irony often appears when experience is viewed after-the-fact or in opposition to another's subjectivity. In this essay, I would like to explore the ironically erotic dance that Castillo's speaking subjects often take up with men. Thus, my exploration will follow the trajectory of the traditional heterosexual, female speaking subject in Castillo's published works: *Otro Canto*, *The Invitation* (1979), *Women Are Not Roses* (1984), and *The Mixquiahuala Letters* (1986).

Otro Canto portrayed the burdens of the urban poor through the voice of a young woman who had learned the bitter lessons of disillusionment early in life. Thus, in the poem "1975," we hear a sign of relief when all of those "proletarian talks"—the nemesis of many a left-wing activist—are finally translated into action. The speaker underscores the repetitiveness of mere talk by starting off every stanza with the line, "talking proletarian talks," which subsequently opens the way for details that give rise to such talk. We are not relieved from this tactical monotony "until one long awaited day—/we are tired/of talking" (1977, 49-51). Though in "1975" the speaker is not gender-marked but is revealed as being in a "we-us" speaking position within a Marxist revolutionary stance, that speaker is transformed into a "we-us" who makes "A Counter-Revolutionary Proposition." In this poem we are called upon to make love and "forget/that Everything matters" (1984, 63). Given the litany of the things that matter in the stanza preceding the call, however, the poem urges me to ask if the speaker is wryly alluding to the well-known Anglo counterculture slogan of the sixties: "Make Love, Not War." As the poem notes, what matters to the proletarian (i.e., Marxist) revolutionary speaker is the struggle to overcome class oppression, a struggle that is spoken through a supposedly non-gendered we. However, juxtaposing the poem's title, "A Counter-Revolutionary Proposition," with the implicit allusion to the slogan "Make Love, Not War," may help us to unravel a story with a difference for the underclass female speaker who addresses her partner, "Let's forget. . ." (1984, 63).

Notwithstanding the recent involvement of women in revolutionary struggles (i.e., Cuba and Nicaragua), it is still the case that in opposition to the erotic, a revolution or a war is especially marked with a traditional male subjectivity that awaits analysis. In order for a female speaker to recover the full meaningful impact of herself, she still must address how that self figures in the "heterosexual erotic contract," revolutions not excepted. Within this contract, the female body continues to be the site of both reproduction and the erotic; despite class position, a speaker and her gendered social experience are imbricated in that age-old contract. Thus, "A Counter-Revolutionary Proposition" may now be understood as a call to explore the politics of the erotic. Let us actively explore the neo-revolutionary implications of erotic relations that have been constantly displaced, undervalued, and even erased by masculine-marked militancy, or at best rendered passively by the male poet, with the woman as the muse, the wife, the mother.

From this point of view, the poem's title acquires a polyvalence that goes beyond the private, where the erotic has often been held "hostage," and is placed in the political arena. In a sense, then, "Let's 'make love'" is taken from the lips of an Anglo, male, left-wing activist by the most unexpected speakers—Ana Castillo's poetic persona. In retrospect, Castillo's early work stands out as one of her first attempts to appropriate the erotic and its significances for the female speaker, with ironic repercussions. Given the assumed class position of the speaker herself, affirming the erotic, as she takes pause from the class struggle, is tantamount to speaking against herself, or so her "brother/lover" may attest. The implicit suggestion that the erotic and the class struggle may be incompatible in a patriarchal world, when both are made public, places the underclass female in a double bind, since she may be forced to choose between areas of life that, for her, are intertwined or indivisible. In my view, the speakers in Castillo's work refuse to make such choices. Choosing one or the other splits the subject into the domains that heretofore have been symbolically marked feminine or masculine.

In the seventies, Chicanas and other women of color had a difficult time within their fraternal group when they insisted that feminist politics, with its commitment to the exploration of women's sexuality and gendered identities, also applied to them. The supposed contradictory position of women of color, one that was between a male-identified class liberation struggle and a middle-or upper-class, white, female-identified sexual liberation struggle, forced women of color to walk a tightrope in their quest for an exploration of gender (Moraga 1983; Pineda 1986). Thus, a poem such as "A Counter-Revolutionary Proposition" was politically risky, as the speaker addresses another, ostensibly male, and asks that he forget that "Everything matters." Yet, it is only within this apparent self-contradictory situation that such a speaker may be able to claim sexuality for herself and explore the significance of the female body that is always, and already, sexually marked. Such a "proposition" simultaneously opens up a gap between the fact of economic oppression and the desire for erotic pleasure and significance that faces us when we perceive the separation between the first and the second stanzas in the poem.

In *The Invitation* (1979), a chapbook-length collection of erotic poems and vignettes, Castillo's speaker no longer requests that her interlocutor forget that "everything matters" but pursues, instead, a sustained exploration of her erotic, at times bisexual desires. The appropriation of the erotic for the female speaker is again a motivating force. The emphasis, however, is not so much on the speaker's uneasy conjunction with "proletarian politics" as it is with "textual politics." That is, the appropriative process resonates respectively against, and with, two important books of our time: Octavio Paz's *The Labyrinth of Solitude* (1950), and María Teresa Horta, María Isabel Barreno, and María Velho da Costa's *The Three Marías: New Portuguese Letters* (1975). Consider, for example, that in the second chapter of this book, Paz affirms women's dormant and submissive sexuality that awaits discovery through male efforts, while "The Three Marías" reject this view throughout their book and protest women's political bondage that, at the core, is based on their sexuality. Notwithstanding the different approaches that each of "The Three Marías" would take to liberate women, there is very little doubt that they agree that male perception of women's sexuality pervades all levels of women's existence.

The erotic thematics of *The Invitation* openly declare the influence of those two books (1979, iii, 9). Castillo's text, when viewed in their light, becomes a purposefully glossed negation of Paz's view and an extension of the authors own erotic vision. It is as if the relative absence of any sociopolitical debate of the Chicana/ Mexicana's sexuality had made it imperative that Castillo explore instead her speaker's desire in the light of a textual milieu. Moreover, reading Castillo's work in this fashion enables us to clarify her struggle to place her erotic thematics and voices in the interstice of both her sociopolitical and textual experiences. In other words, if, due to her social position, the underclass female is called upon to address her oppression with a ready-made, class-struggle rhetoric, attempting to address her sexual/erotic oppression forces her to see it in relation to texts. Her own response to those texts enables her to give voice to her experience and make it public. If she does not make an effort to bring out that voice herself, it will remain muted, as she is forced to align herself with the heretofore masculine-marked class voice. Thus, she is reconfirming, from another angle, Gilbert and Gubar's call in *The Mad-woman in the Attic* for our critical need to explore "the metaphor of experience" (in "1975" and "A Counter-Revolutionary Proposition") and "the experience of metaphor" (in *The Invitation*) (Gilbert and Gubar 1979; Wigel 1986, 59-80). The speaker/writer and the critic must discern, insofar as it is possible, between the metaphors female speakers create to represent our sociopolitical and erotic experience and the metaphors these speakers inherit and that *a priori* inscribe our potential experience. Thus, a writer/speaker can unwittingly live out the experiences that the metaphors call upon her to duplicate (i.e., Paz's description of female sexuality) or she can struggle to lay them bare and thus reinscribe her evolving position (i.e. "The Three Marías" struggle to reinscribe women's sexuality).

Paz's work, as well as "The Three Marías" and *The Invitation* it-self, are, in a sense, all glossed over in Castillo's epistolary narra-tive, *The Mixquiahuala Letters* (1986), which more closely approxi-mates the sociopolitical images of *Otro Canto*. In a sense, *Letters* is more aggressive in its conjugation of "the experience of meta-phor" and "the metaphor of experience" as it pertains to the erotic, for it is yet another link in Castillo's exploration of sexual-ity and its significance for women. If in *Letters*, however, the nega-tion of Paz's view of women's sexuality continued, even as it is ironically reconfirmed by some of the males represented in the text, the work of "The Three Marías" is honored by adapting it's epistolary form. However, the letters of "The Three Marías" are also supplemented by Castillo's Anglo-American political and sex-ual angle of vision. Castillo's sole speaking protagonist—Teres ("Tere")—takes up the position, initially, of a free agent, while the narrative web of "The Three Marías" starts out by recognizing that women are not free agents in any sense whatsoever. More-over, as Darlene Sadlier's essay (1986) makes clear, "The Three Marías" did not have the political freedom to explore women's sexual oppression or question its nature even textually, let alone in practice. As a result, they were placed on trial for publishing their book. Ironically, the trial itself corroborated their point; women have not been free to express an uncensored subjectivity. Ana Castillo's *Letters* supplements "The Three Marías" insofar as her protagonist projects a subjectivity, free to express and practice her sexuality, but still imprisoned by an intangible heterosexist ideol-ogy, a heterosexist ideology for which we may posit Paz's view as the model. Thus, in *Letters* we have a protagonist who, by virtue of North American political practices and feminist influence, had "forgotten" what it is like to live in the world of "The Three Ma-rías" or even in Paz's world. As a result, Tere, the main speaker in *Letters*, undergoes a trial by fire when Mexico's cultural configu-ration is put into play. She is forced to recall that she is not as free as she thought. Since Teresa is a woman of Mexican descent (a Chicana), she should not have forgotten but, insofar as she wants to be a freer agent, she would want to forget. The complexities of her diverse levels of consciousness may be located in the push and pull of divergent political countries, i.e., the United States and Mexico. As Gloria Anzaldúa states in "La Conciencia de la Mes-tiza: Towards a New Consciousness":

> Within us and within *la cultura chicana*, commonly held beliefs of
> the white culture attack commonly held beliefs of the Mexican
> culture, and both attack commonly held beliefs of the indige-
> nous culture. . . . In a constant state of mental nepantilism, an
> Aztec word meaning torn between ways, *la mestiza* is a product
> of the transfer of the cultural and spiritual values of one group
> to another. . .and in a state of perpetual transition, the *mestiza*
> faces the dilemma of the mixed breed: which collectivity does
> the daughter of a dark-skinned mother listen to? (1987, 77-91)

Indeed, this may explain the rationale behind addressing the letters to Alicia, who was Tere's traveling companion and ought to
have known what they experienced. Nevertheless, the technique
enables Tere to bring out, through Alicia, the Anglo-American
cultural influence that, in any case, does not save either of them in
the face of the erotic, as we shall see.

Before further consideration of the *The Mixquiahuala Letters*, however, other important points must be brought up that will clarify
its social and literary importance as well as my necessarily complex critical approaches. The critical conjugation of "the metaphor of experience" and "the experience of metaphor" is as complex as its literary elaboration.

Selections from both chapbooks, *Otro Canto* and *The Invitation*, as
well as sixteen new poems, have been made available to a wider
audience in Castillo's book, *Women are Not Roses*. As happens in
"selections" books, the evolution of a writer's work is often cut
short in favor of the "best" that a writer has produced, a factor
that is the prerogative of editors. As a result, *Women Are Not Roses*
does not provide the reader with many clues to the intertextual
observations made above. Theorists of the text, of course have
taught us that one does not have recourse to direct intertextual
sources for the pursuit of such considerations. However, it is also
the case that writers do respond consciously to their textual mi-
lieus and effect a revisionary dialogue. As such, it is of paramount
political importance to identify the textual milieu of culturally
marginalized writers such as Chicanas, as well as to clarify the appropriative strategies at work in the struggle to construct and reconstruct an identity despite its instability, lest a writer appear to
speak in a vacuum. Moreover, writers and critics often rely on a

textual milieu and an actual experience, insofar as that milieu assists with the verbal translation of our cultural experience. In this fashion, a variety of discourses can be negated, supplemented, modified, and repeated, though it may not always be possible, or even necessary, to make clear-cut source identifications (Kristeva 1984, 59-60; Roudiez 1980, 15; Bakhtin 1981, 259-422).

Women Are Not Roses does not provide any clues to Castillo's appropriative strategies and experimentations, though the word "rose" in the title points to, and plays upon, the masculine textual production in which women are represented as flowers/nature. In this book, however, there are at least two poems that resonate intertextually and intratextually, and their examination may also help us in the reading of *The Mixquiahuala Letters*.

Both "An Idyll" (1986, 8-10) and "The Antihero" (1986, 24) warrant a closer look because they not only evoke the Western romantic tradition that has underpined women's erotic image within patriarchy but also, in this instance, further the female speaker's appropriation of that tradition to explore her sexuality and revise the image. Moreover, since Tere, the letter-writing protagonist of *Letters*, does not explicitly speak of her erotic illusions and ideals but instead reconstructs, from a ten-year distance, a period of her life that she calls a "cesspool" (Letter # 2), a consideration of these two poems may help us come to terms with the nature of her failed erotic quest. Though *Letters* represents sexual encounters with men, Tere often assumes a sarcastic, pragmatic, and even distant tone that contrasts sharply with whatever illusions and ideals may have led her (Letter # 1) and her friend Alicia to actively explore their sexuality. This is an exploration that falls short of erotic bliss, to say the least: hence, the label "cesspool." In a sense, the expectations of heterosexual erotic bliss constitute the partially repressed aspects of *Letters*, which on occasion contains such startling confessions as "i was docile" (1986, 113) or "i believed i would be placed in the little house and be cared for..." (1986, 118).[1] These occasional confessions are barely audible. They tend to get lost in Tere's latter-day, after-the-fact sardonic anger. As we shall see, she has been framed *a priori* by certain "semantic charters,"[2] and Castillo mocks her further by framing her with the "reading charts" offered to the reader.

"An Idyll" and "The Antihero" reinscribe two aspects of the erotic/romantic hero—the god-like and the demonic—from the point of view of a female speaker. Their representation, however, is complicated by the different spatio-temporal positions that the speaker takes, consequently putting into question how one translates and interprets (writes/reads) the experience. Since "The Antihero" is a significant inversion of the hero in "An Idyll," the speaker's relational position to each becomes very important, adding another dimension to their inscription. A speaker's position in relation to such monumental and heroic figures cannot be all that simple. The speaker is probing not only a relationship to the symbolic, that is, how the romantic hero has figured in textual tradition, but her social experience as well, that is, how she has lived her sexuality in, and through, such figurations.

In these two poems, the speaker filters her position through an intricate use of the first- ("An Idyll") and third- ("The Antihero") person pronouns in combination with temporal distance and proximity, respectively. These spatiotemporal, positional techniques are employed in *Letters* as well; though most of the letters are first-person accounts, Letters # 21 and # 32 are examples of speaker shifts. "An Idyll" is a first-person narration of past experience that is represented in fantastic terms, a virtual parody of male literary figurations:

```
            now
i      can      tell
of  being  swept  b
y  a  god  a  michael
angelo's    david    a
man  of  such  phys
ical        perfection,
one  could  not  be
lieve  him  human.        (8)
```

In this poem, the very columnar shape points to a phallic symmetry that distorts the potential plasticity of language for its own sake. It takes a very well programmed machine to reproduce that form. It is akin to a divine hierarchical account that only "now," by stepping outside of it, can be apprehended. The narrator, who only "now" can represent her enthrallment with the beautiful stony hero, assesses that erotic dance as "truer" because it was satisfying, in some measure. Enthrallment itself may have its own temporary erotic rewards. The romantic interlude—an idyll—as a symbolic fantasy may be spellbinding, but the effort to transform it into a social reality literally enslaves her:

> i ate
> with it slept wi
> th made its b
> ed in the mornin
> g when it disapp
> eared. . . . i waited
> for its return—
> each night.   (9)

Indeed, like language, she is immobilized and transfixed by "it," a god-like man. "It" has turned her into a robot. The murder of this fantastic being is due to her almost sudden awareness that her union with him, despite its insane and masochistic pleasures, is tantamount to her own self-destructive collusion. In the poem, his murder is anonymous, perhaps collective. As a crowd gathers to demand his expulsion, one of them shoots him when he refuses to leave:

> until one of us c
> ould not stand it
> any longer and
> shot him.   (10)

Now that the fantasy, with its perverse truth, is over, the first-person speaker is free to recall her delusion. Indeed, it is the newer, after-the-fact consciousness that makes it possible to see the enthrallment as a delusion. The one who narrates, however, is distanced from the one who lives the fantasy, that distance itself muting the emotional charge of the actual experience that was once lived as true and is now viewed through the lens of fabulous fiction. It is as if there was something inherently ironic in an experience recollected from the now-distant point of a changed consciousness. This is precisely the ironic tone effected in many of the letters (see, for example, Letter # 16 where Tere's attraction to Alvaro is later viewed as a weakness). Tere mocks her initial enthrallment. She "Believed that beneath his rebellion was a sensi-

tive human being with an insight that was unique and profound."
(1986, 48). Years later, however, either Tere's narrative hindsight
or that of an unidentified narrator reports, "This is a woman conditioned to accept a man about whom she has serious doubts. . . ."
(1986, 48).

The ironies of "An Idyll" take a more cruel turn in "The Antihero," who exhibits a reckless disregard for his partner's erotic desires: "the antihero/always gets the woman/not in the end/an anti-
climax instead" (1986, 24). If the heterosexual dance in "An
Idyll" is paradoxically viewed as a true fiction by the first person
narrator, the lyrical speaker of "The Antihero" views him as pur-
posely playing his partner false. He obfuscates erotic desire by
rendering sexual experience anticlimactic, as against pressure and
denouement. He manipulates her desire so as "to leave her yearning lest/she discover that is all" (1986, 24). She is double-crossed
by the anticlimactic ruse into continuing to conflate desire with
him. It is clear, as Luce Irigaray comments in another context,
that "man's desire and woman's are strangers to each other"
(1985, 27). If she discovered the infinite power of her own desire,
then certainly the cruel dance would undergo transformation or
come to a stop. The poem presents the anticlimactic sexual event
in the present-tense lyrical mode, through the lens of the third
person. The couple is objectified in the present tense to suggest an
ongoing, unsatisfactory scenario of desire that brings them together, yet keeps them apart. Thus, contrary to the dictates of the
lyric, which calls for a personal account of sensual experience, the
poem switches the speaker position to suggest a model of contemporaneous behavior that distorts erotic desire. For Castillo, then,
angles of perception, which may be both spatial and/or temporal,
are sites for discrete eruptions of meaning that may be subsequently juxtaposed, thus effecting additional meanings. In a
sense, the significance of any one thing is highly unstable and
much depends on the angle of vision.

Conventionally, the letter form has shared at least two important
features with the lyric, notwithstanding the fact that the first is
prose and the second is poetry.[1] Both reveal the intimate events in
the life of the speaker, *combined* with the speaker's emotional response to them, thus exploring the personal states of mind at the
moment of the event or with respect to it. It should be noted, in

passing, that *Letters* is a mixture of poetic and prosaic forms, but the speaker, who may not always be identified with Tere, does not feel bound by conventions. This disruption of conventions signals, in my view, a pursuit of narrative approaches that may be beyond Tere's simple "i." In a sense, she is undergoing an inquisition that makes her both the subject of her narrative and the object of someone else's.

Consider how, in recalling events shared with Alicia, her sole interlocutor, Tere almost consistently shifts to a third-person, present narration to explore emotional responses to an event. Letter # 21 is an example of such an instance, an account telling of Tere's breakdown as a result of her misalliance with Alexis: "After a while, she adapts to neglecting herself more than he can. Her nails are bitten to the quick. She forgets to eat or eats when she's not hungry. Her inability to sleep makes her face droop like the jowls of an old hound dog. She is twenty-six-years-old. With nervous gestures, she tears an invisible thread from the edge of her slip. If she doesn't watch out, she will quietly go mad and no one will have noticed" (1986, 112).

As in "An Idyll," enthrallment again leads to a slavish madness, but it cannot be stated in the first person. Who narrates? An older Tere, who fears to re-enter that period of insanity with a personal "i"? Also, as in "The Antihero," the speaker shifts to the third-person account, thus creating distance with regard to speaking positions, but not to time. As a narrator of her letters, Tere reveals that she occasionally shifts personae to "create distance with the use of a personal 'i'" (1986, 64). As such, it would appear to be an admission that, emotionally, events have a dangerous, contemporaneous power that must be objectified, displaced to a "she/her." Often, Tere can only re-present what has lost the power to hurt her. Romantic love, however, cannot be spoken of, intimately or directly. As she—or is it she?—coldly says: "Love? In the classic sense, it describes in one syllable all the humiliation that one is born to and pressed upon to surrender to a man" (1986, 111). In our time, "the classic sense" of love is the erotically romantic one that has been popularized *ad nauseam* through romance novels or, in the case of Mexico and Latin America, *foto-novelas*—as Tere knows (1986, 50). It is a genre that cuts across classes and makes many women, regardless of their economic status, sisters under the skin, daughters of patriarchy. In fact, it is the erotic quest that holds Tere and Alicia's friendship together. The true closeness of the friendship is placed in question when we read Letter # 13, in which Tere emphasizes her occasional loathing of Alicia. The wedge between them is Alicia's privilege, color, and worldly-wise airs. Clearly, Tere and Alicia's relationship requires further scrutiny. However, what keeps them together is their shared relationship to the romantic. Letter # 40 serves to additionally reiterate the erotic common ground.

In Letter # 33, to further explore her relations with Alexis, Tere again shifts speaking positions. On this occasion, she switches to her fantasy of his voice. When Tere encounters Alexis five years after the breakup, she imagines what he should be thinking upon seeing her. This is the end to the affair that pleases her (1986, 114). The poem, entitled "Epilogue" and attributed to Alexis, is a tribute to Tere's unequaled charms, a testimonial to his lingering affection for Tere, despite the passage of time and his subsequent involvements with other women: "It was *her*./ . . . *She* /was there, in the same room . . ." (1986, 115). Tere is effectively converted into his Muse, the one still capable of stirring him into poetic reverie. Indeed, she reveals that being the object of his desire is something in which she is well trained, so well in fact, that she can even write poems about that object, herself, and assume his voice. Even as this version of the end pleases her more than the actual reported sordid end of their affair, Tere's self-conscious posing parodies the experience of the romantic metaphor: *She*, the muse, the love object that truly moves him; *He*, the desiring lover/poet. In Tere's relationship with Alexis, the gap between the metaphor of experience, insanity and abandonment, and the experience of metaphor, the enchanting muse, provides us with a variation of the chords struck in "The Antihero" and "An Idyll" (see Letter # 28 for Tere's initial response to Alexis). As Janice A. Radway has told us in *Reading The Romance*, (1984) romantic/erotic bliss is the salient promise that Western patriarchy holds out to women, a bliss that constantly eludes our hapless heroines. Why? I can only conjecture that, while both Tere and Alicia are quite adept at posing as the object of desire, they find it impossible to carry through the subsequent social actualization of that objectification, primarily because it is not an option at all. It spells the death of their subjectivity. Ironically, that is their near-unconscious discovery. The patriarchal promise of romantic/erotic bliss, re-presented in all manner of popular literature, is an ideological maneuver to kill their subjectivity and any further exploration of their own desire.

The understated, failed quest for romantic/erotic bliss effects a blisteringly sardonic tone in the *Letters*, which are an exercise in hindsight. If, in fact, *Letters* represents the struggle to move beyond the quest, the irony is Tere's inability to succeed. In part, this is due to the fact that both the women and their string of men are still operating under a romantic/erotic heterosexist ideology that is hard to shake, notwithstanding Tere's latter-day awareness that this is so. Consider what she says ten years after the quest for "womanhood": "Destiny is not a metaphysical confrontation with one's self, rather, society has knit its pattern so tight that a confrontation with it is inevitable" (1986, 59). The quest for "womanhood" is still socially defined in sexual terms under the popular emblem of the romantic/erotic. Both Tere and Alicia are pressed to fulfill the pattern. In a sense, *Letters* offers us a different version of the so-called "star-crossed" lovers.

Destiny, as such, is a socially enforced misrecognition under the guise of love that places Tere in a double bind: on the one hand, a desire for her own sexual definition, and on the other, an overly determined script in which she takes part. Tere, in short, is bitter over her unwitting, yet unavoidable, folly. The appropriation of the erotic, as enjoyed and desired in the more symbolic book, *The Invitation*, is betrayed in *Letters*. *Letters* makes evident the possibility that an appropriation of the erotic in a heterosexist society may only end up being revealed as a misappropriation.

Castillo's experimentations with shifting pronouns and appropriative techniques for the purpose of exploring the romantic/erotic does not stop with Tere's letters, however. If we return to the "real beginning" of *Letters*, we must note that the first letter is to the reader, penned by Castillo. We are directed to undertake a Latter-day of unconventional readings—"The Conformist," "The Cynic," and "The Quixotic"—each tailed to our reading needs. We are also given the option to read each of the forty letters separately, as if they were short fiction. We are alerted that we are in for a variety of ironic and parodic plays but we are ignorant of what they might be. In short, the book brings into question our own reading practices, for the apparently unconventional suggested readings actually lead to resolutions that are more conventional than the handful of letters attributed to Tere. Insofar as each suggested reading by Castillo presents us with a resolution, we are handed an ideological nexus (i.e., The Conformist-idyllic conjugal life) that forces us to reconstruct the meaning of Tere's letters as always and already leading in that direction.[1] Was that Tere's desired end, or is it The Quixotic, or The Cynic's? If, as readers, we play along with the suggested charts, we are forced to come to terms with the notion that Tere is very much trapped by a variety of ideological nexuses that she, and we, need to question and disrupt.

But it is not only our reading and interpretive practices that are in question; Tere's are, too. She constantly shifts voices in an effort to "read" and interpret her own experiences. Which one of the various selves that she explores is she? Is she the vampish one, the docile one, the clever one, the fearful one, the liberated one, or the oppressed one? Insofar as each is connected with her sexuality, she is all of them, and more. Above all, I think she is betrayed by a cultural fabric that presses its images of her upon her, and her response (as well as Castillo's) is to give them all back to us, albeit sardonically. Tere is no longer a sitting duck, as Paz or even "The Three Marías" would have it, but she still inhabits a shooting gallery in which she must wear many a mask to survive and to understand where she has been.

Notes

1. The use of the small "i" pronoun throughout *Letters* is disturbing but something other than an affectation. Weigel (1986) suggests that to use the "I" in public, women will have to learn to speak "without having first to acknowledge the male definition of their gender role."
2. Pierre Maranda (1980, 184-85) suggests that "Semantic charters condition our thoughts and emotions. They are culture specific networks that we internalize as we undergo the process of socialization." Moreover, these charters of signifying systems "have an inertia and a momentum of their own. There are semantic domains whose inertia is high: kinship terminologies, the dogmas of authoritarian churches, the conception of sex roles."
3. Ruth Perry (1980, 117) discusses at length the enactment of "a self-conscious and self-perpetuating process of emotional self-examination," as well as the history of the epistolary genre, in her book.

4. Frederic Jameson's commentary (1975, 225) on "the kind of reading which attaches itself to finding out how everything turns out in the end" provides a helpful perspective for understanding Castillo's parodic plots.

The "Wild Zone" Thesis as Gloss in Chicana Literary Study

Cordelia Chávez Candelaria

One of the difficulties faced in the feminist project undertaken by women of color in the United States[1] has been to avoid privileging gender over race because Chicanos and other men of color are themselves members of politically and economically subordinated classes. Yet, to recognize the compound oppression referred to as "double" or "triple" jeopardy (Millman and Kanter 1975; Candelaria 1978; Melville 1980) of Chicanas, Latinas, and other women of color demands recognition of the additional burden of gender for women as it is interpreted within political hierarchies in all patriarchal societies. One approach to addressing the tension between race and gender, both that experienced in material political reality and that evident in U. S. American analytical feminist discourse,[1] is suggested by an influential essay in *Perceiving Women* (1975), a book on the anthropology of gender written by anthropologists Edwin and Shirley Ardener to analyze their ethnographic field experiences. In it, they describe as a "wild zone" the separate political and cultural space that women inhabit in the societies they studied.

In the societies described by the Ardeners, that space was perceived to derive from certain physiological circumstances which then became defined and affected by societal and cultural responses to those circumstances. Because among humans only women produce ova, experience gestation, childbirth, and how it feels to suckle an infant born of one's body, within historical time this physiology was interpreted and described socioculturally by the societies the Ardeners researched, as it has been throughout history, in a variety of ways (e.g., as saintliness, nurturance, docility, weakness, mental deficiency, and other now established stereotypes of femininity). Civilization's (that is, the patriarchy's) elaborate social conventions and political systems based on learned gender difference are traceable in large measure to the physiology of sexuality and the acquired stereotypes of femininity and masculinity. Even when women have been revered for specific, discrete attributes like maternity, traits that have been generalized metonymically to all women and to essential femaleness, these gendered identities subordinate women as a class to the definitions of male-wielded power and patriarchal institutions. The Mexicano/Chicano cultural archetypes of the Virgin of Guadalupe, La Malinche, La Llorona, and La Adelita exemplify this stereotypification (Candelaria 1980; Limón 1990; Pérez 1991).

The Ardener "wild zone" thesis posits that women's experience has evolved distinct female-identified cultures necessarily marginalized within, and simultaneously outside of, the dominant male-identified patriarchy. The thesis asserts that:

> The real problem is that all world-structures are totalitarian in tendency.... The englobed structure [of femaleness] is totally "muted" [i.e., both marginalized and silent] in terms of the englobing one. There is then an absolute equality of world-structures in this principle, for we are talking of their self-defining and reality-reducing features. *Dominance* occurs when one structure blocks the power of actualization of the other, so that it has no "freedom of action." ...[T]he articulation of world-structures does not rest only in their production base but at all levels of communication: that a structure is also a kind of language of many semiological elements, which specify all actions by its power of definition. (E. Ardener 1975, 252)

The citation stresses that "dominance" of one structure over an/other produces disproportionate socioeconomic (i.e., production base) and cultural (i.e., language and semiotic) effects. The interwoven connection between social norms and individual identity that results in patriarchal dominance over women in turn produces a greater distance between female *desire* and actual choice— between personal identity and the sociocultural power to begin even to approximate the actualization of that identity.

The Ardeners labelled women's separate space as a "zone" to denote both its *physiology-derived* bounded space, as well as to capture the idea of the learned, *stereotype-derived* female space defined by the dominant structure. (Analogous examples include climate zones which typify areas identified by actual, geography-derived characteristics, and traffic parking zones which illustrate areas designated according to abstract ideas [like stereotypes] arbitrarily circumscribed.) To distinguish women's space from the societal hegemony that contains it, the Ardeners applied the term "wild" to suggest an emphatic pristine nature (of geography, physiology, and sexuality) free of the inscribed assumptions and definitions of traditional patriarchal civilization. Although the sign *wild* might be considered problematic because of its perceived pejorative connotations, it is intended to be understood as continuing the feminist project's recuperation of reductive, distorting anthropomorphic labels (e.g., bitch, spinster, witch, dyke) according to feminist-defined primary values of proto-herstory and originary women's experience. Accordingly, "wildness" and "wilderness" not only express conditions of nature in a non-technologized unconquered state, but they also describe certain required conditions and activities of life-generating experience (e.g., sexuality and emotion) in organized society.

The "wild zone" thesis thus identifies a fundamental paradox of female identity: on the one hand, a distinct female experiential, cultural space derived from an unrestricted ("wild") existence unmediated by inimical, imposed definitions of identity, and on the other the restricted women-space defined by and located within the englobing historical patriarchy without recognition of women's human potential or achievement. To Kristeva (1981) and other intellectual descendants of Lacan (1958 and 1977), this paradox is explained by the historical power of the patriarchy to define language and to subsume within itself the evolved significations of language thus invalidating concepts based on any "real" or "true" categories of "woman" and "femininity." To Jardine (1985) and what she calls the "fundamental feminist gesture" within both Lacanian concepts *and* the political materialist categories identified with U.S. feminism, this paradox is explained by focusing on the "space" between masculinized perceptions (whether perpetuated by men or women) and the Other, "*a space coded as feminine*" [her italics] within her theory of "*gynesis*—the putting into discourse of 'woman'" (1985, 25).

The "wild zone" schema, with the theoretical nuances and anthropological observations contained in *Perceiving Women* only briefly outlined in this essay, offers a gloss on the partially divergent views of Kristeva and Jardine, a gloss that apprehends validity in both viewpoints contingent upon the function of the discourse. The "wild zone" schema acknowledges the legitimacy of questions regarding the idea of *an essential woman-ness* and the critique that dismantles such an idea, but it simultaneously recognizes that a crucial consequence of patriarchy is the persistent *and empowered* "perceiving" of "women" in essential(ist) terms. Further, the schema provides a useful perspective on the fundamental paradox of female identity (and that of other disempowered classes). As politically subordinated subjects, women (and other marginalized political subordinates) must, for survival, know and practice the dominant patriarchal discourse and conventions. But equally manifest is that for survival and maintenance of an unmediated, affirmative identity of self and class, women and other marginalized groups develop an/other culture and discourse—one not required for the survival of, and therefore largely unavailable to, the empowered members of the dominant class. The central point here is that *the power of the patriarchy itself* impedes and frequently precludes members of the dominant class from perceiving, understanding, or accessing "wild zone" values and codes, or what Kolodny has identified as gender inflections outside the canonized norms of patriarchy (1985, 47-50). The empowered statuses and valorized identities of dominant class members—that is, their power—both bind them to the hegemonic order and also blind them from either apprehending or comprehending the separate experience and values of the disempowered classes.

To return to the issue presented in this essay's introduction— the privileging of gender over race given that Chicanos and other men of color are themselves members of subordinate classes—the "wild zone" again offers a useful gloss for reading the Chicana/ Latina experience in the United States. The "wild zone" facilitates the examination of gender as a discrete attribute because its very conceptualization is based on a recognition of multiple and distinct *cultures* of experience that develop from such fundamental categories as gender, race, and ethnicity, as well as according to political-economic categories of class and wealth distribution (Candelaria, 1989). This is salient to Chicana studies (and other studies of politically oppressed groups) for it encourages gender-specific analysis without denying of the importance of ethnic-or race-specific or class-specific analyses. Unlike traditional academic studies by Chicanos and non-Chicanos which uncritically focus primarily on male-defined subsets of the patriarchy, the "wild zone" thesis encourages the examination of gender as a subject of critique within the analysis of ideology, power, and culture without privileging it over the defining attributes of other categories of identity.

The conceptualization of an affirmative culture and discourse originating in the "wild zone" distinct from, but also in relation to, the hegemonic culture complements and enhances other conceptualizations of supra/subordinate societal relationships. Dubois' idea of "double consciousness," for example, recognizes the requirement for political minorities within a culturally different polity to be fluent in the language and social behaviors of the supraordinate "masters" even as they develop their own group-affirming idioms (1965). Freire, too, describes a "bifurcated vision" that political minorities possess as "victims" of dominant/dominating structures whose public rhetoric articulates principles and ideals remote from their "concrete victimization" (1970). Beauvoir's "second sex" idea of female gender reflects a similar perspective that defines women and womanhood in relation to the patriarchy, men, and the *doigt du seigneur* (the right of the master) (1949). Emphasizing the important dimension of the subjective consciousness of particular individuals or classes, these conceptualizations focus on "minority" subjectivity in relation to the culture of dominance. The "wild zone" idea problematizes that dimension, as Bakhtin does in his reading of the multiple codes of medieval folk culture (1964), by emphasizing the collective culture(s) from which individuals and classes emerge. Further, it focuses on the interactive dynamics of relationship, on the nexus between private and public spheres and between power and disempowerment, and on evolving social forms and patterns.

Another utility of the "wild zone" concept is its forefronting of the substance and affirmative aspects of marginalized cultures. By identifying Chicanas, for instance, as part of a zone of experience and power inaccessible to the agents of patriarchal power or to those lacking critical awareness of the patriarchy, the authority of Chicana expression in language and other mediums of creativity is defined from *within* Chicana experience and not solely *in relation* to the dominating political hegemonies, public or private. This is crucial both in Chicana/o studies and in policy-making arenas for it neutralizes the often voiced reluctance by both women and men to focus on the needs, desires, achievements, and oppressions of

woman-identified Chicanas (and other women of color) in order
to avoid diminishing issues of race, ethnicity, and class. The very
terms of its definition as a space among others underscores the
"wild zone's" explicit acknowledgment of the authority, but not
superiority, of a multiplicity of other zones of experience, idea,
and culture.

Conceptualization of the "wild zone" also complements other
descriptions of Chicana-identified creative expression. Literary
scholar Rosaura Sanchez, for example, in "The History of Chicanas: Proposal for a Materialist Perspective" calls for "subject-
identified" analysis; that is, analysis that valorizes the Chicana
subject's "multiple subjectivities" of gendered identity, ethnoracial
experience, and material class situation (1990, 5-23). Similarly,
historian Emma Perez in "Sexuality and Discourse: Notes from a
Chicana Survivor" calls for perspectives that seek to comprehend
from inside *un sitio y una lengua* of the subject (1991, 161). Implicit
in both of these appeals is a recognition of the distinctly separate
experiential and political space of Chicanas and other women *as
subjects*; in the Ardeners' thesis, the subject-identified "wild zone"
asserts both the appropriateness *and necessity* of gender-specific in-
terrogation in the research and study of all peoples of color.

As the feminist/ethnic studies revisionary project of the past two
decades has demonstrated, Chicana/Latina and other women
writers have struggled for centuries to express and assert the validity of womanspace and the textured zone of women's experience.
In America at least as far back as Sor Juana in the seventeenth
century we find vigorous protest against the accepted hegemonic
principle of "silencing women" in her era. Her carefully reasoned
and impassioned analysis in *La Repuesta* argued that the effect of
barring women from access to formal education resulted in the total disempowerment of women in society. Later women writers of
the Americas have echoed Sor Juana by tracing a similar link between gender and genre, between female experience and its expression in literature, the arts, and other discourses.

Examples of these tracings from the "wild zone" include the
majority of contemporary Chicana writers. Significantly, many of
them have chosen to configure their stories with images and
themes of place—that is, in terms of thematic *zones* that intercon-
nect experience and imagination. Sometimes that configuration
centers on the geography of birthplace and homeland; sometimes

its center is the home and personal surroundings. Whatever the center of origin, these external spaces also serve to inscribe aspects of the interior dimensions and private spaces of Chicana experience. Three noteworthy illustrations of these inscriptions are writings by Estela Portillo-Trambley, Denise Chavez, and Sandra Cisneros.

Estela Portillo Trambley, one of the first women to gain prominence within contemporary Chicana/o letters (receiving the Quinto Sol Award in 1972), integrates issues of woman-identity and feminism with figures of place in her fiction and drama. For instance, her short story, "The Paris Gown" (1973), highlights in its very title one of the world's premier cosmopolitan cities. More important to a reading of the narrative is that the plot's feminist rite of passage depends for its thematics on the contrast of French and Mexican landscapes and the cultures both places represent in the imagination of the young Theresa, the niece of the story's protagonist, Clotilde, whose life is told in flashback. Paris and Europe represent freedom and choice to Clotilde as she tells her story decades later to her visiting niece, whereas Mexico and home mean suppression under the stifling authority of her father, of the future husband arranged for her, and of the machismo she sees pervading the society of her birth. By inscribing her protagonist's personal desires and choices in terms broader than her private psychology, in the spatial and political dichotomy of place and culture, Portillo-Trambley's narrative expresses one aspect of the paradox of gendered identity described above and usefully glossed by the "wild zone" thesis.

Less dichotomous in its emblematic use of place is *Rain of Scorpions* (1975), the title novela of Portillo-Trambley's first published collection of short fiction. Employing the techniques of naturalism, the author underscores the omnipotence of land, nature, and industrial corporations over the people of Smelter-town, a symbolically drawn industrial town situated between "two propitious mountains where long ago Cabeza de Baca had ciphered the name of El Paso del Norte" (136). The narrative juxtaposes the socioeconomic struggles of the town's downtrodden workers with the personal struggle of Lupe, an earth-mother figure seeking to discover her selfhood and, in the process, to recover her feminine power, particularly over Fito, the veteran who returned from Vietnam with one leg missing but with his political conscience activated. Ever present in the people's lives is the awesomeness of nature with its demanding beauty, its unpredictable weather, and the ubiquitous animals—elements drawn together in the conclusion when the flooding rains arrive along with the deluge of scorpions. Even though the town's smelter is a site of industrial pollution and corporate exploitation, Portillo-Trambley makes it clear (sometimes heavy-handedly) that the smelter and the ore derive from the land that preceded it, and the land's primacy and originary power invests it with spiritual energy. Like the land's precedent spiritual power Lupe's compassion is linked specifically to her womanhood in attributes associated with recuperative "wild zone" definitions of subjectivity.

Denise Chavez's and Sandra Cisneros' work also frequently underscore place, especially home and geography, as metaphor. They share with Portillo-Trambley the portrayal of compelling female figures whose characterizations are closely related to their physical environments. Stylistically, their most well-known titles resemble in their use of short narrative and vignette the major works of several important literary antecedents: Kate Chopin's *Bayou Folk* (1894), Sherwood Anderson's *Winesburg, Ohio* (1919), and Tomas Rivera's *Y no se lo trago la tierra* (1971). The continuity between these titles and Chavez's and Cisneros' extends beyond narrative sketches yoked around a central narrator, for they also portray a similar terrain of psychological alienation and sociopolitical subordination. They share as well a heightened interest in writing the protagonist's self as simultaneous product, observer, antagonist, and embodiment of place—whether bayou, Winesburg, or la tierra.

Chavez's *The Last of the Menu Girls* (1986), a collection of short stories, is united by its New Mexico settings and female perspectives. All of the seven stories in *Menu Girls* present the girlhood experiences and imaginings of Rocio Esquibel, the "menu girl" of the collection's title story. Although plots of the stories collectively focus on Rocio's personal development and emergent writer's consciousness, Chavez etches her personality—and that of many of the other characters—through meticulous attention to the specifics of her surroundings. The closing lines of "Compadre," the last story in the book, exemplify this concern with place. To the query, "What do you write?" Rocio responds offhandedly "Oh, about people. New Mexico. You know, everything" (1986, 190).

Her mother then intrudes, characteristically, into the conversation with a long monologue that captures much of the essence of the preceding stories: "...I say, Rocio, just write about this little street of ours, it's only one block long, but there's so many stories. Too many stories!...but why write about this street? Why not just write about 325? That's our house! Write about 325 and that will take the rest of your life..." (1986, 190)

The Last of the Menu Girls constitutes the author's realization of this advice, for it chronicles the lives, images, events, speech, and human relations of that street and its houses, yards, secret hiding spots, and special landmarks as remembered by the protagonist.

In the title story, "The Last of the Menu Girls," recipient of the 1985 Puerto del Sol Fiction Award, Rocio's character emerges through her exploration of Altavista Memorial Hospital where she works as a menu taker for the patients. Her encounter of the hospital's offices, patient rooms, corridors, smells, and sounds, along with her reaction to the other employees and patients give texture to her natural inquisitiveness and keen observation, just as her part-time job loosens sharp memories of her Great Aunt Eutilia's dying in the Esquibel home a few summers before. Similarly, in "Willow Game" the unnamed narrator we know to be Rocio recalls a pivotal feature of her girlhood, the trees that punctuated her neighborhood and which serve in her adult mind as landmarks of her rite of passage to maturity. As in the other stories which capture the particulars of place, Chavez here painstakingly describes the trees in their physical spaces: "The Apricot tree was bound by the channelway that led to the Main Street ditch;" "the Willow stump remained underneath the window of my old room" (1986, 43, 49) in order to emphasize the persistence of place in triggering memory: "[Today] I walked outside and the same experience repeated itself" (1986 50). Like Portillo-Trambley in "Paris Gown," Chavez forefronts concrete places interconnected with psychological and cultural perceptions to show both how the interconnected zones shape her characters' lives and imaginations and also how they persist as catalysts of memory and idea.

In similar fashion, Sandra Cisneros unites *The House on Mango Street* (1985), a series of vignettes and short stories, by attentive focus to the scenic details of her main character's Chicago home. The book, which won a 1985 Before Columbus American Book Award, is written with a concreteness and vitality that captures the density and rush of the city, external and visible, as well as the interior traffic of her protagonist Esperanza's feelings and imaginings. Whether recounting the people and occasions that are the subject of the chapters entitled "Boys and Girls," "The Earl of Tennessee," and "Minerva Writes Poems," or telling of the yearning and adolescent angst that gird the chapters "Linoleum Roses," "Born Bad," and "Bums in the Attic," Esperanza defines herself in relation to her memories of her childhood living on the move in the houses on Mango, Keeler, Paulina, and Loomis Streets. As important, her later recollection of the houses and the meaning of all the urban places of her girlhood elicits a sociopolitical sense of community in the adult chronicler actually writing the book. Her memories also locate a positive relation between her adolescent desire for a room of her own and her writerly need for solitude and introspection.

Cisneros' third book, *My Wicked Wicked Ways* (1987), a volume of poetry, contains similarly strong references to geography and physical space. Two of the volume's four sections are titled with place names: "I: 1200 South/2100 West," referring to Chicago's street numbers, and "III: Other Countries," relating to the poet's European travels. In addition, she introduces two of the sections with epigraphs (one by poet Gwendolyn Brooks, Cisneros' mentor; the other from *The Three Marás*) that explicitly allude to place. Especially graphic in communicating idea and feeling through tropes of physical place are the poems "Six Brothers," "Twister Hits Houston," "By Way of Explanation," "Men Asleep," and all the pieces in section III. "Six Brothers," for example, contrasts the "earthbound" speaker's search for ancestral roots in palpable places, "castles maybe" or "a Sahara city," with her father's ambitious hope for his family's successful future as achievers of illustrious careers (1987, 24-25). In "Men Asleep" the speaker casts her sad yearning for intimacy deeper than the flesh in terms of place, by describing past lovers "who go room into room into room,/ who shut themselves like doors,/who would not let me in" (1987, 89). Like *Mango Street* and Chavez's *Menu Girls*, these poems give voice to a self-expression firmly bound to home and to homeland, to hearth and to earth, and authorizes the literary page itself with a fresh discovered territory within the "wild zone" of her woman-identified identity.

Many other talented Chicana writers and artists[2] have indicated a pressing interest in the geography of Aztlan, in the multiple Mexican American crossroads of the U.S., in the rich cultural and political outgrowths of other known territories as metaphors of "wild zone" consciousness. These expressions of creativity are part of the feminist project undertaken by women of color in the United States (see note 1) and, while offering woman-identified perspectives of Chicana experience, clearly do not privilege gender over race or ethnicity. Rather, they depict areas of a subject-identified "wild zone" thereby "putting" Chicanas "into [the] discourse of woman" (Jardine 1985) in its multiple meanings.

Notes

1. I refer specifically to the *United States* to delimit this paper as much as possible to feminism considered within the context of American political power and patriarchal hierarchies and not within the philosophical and psychological theories of French (anti)feminist discourse—particularly that posited by and derived from Lacan, Derrida, Kristeva, Cixous, and Irigaray—even though I recognize the salience of that discourse. My intention is to suggest a presumptive rationale for an activist ethnic feminism in response to the increased impact of the reactionary counter-discourse of such high profile, popular culture mouthpieces as for example, Dinesh D'Souza, Linda Chavez, Camille Paglia et al. These ultra-conservatives seek to subvert the radical multicultural project of expanding U.S. education and politics with an inclusive curriculum.
2. Among them are Gloria Anzaldúa, whose *Borderlands/La Frontera: The New Mestiza* (1987) argues with passion that Chicana identity cannot be separated from land base and place, and Angela De Hoyos, whose *Chicano Poems for the Barrio* (1975) examines oppression in urban barrios by showing how the land "belongs" to no one even though it must be respected as if it "belong[s] to all." Poets Lorna Dee Cervantes, Carmen Tafolla, Gina Valdes, and Bernice Zamora; novelist Isabela Rios; and essayist Silvia Lizarraga have also written nuanced treatments of the interactive dynamics of place and psyche and space and politics. Among visual artists, muralist Judith Baca and painter Carmen Lomas Garza are two Chicanas who express a similar theme in their work.

Unveiling Athena:
Women in the Chicano Novel[1]

Erlinda Gonzales-Berry

Si has pensado cambiar tu destino recuerda un poquito quien te hizo mujer
(popular Mexican song)

In her article, "Foucault's Fantasia for Feminists: The Woman Reading," Michelle Thiebaux (1982, 45) affirms that discourses about women find their corollary in Foucault's *scientia sexualis*, according to which "the multiplication of discourses about sex have succeeded in displacing the sexual act." Likewise, she emphasizes, male discourses about women have displaced "what women are, do, or feel," the sign "gaining a more powerful reality" than the signified, the original referent making way for the "verbal machinery" that has acquired autonomy and solidity (1982, 45). It is by now commonplace to acknowledge that this symbolic displacement often has confused women, setting them astray in their own quest for self-definition and, more often than not, keeping them in their place, that is, in the niche designated for them by the creators of cultural and symbolic paradigms.

What specifically are the signs that have displaced the original referents? In an interview, French psychologist and writer Luce Irigaray addresses this issue. To the question, "What are the basic representations in the symbolic world by which the oppression of women is articulated," Irigaray responds: "Virgin, mother, whore" (1983, 231). She goes on to state that "one might also add the mask of femininity that one sees in the mythology beginning with Athena. Athena is always veiled. That is, I think, the basic ornamentation of the female body. And Athena is also called Pallas which means 'wound.' The ornamentation becomes a veil over the wound" (1983, 239). Irigaray's words have prompted the following discussion of my own perception of three stages of development in the portrayal of women in the Chicano novel: 1) Chicana characters cast as types—virgin/mother/whore roles; 2) Chicana characters hidden behind the mask of femininity, cast as the "Other" of male protagonists; 3) Chicanas cast as unveiled Athenas or characters of multiple dimensions.

The first of these stages, the rigid typecasting of Chicana characters, has received its share of critical attention. Judy Salinas, for example, in her early analysis of the role of women in Chicano literature, observes that, for the most part, women have been limited to two basic roles (she obviously merges the mother/virgin roles which Irigiray handles as separate categories): the "good" woman, symbolized by the Virgin Mary and the "bad" woman (1977, 192). Though she limits her description of the evil woman to one who tempts and seduces men, I would state that the "evil woman," "the whore," is an epithet reserved for women who refuse to limit themselves to the sanctioned virgin/mother role. It is not so much because of their proclivities toward sins of the flesh that women become evil, but rather, because of their refusal to abide by patriarchal dictates of ownership. In refusing to accept the ideal pattern of female behavior, women shun the machinery, the main cog of which is respect, designed to protect and consequently dominate them, thereby creating chaos and threatening to destabilize the system by usurping male privilege. In order to discourage such behavior, noncooperative (evil) women are marginalized, stigmatized, and censured: They are condemned to be *La Puta*.

Thus, the triad referred to by Irigaray (virgin/mother/whore) collapses into a binary opposition. Young girls are first virgins who grow up to be wives and mothers who subsequently must continue to act as if they were virgins. The opposite pole in the dichotomy is the whore. It is not, however, an automatically given opposition, but one which depends for its existence on a negation of the virgin/mother pole. Unable to conceive of a society free of this binary system, male writers have tended to create female characters whose behavior corresponds to the familiar pattern. In doing so, they have reinforced the binary phenomenon, ensured its continuity, and contributed to the exclusion of women from participation in the public domain. This pattern represents not so much a case of displacement, as asserted by Thiebaux (1982, 45), but rather, one of limitation. In their propagation of patriarchal ideals, male writers have contributed to the solidification of symbols which in turn have influenced what women of flesh and blood "are, do, and feel" (1982, 45). Thus, we have a vicious cycle of entrapment and limitation in which it becomes difficult to distinguish reality from fiction, fiction from reality.

One interesting treatment of the virgin-mother/whore construct is found in Villareal's *Pocho* (1970). True, the virgin is not concretely present. However, the young Rubio sisters, who should realize this archetype, have chosen the way of the whore and the traditional virgin role is left vacant. Moreover, the ubiquitous presence of "bad girls" highlights the absence of the virgin figure; it consequently acquires prominence through absence, and we are made aware of the fine line that separates these polarized images.

The mother is presented with an interesting twist. In an attempt to become emancipated like her American neighbors, Consuelo Rubio turns her back on the cultural ideal of the self-sacrificing, abnegated mother. When the family finally collapses and her husband and son abandon her, there is really nothing left for Consuelo to do but to become a pathetic *llorona* figure, clad, not in virginal white, but in *luto*, condemned to mourn forever the loss of her men, her *raison d'etre*: "She had lost her men—both of them. And already there was a look of mourning on her face" (1970, 173).

In his treatment of the mother as a betrayer of culture, Villareal continues to propagate the worn out women-as-traitress motif and to use it as a paradigm upon which to mold female characters, a pattern, Herrera-Sobek (1982, 135) reminds us, commonly found in the corrido. That he views the archetype as an inspiring model becomes even more apparent in his treatment of another Chicana mother, Queli Chacón; of *Clemente Chacón* (Villarreal, 1983). In this novel we see the Chicana renege, once again, on the cultural ideal of wife/mother. Consuelo Rubio's peccadillos—her refusal to keep a clean house and her discovery of sexual pleasure (and we might ask, is this the cause of her downfall? Does this discovery move her toward the whore pole?)—pale in comparison to Queli's full-fledged mortal sins: female ambition, refusal to have more than one child, and the crassest type of infidelity. Whereas Consuelo's life simply loses meaning, and she is left to wither behind her mourning veil, Queli is transformed from wife/mother to whore and replaced by a new Anglo wife who, upon bearing him two sons, helps Clemente salvage his masculine pride and honor.

That Clemente chooses the suburban Chicano way rather than the suburban Anglo nirvana favored by the traitress Queli, is alluded to at the end of the novel when he rushes to fetch a *curandera* rather than a doctor for his ill child. This negative treatment of the mother type stands in sharp contrast to the numerous idealized versions encountered in other Chicano works such as Jose Montoya's poem "La Jefita," or Rudolfo Anaya's María Luna in *Bless Me, Ultima.*

Let us now turn to another of Irigaray's symbols of female oppression, the mask of femininity, and examine its relation to the second stage of development alluded to earlier in this paper. While I have concluded elsewhere that the mother/virgin/whore symbols do not necessarily displace, but rather limit women, it should be stressed that it is through the discourse of the *Eternal Feminine* that what women are, do, and feel is displaced. It is through this discourse that woman is posed as "incidental as opposed to the essential" (de Beauvoir, 1973, xvi), as object, outside the symbolic order of culture. Woman is outside the symbolic realm, Helene Cixous argues, "because she lacks any relation to the phallus," the culturally determined "transcendental signifier," which functions as "the primary organizer of the structure of subjectivity" or of "all symbolic functioning" (1981, 546). Athena's veil, as discussed by Irigaray, then, functions as a visual component of a discursive system designed to hide the wound imprinted by her lack of the "transcendental signifier." In order to "cover" women's wound, that is, her condition of lack, man has seen to it that she not simply vanish from the phallocentric construct. He has "included" her by creating a discourse wherein lie all the attributes of the "Absolute Woman." The importance of the Absolute Woman, clothed in her veil of mystery and femininity, is that she can be posed as the "inessential," (yet essential) *Other* of Man.

In response to the growing awareness of women as full-fledged human beings, and to the negative criticism aimed at those writers who indulged in the propagation of virgin/mother/whore stereotypes, more recent Chicano novelists show a sincere attempt to break away from those limited roles and to portray women of more authentic dimensions. Alejandro Morales's *La verdad sin voz* (1975) is one such novel. In it he very consciously sets out to create some female characters who break away from stereotyped roles.[2] Margarita, for example, is a single mother who must make her own way in life. Gone are all the traces of male dependence. Instead she is depicted as a bright young woman, a good worker, in tune with her emotional and physical needs. When the opportunity presents itself to enter into an intimate relationship with Michael Logan, she does so willingly and free of the cultural baggage which, in a more tradition-bound Chicana, might manifest itself as guilt or fear of being pegged a *puta*. Caring not how others might judge her, she responds to the call of Eros, the call of life. And yet, and yet. . . We can't help but ask if she is merely a backdrop for the development of the male protagonist. Is it Margarita's role to function as a pool into which Michael Logan can narcissistically gaze at his own reflection? Do we ever get close enough to Margarita to know what motivates her actions, what she wants from life? The truth is that Margarita is everything a man could dream of in a woman—but nothing more than that dream. She is posed as the Other of the male protagonist, transfixed as object rather than subject. And as object she merely exists as the projection of someone else's needs and drives, as Athena wrapped in the veil of male-edifying alterity.

The same could be said of two female characters in Villareal's *The Fifth Horseman* (1983). Carmen and Otilia are women who are believable and interesting as characters. Carmen is the saucy and rebellious rich girl who gives herself spontaneously and selflessly to Heraclio Inez, knowing full well that her father will oppose her liaison with someone beneath her station. Motivated by deep passion, she is steadfast in her resolve to marry her father's hired hand until the latter discards her. He does so because the woman he will marry one day must be not only virtuous but humble before her man. Otilia is the smart, independent sister-in-law who understands the historical conditions which have molded the events and individuals surrounding her. Like Carmen, she is motivated by love for Heraclio and is free from fear of the traditional denigrating labels reserved for assertive women who make their desire known to men. However, these women are merely way-stations on the path of a male protagonist in his quest for self-knowledge and a destiny created by his own hand. Because they function primarily as mirrors that assure Heraclio Inez, that yes, indeed he is developing and maturing as a young man should, their own possibilities for development are thwarted. They remain trapped in the nebulous world of the inessential Other.

A third stage of development is to be found in the works of writers such as Arturo Islas, Gloria Anzaldúa, Margarita Cota-Cárdenas, Ana Castillo, to mention but a few. Of particular interest to me are the works of two writers who have been especially successful in presenting authentic female characters, not limited by their lack, or driven by their fear of lack, but rather secure in their lack, that is, in their "womanness" and in the right to be the kind of women they choose to be, thus freeing themselves from the bonds of alterity.

In Viola Barragán, Rolando Hinojosa has created a character who not only flouts tradition but who is allowed to break the bonds of silence and the bonds of propriety. The development of this character takes place gradually in the microtexts of the *Klail City Death Trip Series*. In the first two, *Estampas del valle* (1973) and *Generaciones y semblanzas* (1977), she appears as a mere skeleton of a character and her latent positive dimensions tend to be overshadowed by negative banters such as *la viuda* and *la viudita* which accomplish little more than suggest her kinship to the mate-devouring black widow spider. Actually, aside from her circumstantial involvement in Pioquinto Reyes' death—the latter dies of a heart attack while copulating with her—Viola has nothing to do with the deaths of her two husbands. These pass on quite simply as a result of *esas cosas que pasan*. Their deaths, however, do free her to improve her lot and to cross *ríos y mares* on the road to her maturation as an authentic character.

Viola is presented, from the beginning, as a spirited, independent woman who does what she does "porque le da la gana y no por comer caliente" (1973, 120). That her actions are frowned upon by *el pueblo* does not escape us. Disdain toward her, and the general view of women as sex objects, are expressed thus by the narrator: "hace veinte años fue carne de cañon de lo mejor" (1973, 118); "se retiró de su vida andariega y aventuerera" (1973, 119); "La vuidita fue reemplazada por otro cuero" (1977, 159); "La Viola se puso tan buenota como Gela pero todavía le faltaba espabilarse y ponerse como tren" (1977, 157). The narrator nonetheless, does express some admiration for Viola: "Lo del anillo, ni para que decirlo, fue un gesto de primera, un gesto de desprendimiento digno de enseñanza a los de poco corazón" (1973, 120). One is left with the notion that this parting shot represents the narrator's true feelings and that the negative comments cited above form an embedded subtext which reveals an entire community's bias toward women like Viola Barragán.

There might be those who would argue that, in his treatment of Viola Barragán, Hinojosa has resorted to highly stylized colloquial speech to elicit cheap laughs at the expense of his female characters. If this is the case, he certainly redeems himself in *Mi querido Rafa* (1981). In the first place, it is now Viola's discourse that is characterized by the bawdy sort of language used earlier to describe her: "Te apuesto que Jehú, flaco cabrón, se echó a la Sammie Jo también. Y creo que voy bien cuando digo que de ahí que se enojara la Livita San Esteban. ¡Ja! Estas muchachas que no saben nada de nada; creen que porque ellas no aflojan, que las demás no debiéramos tampoco" (1981, 64).

In portraying Viola as a successful businesswoman who adopts the crude speech of men, Hinojosa could appear to have fallen into the trap of creating a female character who imitates the worst in men, a veritable virago. I would suggest instead that Hinojosa understands that if women are to gain control of their own lives, they must invade the "sanctuaries of existing language, the treasuries where our meanings for 'male' and 'female' are themselves preserved" (Ostriker 1982, 71), if for no other reason than to demystify and disempower men's discourses about women.

In *Mi querido Rafa* Viola has not shed fully her reputation as black widow spider. In fact, Jehú subtly informs Rafa in a letter that her husband, Harmon, "se ve mal, decaído." Later we learn that he in fact has died, and Viola is once again a widow. The men in town continue to view her as a sex object; she, however, assumes the aggressive stance of subject when she tells Jehú, "lo que quiero saber flaco cabrón, es cuando te casas para darte un arrejuntón la semana antes" (1981, 27). Later we find out that she is all talk and no show: "Se asegura que lo único que se tomó enquese Viola fueron sendos vasos de te. El escritor también confiesa que lo único que se gastó en campañía de esa mujer sin par fue el tiempo" (1981, 65). One wonders if the intent here is to redeem Viola from the negative image of "aventurera" that she has gained over the years (and over the texts). Implicit in such a reading is the notion that women's engagement in non-sanctioned sex is pernicious, a world view held by those who insist on measuring women's behavior with the proverbial good/evil yardstick. *El escritor* may, of course, be saying other things, such as, that Viola has substituted business for sex, that she is over the hill, or that she is merely selective, in which case P. Galindo—in good Hinojosa ironic form—casts suspicion upon himself. At any rate, *el escritor* has no reservations in his admiration for Viola:

> ¿Qué se puede decir de este fierro sin moho? Sostenedora del *status quo ante*, del *American free enterprise system*, fiel seguidora de *laissez-faire entre nous*, amigo de sus amigos, leal y luchadora, independiente, descobardada y firme repositorio de todo lo bueno y lo malo del valle. El esc. (obvia y descaradamente admira a este ejemplo sui generis). (1981, 63)

Should we find P. Galindo's valuation of Viola Barragán a bit patronizing or distrust his sincerity, we need only examine the role she plays in this text in order to convince ourselves that Hinojosa indeed was sincere in his efforts to unveil Athena.

Hiding behind a feigned mask of objectivity, P. Galindo conducts his search for truth, listening to all opinions regarding Jehú's disappearance. However, the short-sightedness of most of the characters, thus the unreliability of their testimonies, is as obvious as each one's position on the assimilation continuum that functions as the underlying structuring devise of the microtext. As regards Viola, however, the fact that she has crossed the sea twice-over has not impaired her ability to read Anglo manipulation of raza and the latter's collusion or resistance. Viola Barragán is, in fact, on the side of "los que saben" as opposed to "los que suponen." Actually the only other person who knows the facts, is Jehú himself. P. Galindo nonetheless, seems a bit skeptical about Viola's testimony: "Aun así se complica más el caso porque Viola misma, con todo eso en su favor, no sabe si sabe todo o no" (1981, 65). We must keep in mind, however, that when *el esc* makes these judgments concerning Viola's testimony, he himself is not privy to the whole story. In fact it is much later—after he conducts the interviews—that he gains access to Jehú's letters to Rafa. The reader, however, has access to the letters the moment s/he begins to read the text, and by the time s/he reaches Viola's disclosure, it is obvious that it, in fact, does coincide—except on one minor point: the affair with Olivia—with Jehú's. It is, therefore, not Viola's testimony, but rather P. Galindo's valuation of her testimony which is unreliable. Hence, of all the interviewees, it is a female character who speaks with most authority. Consequently, in this novel, at the core of which lies an ostensibly phallocentric society in which men compete for political and economic power and women are used as pawns in the game, there is a pleasant surprise: Viola Barragán emerges as a woman who not only is in control of her own life, but as one who speaks the truth. Since *Mi querido Rafa* is based on the premise of a quest for truth, Viola becomes indispensable to P. Galindo's search and discovery. This representation of a female character is a far cry from the image of the silent women, the passive Other.

Another writer who has taken great strides in the creation of a female character who consciously struggles against the role of Other, is Sandra Cisneros. There is in *The House on Mango Street* (1983) a powerful metaphor that obviously haunts the young female protagonist. Everywhere that Esperanza looks, she sees women in tenements, sitting at windows, gazing at the world beyond, "Their sadness on an elbow" (1983, 12). This image synthesizes all the impressions of the many female *bildungsromans* in which young female characters, instead of maturing and achieving knowledge of the world, end up trapped in second childhoods, passive and dependent on husbands or lovers.

Cisneros counters the leitmotiv of women at windows, like passive portraits, with the strong-willed actions and observations of young Esperanza who "refuses to grow up like the others who lay their necks on the threshold waiting for the ball and chain" (1983, 82). And though she is motivated at a very early age by a vision of her own house, she must experience a number of rituals, either directly or through observation, which test her ability to realize that vision. A rebellious spirit inherited from her great-grandmother, "a wild horse of a woman" (1983, 12) allows Esperanza to observe, evaluate, and reject paths chosen by women of her family and her neighborhood, paths which ultimately lead to Rapunzel's prison tower. Let us examine some of those paths.

Marina, the Puerto Rican girl who is older "and knows lots of things" (1983, 27), sells Avon products while she waits for a real job downtown that will allow her to "wear nice clothes and meet someone on the subway who might marry and take her to live in a big house far away" (1983, 27). This young women remains imprinted in Esperanza's memory and when she writes, in later years, she remembers her this way: "Marina, under the street light, dancing by herself is singing the same song somewhere, I know. Is waiting for a car to stop, a star to fall, someone to change her life. Anybody" (1983, 28).

Another young girl, beautiful Sally, learns early the tricks which will enhance her femininity and buy her a one-way ticket away from her father's physical abuse. Esperanza admires Sally and views her as a role model: "Sally, who taught you to paint your eyes like Cleopatra? And if I roll a little brush with my tongue, and chew it to a point and dip it in muddy cake, the one in the little red box, will you teach me?" (1983, 77) The appeal of Sally's path, however, vanishes when Esperanza discovers that her fate is far worse than Rafaela's who drinks coconut and papaya juice (metaphors for her erotic desires) and whose husband locks her up on Tuesdays, leaving her at the window to lean "on her elbow and dream her hair is like Rapunzel's" (1983, 76). After Sally marries, Esperanza learns that she is happy except her husband "won't let her look out the window" (1983, 95).

Trials leading to sexual maturity are important components of the *bildungsroman*. In the female version, however, coming to terms with sexuality is often more difficult and painful than it is for male protagonists.

True, it is in the spirit of play that Esperanza and her friends don the symbolic accouterments of femininity. "It's Rachel who learns to walk the best all strutted in those magic heels. She teaches us to cross and uncross our legs, and to run like double-dutch rope, and how to walk down to the corner so that the shoes talk back with every step. Lucy, Rachel, me tee-tottering like so. Down to the corner where men can't take their eyes off" (1983, 39). But even in play, a lesson regarding the implications of this particular game are implicit. When "bum man" says, "If I give you a dollar, will you kiss me" (1983, 39), the young girls run away and hide the lemon and red shoes, the magic of which transformed them into objects of lascivious desire. The primeval ambience of the story called "The Monkey Garden" is a perfect setting for staging a story about the mythical loss of innocence:

> There were sunflowers big as flowers on Mars and thick cockscombs bleeding the deep red fringe of theater curtains. There were dizzy bees and bow-tied fruit flies turning somersaults and humming in the air. Sweet peach trees. Thorn roses and thistle and pears. Weeds like so

many squinty eyed stars and brush that made your ankles itch and itch until you washed with soap and water. There were big green apples hard as knees. And everywhere the sleepy smell of rotting woods, damp earth and dusty holy-hocks thick and perfumy like blue-blond hair of the dead. (1983, 87)

After Sally begins to play kissing games with the neighborhood boys in the garden, Esperanza struggles against that which Sally accepts with ease. Perhaps it is the fact that "one of the boys invented the rules" (1983, 89) that makes Esperanza so angry that she runs to tell Tito's mother that the boys are forcing Sally to kiss them. Tito's mother utters a conspiratorial "That's all?" Devastated by the discovery that she can't count on women to defend young girls, and that young girls collude in their own abuse, Esperanza lies down and cries.

And though Esperanza anticipates and dreams of erotic love— "I want to be all new and shiny. I want to sit out bad at night, a boy around my neck and the wind under my skirt" (1983, 70)— her actual initiation into sex is traumatic. Once again, Sally's failure to act in the spirit of sisterhood and her passive acceptance of sexual victimization move Esperanza to cry out in pain and disillusion: "Why did you leave me alone? I waited my whole life. You're a liar. They all lied. All the books and magazines, everything told it wrong. Only his dirty fingernails against my skin, only his sour smell again. . . . Sally, you lied, you lied" (1983, 94). The last words are uttered not only at Sally, but at all the discourses that have constructed sexuality in such a way as to include, at one end of the spectrum, romantic fantasies, and at the other, sexual violence. This is perhaps the most painful trial encountered by Esperanza on her journey to womanhood.

In *The House on Mango Street*, Sandra Cisneros presents a rare phenomenon in the Chicano novel. She makes women the central focus of the narrative and presents a firmly centered female protagonist who acts, not as the Other of a male protagonist but, rather, as a subject who dares to confront lies and to deconstruct myths. Mothers and virgins are certainly still present, as are women content in their role of the Eternal Feminine, but these are viewed with a critical eye. Are they the only roles available to Chicanas? What price have women paid for protection and dependency? Are the fairy tale castles all that they promise to be, or are they prisons? Can eroticism exist free of abuse and humiliation?

These are some of the questions that the Chicano novel, written by males or females, must continue to address if the material and spiritual reality of women is to regain primacy over discourses and symbolic constructs based on fear, half-truths, and masculinist prerogative. With *The House on Mango Street*, Sandra Cisneros invites Chicana and Chicano authors to open new horizons for female characters by allowing them to create houses of their own, houses in which they may wander like naked Athenas.

Notes

1. A Spanish version of this article, "Imágenes de la mujer en la literatura chicana," first appeared in Lia Tessorrolo Bondolfi's *Dal Mito al Mito; La Cultura d'espressione Chicana: dal mito originario al mito regeneretore*. Bergamo: Jaca Books, 1988, pp. 129-141. If some of the ideas developed in this article seem dated to today's reader, I ask that she keep in mind that this is a reprint of an article written five years ago. Chicana feminist criticism has indeed come a long way since 1987. Also, bear in mind that the specific texts chosen for analysis are not the only novels that exemplify the phenomena discussed; they are novels that are of special interest to this writer.
2. Despite his effort to create alternative roles for women, Morales unfortunately, does not free himself totally of his sexist baggage, as an appraisal of the narrator's attitude, expressed via his choice of descriptive language of Silky, will reveal. Teresa's change of heart toward Pistola Gorda, the man who rapes her, is also questionable, and is so not only from a feminist perspective.

Sexuality and Discourse:
Notes From a Chicana Survivor

Emma Pérez

> Don't remain within the psychoanalytic closure. Take a look, then
> cut through.
> —Hélène Cixous, The Laugh of the Medusa

My socialist feminist bias has spurred me in this direction. When
I was a budding graduate student in Chicana/o history and Wom-
en's history, I tried stubbornly to show that class-based movements subsumed gender.[1] While Chicano scholars argue that race
must be integrated into a class-based revolution, many Chicana
scholars defend that the secondary status given to women's issues
in a race and class-based revolution cheats the revolution (Barrera
1978; Montejano 1987; Zavella 1987; Ruiz 1987; González 1985;
Castañeda 1990). We are tired of debating the same questions that
plagued Alexandra Kollontai in Russia to Hermila Galindo in Yucatán in 1917. The global socialist movements in the early twentieth century in Europe, Russia, China, and the Americas inevitably found women forced to place gender issues as secondary to
male-defined arguments. Ironclad men assumed they knew what
was good for all workers. Women wrote and women spoke. But
they were not heard.

I turn from the socialist feminist debate and assume that those
of you reading this essay agree that the "unhappy marriage" between Marxism and feminism remains the chosen marriage given
that the alternative for feminists is capitalism, a deadly, destructive
"husband."[2] We opt for the man, who, as our mothers point out,
"sí toma hita, pero no te golpea" (yes, he drinks, but he doesn't
batter you). He is far from perfection, but as socialist feminists we
tenaciously hitch ourselves to the man we are desperate to change
to improve the marriage. This "husband" has potential if he quit
his ego-driven anxiety that defines his world on his terms. But, at

least with him, there is the potential for equality and freedom. With the capitalist, we are battered, raped, and left to die in the factories, fields, bedrooms and boardrooms. From the Marxist, we hear that "women are oppressed," as he gathers with his male cohorts, then yells to you, "hey honey, bring me another beer." Lip service is worth something, whether it's in the boardroom or the bedroom but it is not a revolution.[3]

I reassert beliefs that evolved in my young days as a radical feminist, that is, that sexuality and our symbolic reading of sexuality is the core of the *problem*. The problem: before the revolution, political, Marxist men refuse to give up their *power*, during the revolution, men refuse to give up their *power*, after the revolution, men refuse to give up their *power*.[4] And what power do we mean? Social, political, economic and yes, sexual power.

In this essay, I want to take us beyond the antiquated Marxist-feminist debate, assuming we agree that class struggle is unavoidable and assuming we agree that race-gender analysis and sexual autonomy must be the vanguard of a victorious revolution.[5] The question is, how are we going to achieve such a revolution given the strength and persistence of the patriarchy? I define my analysis of the patriarchy by invoking Freud, Lacan and Foucault, if only briefly. I take from the French feminists who deconstruct male-centered   psychoanalysis—Hélène   Cixous,   Marguerite Duras, Luce Irigaray, et al. I take from them what is useful to me, and I find their aphorisms often brilliant. Deconstructing white European feminism to reconstruct Chicana feminism may appear inorganic. It is as inorganic as taking from Marx, the quintessential white, middle class, European man, to explain the exploitation of a Chicana in the cotton fields of Texas. Consciousness is born out of one's intimate awareness of one's oppression. Theoretical models can often provide short cuts to dissect exploitation.[6] Just as Marx provided a paradigm to grasp the relationship between worker and capitalist, I claim that Luce Irigaray, particularly, and other French feminists offer a paradigm for me to interpret sociosexual relationships and hierarchical structures between and among heterosexuals, lesbians and gay men.[7]

But, where does culture, race, and colonization fit into the paradigm? Neither Marx, Freud, Lacan, nor Irigaray explain colonization and its effects upon people of color. Hence, I am drawn to writings by women of color who deconstruct the male-European tradition that has usurped our power since Columbus landed in the Americas. Gayatri Spivak dissects colonization as she deconstructs the power-wielders, Jacques Derrida, et al. She takes issue with the French feminists, and for good reason. What I hope to do, however, is to highlight the significance of sexuality to observe how sexuality is expressed for colonized people, especially women. How do we, as women of color, integrate an analysis of sexism with racism to deconstruct their pervasive ideology? How do we liberate ourselves from the sexism in our Chicano community while we combat the insipid racism in Anglo society? How do we respond to sexism within colonization, given that men of color experience racial oppression and displace their frustration on to women of color? I cannot begin to answer all these questions, but I articulate them to acknowledge the complex problems we face as women of color. I turn to French feminism to place the argument back upon sexuality, because sexuality remains an obscure controversy in our Chicana/o academic community.

I also turn to writings by radical women of color. Gloria Anzaldúa and the writers in the important document *This Bridge Called My Back* reaffirmed the organic movement that has been alive in the women of color community since the 1960s.[8] Third Woman Press, Kitchen Table Press and Arte Público Press's publications by Chicanas and Latinas, and other journals that I have not named, are vital mediums for women of color who publish work that is rejected by "mainstream" presses. My Chicana colegas de MALCS know this dilemma only too well. Chicana scholarship in mainstream feminist journals like *Signs and Feminist Studies* is grossly underrepresented. As Chicanas, we face the same problems that white women face when they attempt to publish in male-centralist journals. The arguments that men pass down to white women are passed down to us. We are forced to address issues as they define them, not as we define them. And, of course, the issue of "academic standards" haunts us. This essay does not address this publication problem directly, nor will it deconstruct writings by women of color. Indeed, our work reconstructs as much as it has always deconstructed the white-male order and white-feminist assumptions about women of color.

Ultimately, when women of color break the silence, our words are rejected. I wish to point out that our works emerge from *un sitio y una lengua* (a space and language) that rejects colonial ideology and the by-products of colonialism and capitalist patriarchy—sexism, racism, homophobia, etc. The space and language is rooted in both the words and silence of Third-World-Identified-Third-World-Women who create a place apart from white men and women and from men of color, if only for a weekend now and again.[9]

The essay has three parts: (1) it will reevaluate the Oedipal moment when men recognize they have sociosexual power, and it will amusingly speculate on how Chicano males hold that power ambivalently; (2) it will assess "the molestation memory," or "memory of origin," when girls recognize they do not have sociosexual power in relation to men; (3) after moving from male power to female powerlessness, the essay asserts female power— how Chicanas seize sociosexual power that creates our own *sitio y lengua*. So I move from deconstructing male centralist theory about women to reconstructing and affirming a Chicana space and language in an antagonistic society.

As a historian trained in Western European tradition, I ardently question white male ideology and white women's assumptions about women of color. Hence, I deviate to the French feminists with a degree of ambivalence. Theirs is not my "language" and theirs is not my history, exemplified by conquest and colonization. Indeed, Europeans acted a history as conquerors and colonizers. French feminist discourse deconstructs white-male language, but the method also builds upon what they destroy, one of the pit-falls of deconstruction. They argue for women's method and culture, yet ignore racial memory. The French feminists, however, rebel against that which I, as a Chicana historical materialist, also resist—the male symbolic order. The way the French school dismembers male dominion is what intrigues me. By scrutinizing their offerings, I attempt to supplement an analysis for Chicanas that chiefly summons sexuality and embraces sexuality's relationship to race, class and gender within our culture.

Implicitly, the analysis questions choices we make about lovers based on race, or ethnicity, class, and gender. Who do we choose to love and to have sex with, and how do we make those choices? I imagine that we each have fundamental, core issues that help us decide who to choose as our lovers. Those core issues can be traced to a precise historical moment, usually at childhood, when something occurs to push us in a particular direction.[10] Heterosexuals who choose to love heterosexually within their own race and class do so for what reasons? Because society constructed them as such or because they desire it? Or because they desire what society desired for them? Lesbians who love women within their race and class do not do so because they were socially constructed to love their own gender, or were they? Lesbians may have been constructed to reflect culture, but gender?

As I address sexuality, I also pose that pervasive homophobia constructs sociosexual power relations in society and pervasive homophobia in our Chicana/o community limits the potential for liberation and revolution. For most heterosexual Chicanos and Chicanas, internalized homophobia and bisexual ambivalence frightens them into a rigid analysis of our community and of the Chicana/o family.[11] Studies in the social sciences on the Chicana/o family which ignore the existence of alternative life-styles and "women-without-men" only serve to perpetuate Anglo perceptions about our community.

Many Euroamericans, particularly white feminists, insist that the men of our culture created machismo and they conveniently forget that the men of their race make the rules. This leads to problematic Chicana discourse within feminist constructs. When white feminists ardently insist upon discussing machismo, they impose phallocratic discourse. By "centering" and "focusing" upon the phallus, they deflect from their racism. This evasion is both racist and heterosexist.

After providing what I hope is simple criticism in simple terms, I despise mystified abstractions about the obvious, the oppression of women of color, I hope to offer simple solutions to daily antagonisms—faith and hope for our future embodied in our spoken words and in our writings.

> Men must cease to be theoretical imbeciles.
> —Margarite Duras, *New French Feminisms*

To address sexuality, discourse, and power, I digress briefly to male theoreticians who, I believe, best defined male behavior.[12] Freud, Lacan, and Foucault classify male behavior, exalt it unknowingly, but where women are concerned, these men were and are "theoretical imbeciles."

Let me begin with Freud, the omnipotent father. The Oedipal

moment is basic to his discourse. The moment occurs when a boy, the son, realizes he cannot have his first love object, his mother, because she belongs to his powerful father. He fears this man whose phallus looms larger than his. Inadequacy and fear ensue because "his" is smaller, but the son's fear swells when he realizes that his mother does not have one. Therefore he, like a woman, could dreadfully lack one, hence castration anxiety is linked to his dread of women. The son repudiates the mother and allies with the father because they both have a penis, but he still competes with this powerful father. He spends his life proving his is "bigger" and "more powerful" than any man's or than any symbolic father's.

But he also preoccupies his life with renouncing his mother at the same time that he searches for her. Hence, his Oedipal complex is never resolved, and in this fear and anxiety he acts out against women. As Luce Irigaray (1985b, 81) elucidates, "The little boy will never cease to desire his mother." His acting out, so to speak, is found repeatedly in his making a society where the laws, ideas, and customs permits him to reenact the Oedipus complex. All he has to do is give up his desire for one woman.

> Thus the—fictional—disappearance of the Oedipus complex would resolve itself into the individual's ability to make capital out of ideals and (thereby also) out of mothers, wives-mothers, laws, gazes. . . . Oedipus will have all the mothers he wants, all laws in his favor, and the right to look at anything. . .all, or most, mothers, laws, views (or at any rate points of view). Oedipus will be rich and have no complexes about it. All he has given up is the desire for a woman, for a woman's sex/organ because in any case *that had no value.* (1985b, 82)

Irigaray links capital with the persistence of the Oedipal complex. Men must reify their desire for their mother in rules, laws, and social constructs that deny women their existence. Pornography, a result of his "gaze," helps him swear that he no longer suffers from Oedipal anxiety. Women become his idea—castrated, passive, and eternally feminine in his eyes, in his gaze. As long as he can "gaze," as long as his "love of looking is satisfied, his domination is secure."[13]

Lacan (1977) imparted to us the "symbolic law of the father" entrenched in language. Language, he argues, is ensconced with symbols that dictate patriarchal power. But in his discussion he, like Freud, dismisses women, and exalts the phallus, again because women do not have "one."

The French feminists argue that Freud and Lacan place woman "outside the symbolic" . . . outside language, the law, culture, and society because she "does not enjoy what orders masculinity—the castration complex" (Cixous 1981, 46). To the French feminists, the patriarchy is a law of death, of destruction, of violence. Maleness is socially constructed to be competitive, maniacal, and violent—all rooted in the castration complex and evident in war, violence against women and children, rape, battering, sexual molestation, and nuclear weaponry shaped like penises that ejaculate death. The violent conquest of Third World people mastered. Femaleness, on the other hand, is socially constructed to be collective, intuitive, creative, life-affirming—the other.[14] But women who accept the symbolic law of the father perpetuate it and in essence become like men, women in drag.[15] They might as well be men because they defy bonding with women, allude that men are superior and therefore more worthy of their intimacy. Women, however, even when they accept the law of the father do not rape, batter, and sexually molest children in the horrendous numbers that men do. Hence, it is the symbolic phallus, the tool of oppression, reified in their guns and bombs, that reduces men to dangerous imbeciles. Their death drive tested.

Foucault, finally. Foucault transcribes historical documents to ventilate "the power of discourse." He argues that "through discourse power-knowledge is realized" (Weeks 1981, 7). Language, after all, is power. Third World people know that to learn the colonizer's language gives one access to power and privilege, albeit controlled, qualified power. As a historian, I explored Foucault because he scans the history of discourse on sexuality. I read *The History of Sexuality, Volume I* with curiosity, but soon discovered that Foucault (1978), like Freud and Lacan, spoke to men, about men, and for men in male language. In a single paragraph, Foucault "thrust" "penetrated" "rigidified" and "extended" power.[16] By the end of the page, I felt violated. Such imagery of "seminal" ideas "ejaculating" on paper made the reading painful at first and then comically apparent. Are these male theoreticians so pained with castration anxiety that they must spurt on paper at every given opportunity? It is precisely this kind of male writing and language that rapes, numbs, and dismisses female experience at every stage.[17]

Because Foucault commits his study to the *history of discourse*, he restricts himself to male-defined arenas where women are both absent and silent. Surely, he knows that, but he does not seem concerned. When he argues that the discourse changes through the centuries, I am suspicious because he informs how men's language about sexuality and power has changed. But he doesn't say this. Like Freud and Lacan, he would like women to absorb patriarchal interpretations at the expense of sanity to reconfirm hysteria. As the other, the object, and not the subject, women remain objectified in Foucault's discourse.

My impatience with Foucault, however, is in what he neglects to say *The History of Sexuality*.[18] While in the last chapter, he finally discusses power and its relationship to sexuality, he overlooks the obvious. Like male theoreticians who build abstractions to mask the simple, he does not say: men, especially European white men, hold political, social, racial, and sexual power over women; and men use that power throughout history to control women and to sustain patriarchal power. *Punto.* Is this premise transhistorical? Is it cross-cultural? Yes and no. Every aberration of sexual abuse against women and children of all races and men of color has its historical antecedents.[19] This, I believe, is a point of departure for women historians.[20] For Chicana historians, we begin with what Foucault does not say.[21]

Why can't Foucault declare the obvious? Because he is blinded by his privilege, his maleness, or because he cannot chip away at his own power? Surely, it's not that simple. But I cannot spurn Foucault so easily. Again, as a historian, I appreciate his historical specificity, because within his constructs he forces me to ask if indeed patriarchal power is transhistorical. And, is the Oedipal complex transhistorical and transcultural? Is it useful to Chicanas writing history when sexuality is so inextricably enmeshed in our history of conquest and colonization? The question leads to the next section.

As an aside, I acknowledge that male theoreticians, whether Marxist, deconstructionists, or traditional social scientists, often dismiss feminists and our analysis as bias, especially if the analysis is from radical women of color. I invert that arrogance to dismiss most male perspectives about women because they are much too self-indulgent to comprehend our oppression—that intimate place where theory is born. Men of color understand their own tyranny just as white working-class men potentially understand their class exploitation, but many working-class men and men of color refuse to take that sensitivity to its logical conclusion where women are concerned. Working class men of color often bond with white men based on patriarchal privilege even though white men do not see them as equals. They (men of color) are eager to please the father (white man) who despises him and that the man of color also despises and fears. This leads to the next section where I invert Mexican male philosophy about la india and I hand it back as offensively as it has been handed to us.[22]

El Chingón: Octavio Paz and the Oedipal-Conquest-Complex

> The worst kind of betrayal lies in making us believe that the Indian woman in U.S. is the betrayer.
> —Gloria Anzaldúa, *Borderlands/La Frontera*

Perhaps Lacan is to French Feminists what Paz is to Chicanas. Inevitably, we invoke Paz's *Labyrinth of Solitude*, where he unites us metaphorically with *La Chingada*, La Malinche.[23] We react, we respond repeatedly to his misogyny. But, misogyny alone is not what we contest. We dispute a historically specific moment which denigrates us, immortalizes us as "the betrayer" for all time, eternally stuck in an image, *la puta*, the whore. Long before the arrival of the Virgen de Guadalupe, we were *La Chingada*. The metaphor cuts to the core of each Chicana; each mestiza is flaunted as the India/whore. Worse yet is that the India is our mother and Paz slashed away at her beauty. He subordinates our first love object by violently raping her in historical text, in male-language.

To Paz, the Aztec princess Malinche "gave" herself to Hernán Cortés, the symbol of Spanish Conquest, therefore, Paz charges her with the downfall of Mexico. In Paz, we have the symbolic son, the mestizo, repudiating the symbolic father, Cortés. The Oedipal triangle is completed by *la india* that they both raped and tamed, literally and metaphorically. Malinche, the "other," the inferior, disdainful female was not worthy of marrying, so Cortés passed her down to a soldier. With the soldier Jaramillo, Malinche bore the first mestizos. For Paz, *la india* personifies the passive whore who acquiesced to the Spaniard, the conqueror, his symbolic father—the father he despises for choosing an inferior woman who begat an inferior race, and the father he fears for his powerful phallus.

Paz's essay reveals more about his own castration complex than about Malinche. Obsessed with *chingar*, he expounds upon a theory to explain the inferiority-complex of mestizos/as. But self-hate, the internalized racism with which Paz must contend, emanates. After all, the mighty Cortés was the white Western European male conqueror, the symbol of power that Paz was a step away from, not just as the son, but more importantly as the bastard mestizo son. Paz exhibits his own internalized racial inferiority. He holds far less power than that of his symbolic white father, *el conquistador*. On the other hand, his hatred of women, *las chingadas*, and all that is female, symbolically begins with this Oedipal-conquest-triangle. Here, the sexual, political, social, and psychological violence against *la india*—the core of the Chicana—is born. This core has been plundered from us through conquest and colonization. We reclaim the core for our woman-tempered *sitio y lengua*.

Lacan's symbolic order of "language and meaning" (Weeks 1981, 3-4) is epitomized in the Oedipal-conquest-triangle when the mestizo enters the pained moment of castration anxiety, but for the mestizo male the entry into the symbolic order is even more confusing because he does not know the white father's language. He cannot even guess at the meaning of symbols between himself and his conquering/colonizing father. Cultural differences divide *el español y el indio*, who were thrown together at the moment of Spanish Conquest and who misunderstand each other's symbols and language.[24]

Mestizos/as master the conquerer's language as the language of survival, but it never belongs to the conquered completely. For people whose language has been swindled twice, first the Native tongue, then the appropriated tongue, we are forced to stumble over colonizer language. As an adult, the Chicano male is perceived as the powerless son of the white Oedipal father who makes laws in his language. (African American men referred to as "boy" by white men and women reduces them to this symbolic son, but African American history of conquest and enslavement is unlike ours and I am in no position to conjecture.) Within a racist society, the mestizo male is a castrated man in relation to the white-male-colonizer father. His anxiety is not only reduced to the fear of losing it, but also to the fear that his will never match the supreme power of the white man's. While the white son has the promise of becoming the father, the mestizo, even when he becomes the father, is set apart by his skin color and by a lack of language, the dominant language of the colonizer. Moreover, he must repudiate *la india y la mestiza* for fear that he could be like her, a weak, castrated betrayer of his people. Hence, he colludes with the white-colonizer-father as they both condemn la Chicana.

The conquest triangle dictates the sexual politics of miscegenation in the twentieth century. For example, Chicanos are usually incensed when Chicanas marry the "enemy"—white men. They, on the other hand, practice male prerogative and marry white women to defy, and collaborate with, the white father, and in having half-white children move their sons a step closer to the relations of power—the white-colonizer father. For the Chicana who marries the white male, she embraces the white Oedipal-colonizer ambivalently, because now she has access to power theoretically, but practically she is perceived as *la india* once again. She is not her half-white children, nor will she ever be. Her half-white sons will always have more power than she could imagine. Certainly, the same principle applies to the Chicano with a white wife, but his male privilege has already granted him rank that a Chicana cannot earn. The daughter of a white male and a Chicana has the father's white name to carry her through racist institutions, placing her closer to power relations in society.[25]

Paz's phallocratic discourse casts the Oedipal-conquest-triangle. The triangle symbolizes sociosexual-racial relations between Chicanos and Chicanas and among the white women and white men who oversee the dilemma. It is a metaphor which dictates sociosexual-racial relations. That the Oedipal moment is historically or culturally inaccurate is not the issue here. The point is that it is a symbol unconsciously perceived by Paz, who imposed the psychodrama of conquest upon the Chicano, who in turn inflicts misogyny in the image of "La Malinche" upon Chicanas/Mexicanas. But Paz cannot be held responsible for the conquest, he merely interprets history from masculinist ideology.

The law of the white-colonizer-father conditions our world in the late twentieth century. Our challenge is to rebel against the

symbol of the white father and affirm our separation from his destructive ideology to create a life-affirming *sitio*. But before defying
the law of the father, it is necessary to understand why we are so
stuck and so addicted to the perpetrator of destruction. Why do
we uphold the law of the white-colonizer-European father, knowing the extent of damage and pain for Chicanas and Chicanos?
For example, Chicanos who absorb the white-colonizer father's
ways hierarchically impose those laws on Chicanas. Those Chicanos become a caricature of the white-colonizer father. One has
only to look at any institution where Chicanos have been integrated to see how much many of them emulate the white father
and exclude women, especially women of color.[26]

Breaking the Addiction/Dependency Cycle
to Patriarchal Power

> He has no desire for woman to upset him in his sexual habits. . .
> his rather suspect respect for law and order. He does not want her
> to be anything but *his daughter*, whose gratifying fantasies of seduc-
> tion it is his task to interpret, and who must be initiated into, and
> curbed by, the "reasonable" discourse of his (sexual) law. Or else
> he wants her to be *his mother*, whose erotic reveries he would take
> some pleasure in hearing, whose most secret intimacy he would fi-
> nally gain access to. Unless again some very "unconscious" *homo-
> sexual* transference is tied in there, sotto voce.
> —Luce Irigaray, *Speculum of the Other Woman*

In his theater production, *Corridos*, Luis Valdéz reenacts a provoc-
ative corrido about father/daughter incest.[27] Why Valdéz elected
to depict the corrido fascinates me, but what also intrigues me is
his presentation. He almost condones the arrangement, and he
seems titillated by the possibility. Valdéz's "Delgadina" is an in-
sightful vehicle into the patriarchy, but more importantly, it reveals the dynamic between perpetrators and victims who create
the addictive, dependent cycle between the powerful and the powerless. Like the preceding works by male centralist theorists, the
production exposes Valdéz's castration anxiety through his
"gaze," his male definition and interpretation of the feminine.

I use the corrido to examine and defy Freud's "Electra complex," the inverse of the Oedipal complex. Freud hypothesized the

Electra complex to explain a daughter's recognition that she cannot have her father. But just as Freud could not establish how a
daughter transferred desire for her mother as her first love object
to her father, so she could embrace heterosexuality, I believe, like
many feminists, that he expunged patriarchal law to justify waver-
ing transference. Hence, he rationalized his desire for the daughter's transference.

Patriarchal law dictates the tacit language and behavior of incest, which places fear in the daughter's psyche. At some point,
she unconsciously recognizes the supreme phallus' potential to
harm her psyche. Freud did not consider that even the remotest
possibility of incest victimized the daughter. Her questions according to Freud: Does she repudiate her mother to embrace the father and to be impregnated by him as a substitute for the penis
she was not born with? Does the little girl turn to the father to embrace "normal" femininity? Or, what Freud would not conjecture
was her desire to remain attached to her first love object, her
mother. But, wouldn't this lead to a woman-loving culture? Or
worse yet, lesbianism? wouldn't this press heterosexual women to
examine their bisexual ambivalence?—their occasional desire for
women while gripping the law of the father? (Irigaray 1985b, 72;
Ponce 1989)

The "Delgadina" corrido symbolizes a daughter's painful en-
trance into the law of the father. Her name *de* in Spanish, meaning "belonging to," "a man's possession," is worth nothing.

Briefly, the corrido tells the story of a beautiful young woman
named Delgadina whose father watches her dance by the moon-
light, craves her, and then decides to pounce. As they walk home
from church one day, he commands her to be his lover. When she
refuses, he jails her in a tower (phallic) and waits for her to succumb. While in the tower, she is denied food and water as punishment because she disobeys the father. She begs her mother, her
brother, and her sister for food, water, and to release her from her
prison. Each one fears violating the father's order, his sexual laws,
so they each ostracize Delgadina. Her mother and her sister, who
are "an integral part of a phallic masculine economy" (Fouque
1980, 117), betray her. And yet, what is their alternative? For
women need a moment, a specific moment of consciousness when
they can separate from the law of the father into their own *sitio y
lengua*. Delgadina has nowhere to turn and eventually dies from

hunger for nourishment, for freedom. Her father, a broken man, is left with the memory of never having consummated sex with this young alluring love object—his daughter.

Unlike La Malinche, Delgadina does not succumb. Indeed, she dies a virgin. She is betrayed by an entire social structure that pretends, blinds itself, keeps the secret in disbelief that the father could rape his daughter, or have the desire to. But behavior and language are basic to sexual molestation. A sign, a word, a gesture can be as damaging as penetration by the penis. Patriarchal laws ignore behavior and language when litigating upon cases of molestation. For it is men who dictate that the penis must be present, armed and ready, to penetrate, and it must penetrate before male laws can consider that harm was done. For Delgadina, her psyche was penetrated.

But Valdéz chose to tell us this story—to peek into taboo, to peer into a "secret"—a father's sexual arousal by a young woman —his daughter. This is voyeurism, male gaze asserted. Like Hollywood's pornographic films, Valdéz eroticizes women's victimization to appeal to his male audience. All this is not beside the point. To eroticize the father/daughter incestuous relationship implicitly grants permission to older men who seek young women as lovers and marriage partners. Within this relationship is the reassertion of male sexual power over a younger woman who could very likely be his daughter. Society condones the older man/younger woman relationship, in fact, envies the man who successfully catches one. A younger woman, after all, gives complete adoration, at first. Indeed, there are historical roots to older man, younger woman arrangements. In colonial California the Catholic Church and the Spanish-Mexican settlers colluded when the Church condoned marriages between old men and young women, e.g. uncles and nieces, to keep property within the family (Castañeda 1990, Chapt. 5).

But something else occurs in the corrido that was sung and passed down before Valdéz immortalized it. The corrido does not just pass down the incest taboo to warn against it. The song tells us about a young woman's death when she challenges the sexual law of the father. She cannot, however, break from the law, happy and free to join with women who believe her, or a community who will allow her to be. There is no such community. Instead, a male-centralist society with male-identified women cannot even hear her language, her pain. They just know they cannot defy the father.

But Delgadina does not have the opportunity to resist the father because by the time he commands her to be his lover, the incestuous language and behavior was in motion. The "molestation" was parodied in her perpetrator's behavior hence leading to her "memory of molestation," which by social definition did not occur because physical touch and penis penetration did not occur. But in her memory it happened. The behavior, inappropriate for a father, to say the least, was not challenged by her mother, her sister, or her brother. Not by anyone.

The addictive/dependency cycle had already begun for both of them (Kasl 1989; Shengold 1989). When she tried to break from it, however, she found no support. Like Delgadina, women live in this cycle of addiction/dependency to the patriarchy that has ruled women since the precise historical moment that they become aware that women's bodies are sexually desired and/or overpowered by the penis. A young girl fears its power and tries herself to tame it, manipulate it, adore it, loathe it or ignore it, but in effect she must deal with it in some way. She may feel any variety of emotions toward the tool of oppression, but envy is not one of them. For why should she envy that which symbolically destroys?

This reminder, this memory of molestation, a memory of origin, haunts the young girl even through womanhood. Indeed, the sexual molestation memory dictates sexual desire. Either women/men repudiate the molester/perpetrator or they embrace him/her, most commonly him. Or, victims continue to repudiate and embrace the perpetrator in a persistent pattern through relationships until that addictive/dependent cycle is broken. Not until victims resist the perpetrator and have the courage to abandon the pattern, not until women and men stop assigning the perpetrator power, can women and men finally abandon phallocentric law and order.

When will those of us trying to make a revolution finally let go of these capitalist-patriarchal notions of sexual law and order which dictate a perpetrator/victim dynamic? When will we embrace the real, yet ideal notions of the collective, to work together for the common good? For within capitalist patriarchal ideology, there is no place for the sensitive human being who is willing to transform the world. "If I am the world, and I heal myself, then I heal the world." These are personal, private revolutions, each member of the collective taking responsibility for her/his contradictions within the collective, willing to grapple with the question, "Who am I exploiting?"

Both women and men are addicted to the very thing that destroys them—the patriarchy within capitalist constructs in the late twentieth century. And the sociosexual relations between men and women condoned by the patriarchy are inherently unhealthy and destructive most of the time. Of course, gay men and lesbians who mimic the heterosexual arrangement inherit patriarchy's problems. The dynamic begins, I argue, in the collective memories of Western European conquerors and people of color who are subdued with the memory of the Oedipal-conquest-triangle.

To answer my question at the beginning of this essay, how are we ever to achieve a successful revolution/movement, given the strength and persistence of the patriarchy? At a certain level, the answer lies within this addictive pattern. Perhaps we must begin by modifying our behavior to change destructive patterns today, immediately, with the hope of raising children who do not have to appropriate society's addiction in order to survive. The individual is responsible to the collective, after all. To heal oneself within the collective, heals the collective. But that is only one small integral step. There is much more to do.

Sitos y lenguas

> But what if the "object" started to speak? Which also means beginning to "see," etc.
> —Luce Irigaray, *Speculum of the Other Woman*

> When we speak in a liberatory voice we threaten even those who may initially claim to want our words. . .in the process of learning to speak as subjects, we participate in the global struggle to end domination.
> —bell hooks, *Talking Back*

Un día, mi gëlita me preguntó, ¿Cómo le hablas a tu mamá, de Usted o de tú? Mi mamá le contestó, "Yo no le enseñé de Usted, amá." Curious about their private quarrel, I witnessed how my mother defied her mother and how my grandmother questioned the manner in which her daughter raised her own daughter. Did I respect my elders in the tradition that our culture passes down through language? Or, had I become so *agringada*, so assimilated that I spoke the disrespectful language of a younger generation so imbued with the colonizer's ways?

Like many tejanas/os who attended Anglo schools through grade school, I too was punished for speaking my parent's tongue on playgrounds and classrooms (Anzaldúa 1987). Spanish set my brother and me apart. Anglo teachers peered at us when we spoke Spanish, the way white women peer at me now when they try to interfere in a circle of Chicanas speaking together in Spanglish, reaffirming our mestizaje. As a child in Anglo schools, I realized quickly that I had to learn English, to pronounce it accurately, precisely. I was ridiculed for my accent, I was pushed into dark closets, disciplined for calling a student *gringo*. I practiced at night, staring up at the ceiling in my bedroom, reciting the alphabet. In English. Forgetting *la lengua de mi gente*. Not knowing that the loss of language is loss of memory.

A white lesbian feminist tells me she is offended with my use of the word *gringa*. She tells me she is not a *gringa*. She tells me that if I continue to use that word that she cannot be my friend. I think back to the *gringitas* in my classrooms, the ones the Anglo teachers treated with respect, the ones who stared down at my tanned skin, the ones who ridiculed my accent.

I rage at her arrogance. I rage at her white-skin prerogative, her middle-class dilemma. I rage at her doctrine of reverse racism. She tells me my rage frightens her. Can't we be polite, woman-loving about this? She has just insulted my racial memory. Her implication: there's no room for anger in a feminist community that heals from verbal abuse. My anger about the pain and abuse of racial violence is inappropriate when it is against her. Why can't I take care of her and tell her kindly that she rapes my racial memory just as a perpetrator rapes his victim. Let's do this on my terms, in my language, in my Anglo world, she says implicitly. I'm not a *gringa*, that's a pejorative term, she shrieks.

You're a *gringa*, I thunder. You're white. You will never know how it feels to have brown skin and a Mexican name. You will never know what it is like to watch your mother struggle with white words. You cannot tell me how to define who you think you are to me. You cannot tell me what to think of you.

How many times have I lived this scene, have I repeated these words to Anglos who invade my space, who silence my words.

My boundaries. El Río Bravo was once a life-giving stream that my ancestors crossed to travel north or to journey south. Back and forth, completing cycles. The river was not a boundary. *Gringos/as* built boundaries, fences, for themselves while they invaded our space, our boundaries. The boundaries that I draw to sustain my sanity. We cannot be friends as long as you think you know every part of who I am, as long as you think you can invade my space and silence my language, my thoughts, my words, my rage. *Mi sitio y mi lengua.* Invasion, a deceitful intimacy. The perpetrator wields power over the victim. The colonizer over the colonized. Sexual-racial violence mirrored in language, in words. A speculum of conquest to "penetrate" further.

If discourse reveals the history of sexuality, then women of color face an obstacle. We have not had our own language and voice in history. We have been spoken about, written about, spoken at but never spoken with or listened to. Language comes from above to inflict us with western-white-colonizer ideology. We speak our history to each other now just as our ancestors used oral tradition. A tradition which is minimized. We must write in accomplished English to legitimate our work. We must master the language of the colonizer before our studies are read. *Gringos y gringas* censure our real language which is often born from rage.

The colonizer's language. The French feminists do not recognize my concerns. Marguerite Duras alludes to sexual power relations between an upper class Chinese man and a poor French girl in her novel *The Lover* (1985). Duras wrote alluring, crisp prose about a fifteen and one-half-year-old French girl, whose country colonized Indochina. She tells the story about the Chinese lover and the young French girl. She writes about the way her brothers, European, and older than she, disregard the Chinese man. Treat him as if he is absent, yet they take his money. She takes his money. The narrator, I suspect, recognizes this older Chinese man as an anomaly like herself. She is a woman, the only girl in her family. She is the "other." He is Chinese in a region now overrun by French colonizers. He can speak her language, French, in the colonized land. He too is the "other."

But Duras packs her story with implication. He, a man twice her age, wants sex and love with a child. She is only fifteen-and-one-half-years-old and she goes to rooms with him, sensing the differences between them, their culture, their age, but she tests first love with him, and she needs his money.

I wonder about the Chinese wife the Chinese lover marries, and how she must feel that her Chinese husband still loves the "other," the colonizer, the white skin of indulgence. We know that the narrator envisions the Chinese wife crying because her husband's heart is with the narrator, the French girl. But the Chinese woman is silent, almost absent, just a grieving consequence. She is the extreme "other," the marginal "other." She is someone who cannot understand why her husband loves this French girl. But, for me, the silence of the marginal other burns in my memory. She understands everything. The colonizer is with them in bed, the memory of white flesh pressed between them.

Sometimes, I sense that Anglo women who marry Chicanos must feel some sense of power and equality with men of color. They share an "otherness." They are not marginal others like women of color. She is a woman with white skin together with a man with brown skin. Perhaps they sense social balance in an incredibly imbalanced society. But I can only assume, because I am neither a Chicano nor a white woman. It's only love, after all. Where do we draw boundaries in bed? In sex? How do we interpret sociosexual-racial politics in bed? Rhetorically speaking, of course.

This anxiety that *gringos* have. It is a colonizer-conqueror-anxiety, ridden with guilt about their ancestors' sins. Sometimes, some of them recognize that they inherited the sins of their fathers and mothers and those sins have afforded them this land called the Southwest, this continent called America. Colonizer-castration-anxiety, we can even call it. They fear that Third World people will take from them what they stole and continue to steal—our language, our culture, so they can mirror themselves in us. Force us to become like them, just as the male symbolic order anxiously appropriates and denies the female for fear that he will be like her, without the powerful penis, without his dominant culture as the gauge for all others. Like eating *fajitas* at Jack-in-the-Box or nouvelle *enchiladas*. Appropriate from us to make us more palatable, to continue to conquer and colonize every piece of our differences. You are like me and I am like you. We are all human beings, they would have us believe. We are the same. Just as Irigaray (1985b,

27) points out that male culture desires a woman who mimics him, white society desires Third World people to mimic the colonizers. Our land, our dignity, our rights absorbed by their omnipotent power everywhere we turn. To assuage their guilt, they want to co-opt us, make us like them. Assimilation is their best fantasy. It is best for them when we are light-skinned, but better still when Chicanos/as are half-white and half-Chicano/a. That places half-breeds closer to Anglo language and culture. But these false privileges, many recognize for what they are, a token, a *maldición*.

But to deny the phallus sociosexual power, to deny the *gringo/a* cultural dominance. To revere the Chicana. To invert all power. To love myself and other Chicanas and women of color for who we have always been and continue to be. That is the revolution I speak now.

I phone my mother, I say, "Mom, me peleé con una gringa." "¿Sí hita? Eres tan peleonera." She laughs. We both know she and my father taught me to fight, to have pride for a culture that *gringos* misunderstand.

When I entered the first grade, I cried each day after school. I lay my head on my mother's lap, a woman who was denied the right to read and write the language of the colonizer in a land that belonged to her ancestors. She brushed my hair back, comforting me. I couldn't articulate what I say so easily now. I couldn't say that the woman who comforted me, the woman who held power, beauty, and strength in my eyes, that Anglos dismissed her because she couldn't fill out their damn forms. I couldn't say that the school was infested with white students, so alien to me. And that day the white teacher shoved me against a wall because I didn't recite the "Pledge of Allegiance." I didn't know it. But I knew "El Rancho Grande."

My mother would sing songs to me, Chicana lullabies. "Cielito Lindo" was my favorite. I stared up at her, making *tortillas*, singing. She was my *cielito lindo*. *"Canta y no llores, porque cantando te alegras, cielito lindo, mis calzones."* We sang the last word together and I giggled at what I thought was our private joke.[28]

I seek faithful allies. I have no enemies. I do not perceive white feminists, white men, heterosexuals, or even Chicano males as adversaries. But I see you, who hold sociosexual-racial power, as the subject who objectifies the marginal other—me. Often, I sense you as invasive, conquering and colonizing my space and my language. You attempt to "penetrate" the place I speak from with my Chicana/Latina *hermanas*. I have rights to my space. I have boundaries. I will tell you when you cross them. I ask that you respect my request. At times, I must separate from you, from your invasion. So call me a separatist, but to me this is not about separatism. It is about survival. I think of myself as one who must separate to my space and language of women to revitalize, to nurture and be nurtured. Then, I can resurface to build the coalitions that we must build to make the true revolution—all of us together acting the ideal, making alliances without a hierarchy of oppression. Anglo men and women, heterosexuals, white feminists, men of color, women of color, gay men, lesbians, lesbians of color, etc.

I prefer to think of myself as one who places women, especially Third World women and lesbians, in the forefront of my priorities. I am committed to women's organizations because in those spaces we revitalize, we laugh, we mock the oppressor, we mock each other's seriousness and we take each other seriously. This is a process of support, this is living the ideal, if only momentarily, to give, to nurture, to support each other in a racist, sexist, homophobic Western society. I speak at this moment of historical consciousness as a Chicana survivor who has survived much more than I speak of here, just as we, women of color survive daily. I know that with women of color, particularly lesbians of color, I re-enact the best times that I had as a child, trusting my mother and playing with my sisters and my brother while watching my father battle racism.

I give these words to you now. Like a gift. I tell you who and what I am. This is the gift I offer. Do you understand? *Ya no me van a robar mi sitio y mi lengua.* They live inside my soul, with my mother, my sisters, *mis hermanas del tercer mundo*.

But as Lacan was quick to point out, this is not the whole truth. We can only tell half-truths. No one can know all that another is. Culture denies that. The limitation of language denies that. The signifier, the object, lost in a memory, lost in colonization, but reified in my *hermandad*. We, the subjects, write; we, the subjects, speak. But, do you listen? Can you hear?

Notes

1. In an essay that I wrote in 1982 on the Mexican anarchist group *Partido Liberal Mexicano*, I argued that the nationalist class-based movement placed women-workers' exploitation in the forefront, but dismissed their oppression in the home and in their sociosexual relationships with the male leaders of the organization. The essay should have been published years ago, but "political" circumstances delayed it. In light of current debates spawned by deconstructivists, this essay is dated but perhaps useful because it analyzes the gender ideology within nationalist class-based movements. See Emma Pérez. "A La Mujer: A Critique of the Mexican Liberal Party's Ideology on Women," in *Between Borders: Essays on Mexicana/ Chicana History*, ed. Adelaida Del Castillo (Los Angeles: Floricanto Press, 1990), 459-82. Also refer to my 1988 dissertation, "Through Her Love and Sweetness: Women, Revolution and Reform in Yucatán, 1910-1918." Again, I point out that in a region where socialism was attempted, women's issues were only brought to the forefront to benefit a male political arena.

2. Heidi Hartmann's essay (1981) elucidates the antiquated, unresolved debate. I refuse to identify myself as a "Marxist" and prefer "socialist" because Marxist identifies one with a male, Mr. Karl Marx. While I sanction Mr. Marx's theories and writings, I prefer to call my method a socialist feminist or historical materialist one.

3. Chicano Studies departments that have existed for ten years or more and still have not hired and tenured Chicanas are embarrassments to our community. Lip service.

4. Julia Kristeva (1977) discussed her hope for Chinese women and China's potential for a different revolution that acknowledged women. She found a strong, female affirming atmosphere in China. That was before the massacre in Tiananmen Square in 1989. Kristeva, however, reevaluated her Marxism before this massacre. Within weeks of the Tiananmen Square debacle, the women in Nicaragua suffered a blow to their movement when President Daniel Ortega urged them to place women's issues aside for the revolution, as if women's struggle and the revolution are mutually exclusive. The same time-worn debates.

5. I owe my development of socialist feminist theory to works by Juliet Mitchell, particularly *Women's Estate* (1973), still a superb little book and Michèle Barrett's, *Women's Opression Today* (1988), where she discusses the significance of gender ideology. Numerous socialist feminist writings generated my analysis, but in my Chicana community, historians Deena González, Antonia Castañeda and the Chicana scholars of MALCS help me to imagine our specific, organic movement, especially through our organization. MALCS, *Mujeres Activas en Letras y Cambio Social*, was founded

in 1982 in Northern California by a handful of Chicana academicians eager to affirm our Chicana network within the University.

6. As a historical materialist, I am aware that theory follows practice, but as a socialist feminist I probe theory to apply what is useful and disregard the rest.

7. I agree with Leslie Wahl Rabine, who argues that "Lacanian psychoanalysis is, I think, of greater interest and use to feminist theory than Derridean deconstruction, and, not surprisingly, feminists have a much more intense relation of ambivalence and outrage to this theory" (1988, n. 25). For me French feminists' deconstruction of Lacanian psychoanalysis is useful for feminist theory on sexuality. I also want to point out the importance of Gayatri Chakravorty Spivak's deconstructive essays on colonialism and feminism. For the purpose of this essay, I rely on theoreticians who discuss sexuality directly. For me that is Luce Irigaray. I believe Irigaray's examination of sexuality may provide lesbians with a language to decode our oppression, then invert the language with our command.

8. In the late 1970s, I was revitalized by the women in the organization, Lesbians of Color, active in Los Angeles from about 1978 to 1982. We were a network of Latina and Black lesbians who marched in political rallies and supported each other through daily endeavors (Moraga and Anzaldúa 1983).

9. I use this term, *un sitio y una lengua*, to emphasize that as Chicanas we have always had this space and language, however we assert it now in our exclusive organizations for women of color. For Chicana academicians, the organization is, of course, MALCS, where we create for each other.

10. I realize this is ambiguous, but what I mean to say is that I believe that we can each remember a childhood memory that either drew us to, or pulled us away from, people who could be a "love object." This is not a judgment or criticism about people's choices, but rather an explanation, a Chicana lesbian historical materialist explanation. I have discussed these core issues at length with Deena González and Antonia Castañeda and we hope to publish our conjectures soon.

11. To quote Latina feminist, Lourdes Arguelles, "the person today who is homophobic is a criminal." From her panel discussion on "Latinas and AIDS" at the National Association for Chicano Studies, Los Angeles, 31 March-2 April 1989.

12. I use the definition of discourse put forth by the editors Elaine Marks and Isabelle De Courtivron in *New French Feminisms* (1980). Discourse is "the relation between language and the object to which it apparently refers," e.g. how women have been written about.

13. "Gaze," in Freud's terms, "As phallic activity linked to the anal desire for sadistic mastery of the object." The "love of looking," and the sadistic male, are hence linked to violence in pornography (Moi 1985, 134;

Irigaray 1895b, 47).

14. I want to stress that the French feminists are not arguing that "biology is destiny" anymore than Freud or Lacan argue this. The value of their work is that they understand that female and male are socially constructed. British Marxist-feminist Juliet Mitchell best argued this in her study, *Psychoanalysis and Feminism* (1974), and she was chided for her position in the 1970s. I think we are closer to accepting the value of psychoanalysis in that it provides an understanding of the male-symbolic-order—the Patriarchy. I argue that an examination of the Oedipal triangle and the primal scene can release us finally from its enslavement, from women's and men's addiction/dependency to the patriarchy.

15. Xaviere Gauthier, "Is there Such a Thing as Women's Writing?" in *New French Feminisms* (1980, 162). Gauthier argues that women accept the phallic system to "find their place in male language, law, grammar, syntax." They become "completely divorced from themselves without knowing it." They go crazy denying themselves to accommodate male definitions of what women should be—more like men but still unlike them. The double-messages and double-binds make us appear irrational and hysterical.

16. I read the English translation (1978, 48), therefore the translator may be the culprit. The original may or may not be far from its English translation, but it is disconcerting that the translation should read as such.

17. I am reminded of a male friend who asked if I enjoyed the film, *Dangerous Liaisons*. I responded that I thought it was misogynist, to which he queried, "But, didn't you enjoy it?" He may have well have said "Forget the fact that it was a rape, didn't you enjoy it anyway." I refuse to indulge myself in Hollywood's interpretation of male-female sexual power relations. Even when Hollywood attempts to make a "feminist" film like *The Accused*, about a woman's brutal gang-rape, the filmmakers rely on the fact that the male audience will practice their "gaze," not at all interested in the weak feminist message.

18. Perhaps he clarifies this omission in the other volumes, but I doubt that he appropriates a feminist analysis.

19. The fusion of sex and power is the basis, the foundation for violence against all women and children and men of color. Lynchings, whippings, beatings, and murder of black and brown-skinned men must also be addressed when discussing sexual power relations. I will not do so at any length but I recognize the sociohistorical brutality against men of color and how this damages their psyche and the psyche of our community. When men of color become perpetrators against women and children, and many do, I lose compassion and patience, however.

20. Linda Gordon has written an excellent study about child abuse in the nineteenth-century United States, a different aberration from late twentieth-century sexual molestation cases.

21. Historian Deena González argues, "If we conceptualize most history as written by white males from a white male perspective, then we must start with the premise that it is all biased history." I agree with González's premise that Chicana historians are forced to deconstruct what has been written before we can reconstruct our own history. Small wonder that our work takes longer to produce (Mitchell 1989, 17).

22. For those of you who are already incensed with my use of the Oedipal complex to explain Spanish conquest, I ask that you remain patient and remember that this is about a process which looks at psychoanalysis to move on and away from it ultimately.

23. I refer of course to his chapter on "La Chingada" where he denigrates the Aztec princess, Malintzin Tenepal (1961, 65-88). Adelaida del Castillo's criticism (1977) of Paz's ahistorical account of Malintzin still stands up well. I will not reiterate this history, I assume most already know it. Many Chicana scholars have responded to Paz's misogyny at some point. To list all of the essays, publications, and private gripes is a pointless exercise. Take my word for it. Or, ask any Chicana about Paz's *chingada*. I do recommend Norma Alarcón's essay (1983), "Chicana Feminist Literature: A Re-vision Through Malintzin/or Malintzin: Putting Flesh Back on the Object." Alarcón (1989) argues, and I agree, that we must also delve into the psychosexual exploitation of women of color along with exposing economic exploitation.

24. Tzetvan Todorov (1982) explains the significance of symbols as miscommunication between Spaniards and the Aztecs. Spaniards assumed they understood Aztec symbols and actions and, of course, they did not.

25. Skin color, however, plays an important factor for half-breeds. The lighter the skin, the more possible it is to pass through doors of power and privilege. Of course, skin color gradations do not just apply to half-breeds, but when one has the white skin and the white name of a white father and a mestiza for a mother, then one is likely to have access to more power in a racist society. What one does with that power politically is a different issue altogether and not one I wish to debate. Of course, class status is also a prominent factor to consider in these matchings.

26. For Chicanos, their maleness, offers them the male language since childhood. They must learn to master the colonizer male dialogue, however.

27. Chicana scholars in literature and theater have criticized Valdéz's negative, one-dimensional depiction of women in his productions. I am interested in examining his choice as a symbol which perpetuates the law of the father (Broyles-González 1990).

28. Most of you know that the word in the song is "corazones," hearts, and that it was a fun joke to sing "calzones," underwear. Hah, what do you think of that Dr. Freud?

Political, Social and
Historical Narratives of
Identity and Difference

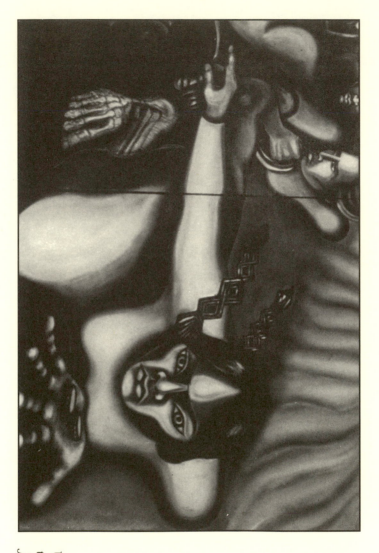

Uprising of
the Mujeres
Judith Baca

Presidarias y Pobladoras: The Journey North and Life in Frontier California

Antonia I. Castañeda

In the chilling, pre-dawn hours of 21 December 1773, Ana María Hurtado and her two daughters, twenty-year-old Cipriana and eighteen-year-old María del Carmen, walked across shaky, torch-lit planks to board *El Santiago*, the supply ship that would carry them from San Blas to Alta California (Serra 1955, 2: 9, 11, 19, 131). Five other women boarded *El Santiago* that morning. Two of them, María Teresa Ochoa, a young servant girl and María Josefa Dávila were also single and of marriageable age. The other three, Josefa María Góngora, María Arroyo Herrera, and Doña Josefa Carvajal came with their husbands. These eight women, wives, daughters, and kinswomen of blacksmiths, carpenters, a storekeeper, and a surgeon, were the first Spanish-speaking mestiza women to arrive in Alta California (Libro de matrimonios 1774, entry 32; Weber 1975, 86-7; Archives of California, 23: 518).[1]

Throughout the journey, sickness and fevers weakened the colonists and caused the death of a young workman. The families celebrated Ash Wednesday and the beginning of Lent aboard ship. On Sunday, the 13th of March, 1774, the ship anchored just outside of San Diego and early the following morning entered the port. After eighty-two days at sea they had finally reached the southern tip of the New California (Serra 1955, 2: 37).

From 1769 until 1774, when this first group of women and families that Father Junípero Serra recruited in Mexico City, Tepic, and Guadalajara to work in the missions arrived, the Spanish *entrada* to California was a militarized venture conducted exclusively by men (Bancroft 1884, 1: 110-25; Bannon 1970; Kinnard 1958; Chapman 1916; Chapman 1930; Richman 1911; Campbell

1977). Sixty Spanish, mestizo, mulatto and other casta soldiers, dispatched to defend the frontier against European incursions, to protect the missionaries, and to pacify the Indians, were garrisoned at the presidios of Monterey and San Diego. In conjunction with nineteen Franciscan friars, the soldiers were to effect the temporal and spiritual conquest of Alta California, peacefully if possible, by war if necessary.[2] The friars, under the direction of Serra, staffed the two coastal and three inland missions that had been built by 1774. This contingent of soldiers and missionaries comprised the entire Spanish-speaking population on the 158,693 square miles of land that was home to an indigenous population of approximately 310,000 persons (Cook 1976a, 1-43; Chartkoff and Chartkoff 1984, 205, 233-35).

The entire California venture, meaning all military and religious installations, was subsidized by the Royal Treasury, under the *Ramo de Guerra* (Department of War), and by the Church, under the Pious Fund (Cook 1976a, 1-43; Chartkoff and Chartkoff 1984, 205, 233-35). Although Spanish explorations had extended to these shores with Cabrillo in 1542 and Vizcaíno in 1602, Alta California was not colonized until the last third of the eighteenth century, when various political forces riveted Spanish attention on this region and compelled the Bourbon crown to extend Spanish dominion over its northernmost territory (Cook 1976a, 1-43; Chartkoff and Chartkoff 1984, 205, 233-35). Specifically, Spanish expansion to California formed part of the eighteenth-century Bourbon Reforms that affected New Spain's northern frontier. It was a defensive measure against both foreign threats from without and Indian threats from within (Cook 1976a, 1-43; Chartkoff and Chartkoff 1984, 205, 233-35).

Who were the women who settled Alta California during the height of the Bourbon reform era? Why were they and their families recruited and subsidized by the Department of War to colonize this frontier? Where and how did women fit within the imperatives of Spain's defensive expansion to this remote outpost of empire? Did the policy of *unidad doméstica* (domestic unity), which Spain employed throughout its American colonies, also extend to Alta California? (Ots y Capdequi 1934)

To answer these questions, as well as others, I examine the social history of Spanish-speaking mestiza women in Monterey, California, from 1770 to-1821. During these fifty-one years, Spain imposed its colonial hegemony on the Indians of California, and Spanish-mestizo soldier families established a presidial society within the confines of the military forts while *poblador* (settler) families developed a nascent agropastoral society in the nearby pueblos. Women, both the Amerindian women who lived on the land, and the Spanish-mestiza women who came to colonize, were central to developments on the frontier.

Incorporating non-European and racially-mixed women into the concept of the frontier is essential to understanding the socio-political patterns that developed in the eighteenth and nineteenth centuries and that persist today in California and the Southwest. Therefore, in my work I seek to develop a theoretical approach to history that places gender, race, culture, class, and sexuality at the center of the historical inquiry, thus allowing me to examine and interpret the role of women in Spanish and Mexican frontier societies (Castañeda 1990, 1-62).

Gender as a category of historical analysis, and sex as a socio-political category, are fundamental to my theoretical approach and to my examination of the roles of women in frontier expansion and development of colonial Spanish society (Castañeda 1990, 1-113; Scott 1988). As a feminist historian, I look closely at the intersecting dynamics of gender, race, culture, class and sexuality in the politics, policies, structures, and relations of conquest and social development in frontier California. I argue that these are pivotal issues in the historical process of Spanish expansion and the development of frontier society in California.

The Policy of Domestic Unity

The arrival of Ana María Hurtado and the first group of Spanish-speaking women in 1774 may be attributed directly to the recruiting efforts of Junípero Serra, who acted within the framework of Spanish frontier politics and policies of sex-gender, conquest, and colonization. From the beginning of expansion in the Americas, Spanish authorities recognized sex-gender as a political issue in the conquest of Amerindian societies and in the imposition of permanent Spanish hegemony in the New World (Machachlan and Rodríguez O. 1980, 236-37; Ots y Capdequi 1934, 206-7; Konetzke 1945; Brading 1973). That is, Spanish or Hispanicized women were essential not only to the biological reproduction of the species, but also to the reproduction of daily life, of the social institutions, and of the ideology that sustained them (Ots y Capdequi 1934, 116-206). Thus, sex-gender quickly became a pivotal issue in emigration and colonization policies under whose broad umbrella the Hapsburg rulers and their advisors incorporated substantive domestic and social policies that reunited spouses separated by the husbands' departure to the Americas or some other part of the colonial empire. These policies, which promoted the marriage of single men and facilitated the emigration of Spanish women, ensured the presence of women and families in the colonies (Ots y Capdequi 1934, 183-206).

The general policy, which scholars term a policy of domestic unity, or unity of residence, was initiated early in the sixteenth century. Spanish lawmakers considered the voluntary long-term, long-distance separation of Spanish men from the connubial household as a serious political problem, and the king and his council responded to it with extensive legislation from the beginning to the end of the colonial enterprise (Ots y Capdequi 1934, 183-206).

First and foremost, the policy of domestic unity was based on the recognition that the economic exploitation of the New World was contingent upon the existence of a permanently rooted, stable, and growing Spanish population and upon the establishment of the entire complex of Spanish institutions (Konetzke 1945, 128). Second, it was based on the perceived threats that the departure of single males to the expanding American frontiers—where new, fluid social conditions were giving rise to unprecedented multiracial, multiclass societies and illicit sexual relations—posed for domestic and social institutions (Martín 1983, 105-12).

A serious consequence of this situation was the increasing number of Spanish wives and families, in both Spain and the Americas, whose husbands and fathers abandoned them, sometimes with no means of support (Martín 1983, 141). In addition to being highly concerned about the economic support of these abandoned families, ecclesiastical and civil authorities were equally concerned about the moral fabric of society and about the strength and development of social institutions (Martín 1983, 142).

Spanish officials especially feared that marriage, one of the principal structures sustaining patriarchal society, would crumble in the face of widespread concubinage, common-law marriages, polygamy, and other illegal unions that Spanish men entered into with non-Spanish women in the Americas (Martín 1983, 141-70). They were especially concerned that both women and men were contributing to the potential downfall of the institution. Cases of Spanish women abandoning husbands, forming illicit sexual relationships, and having multiple marriages were not unknown in the colonies (Martín 1983, 149-50).

To impose order and gain firm control of social development, the Hapsburg king decreed in 1505 that married men living in the colonies without wives and families had to either return to the woman or bring her to wherever he resided and be reunited with her in that location (Ots y Capdequi 1934, 183-84; Konetzke 1945, 125). The policy of domestic unity, elaborated in numerous royal edicts, decrees, and ordinances, was enforced by economic rewards and punishments.

For example, royal edicts ordered that married men with families be given first priority in land assignments and be granted one-third more land than single men; reduced customs duties for men who brought wives and families; gave them access to Indian labor for constructing stone houses; granted them preference in appointments to official posts and in assignments of residential lots; and advised all royal officials to favor and assist married settlers before single men in all matters (Ots y Capdequi 1934, 183-84; Konetzke 1945, 124, n. 4, 139, n. 67 and n. 68, 140, 142, n. 74). Bachelors were encouraged to marry by promises of *encomiendas* (right of tribute from Indians) and *repartimientos* (allotments of Indian labor).

The colonization of California was thus informed by this extensive body of laws, which recognized the centrality of women to Spanish society in the Americas and incorporated sex-gender as a crucial element in the politics, policies, and strategies of frontier expansion and colonization.

Sex-Gender and the Colonization of California

When the first Spanish-mestiza women and families arrived in 1774, California was in a virtual state of war and the existence of the colony was in jeopardy due to the brutal sexual attacks that the soldiers perpetrated against Indian women. In fact, the first recorded acts of Spanish domination and aggression were acts of sexual violence against women (Cook 1976b, 24; Beilharz 1971, 72-73).

In words reminiscent of the sixteenth-century chronicles, Junípero Serra, president of the California missions, described the depredations of the soldiers against Indian women, which began shortly after the founding of the presidio and mission at Monterey in June 1770. The despicable actions of the soldiers, Serra wrote Viceroy Bucareli in 1773, were severely retarding the spiritual and material conquest of California (1955, 1: 361, 363). The native people were becoming war-like and resisting missionization. Instead of pacifying and ensuring order in the colony, the soldiers were provoking the Indians to armed conflict.

Serra was particularly alarmed by occurrences at Mission San Gabriel, where "the soldiers are guilty of the most heinous crimes, killing the men to take their wives" (1955, 1: 257, 361). In 1773 Serra reported recurring incidents: "In the mornings, six or seven soldiers would set out together...and go to the distant rancherías [villages] even many leagues away. When both men and women at the sight of them would take off running...the soldiers, adept as they are at lassoing cows and mules, would lasso Indian women, who then became prey for their unbridled lust" (1955, 1: 363). The Indian men who defended the women were shot (1955, 1: 363; 3: 159).

Although Serra blamed the civil-military authorities in California for the sexual violence of the soldiers, his charges that Pedro Fages, Fernando Rivera y Moncada, and Felipe de Neve were lax about enforcing military discipline and punishing soldiers were not well-founded. The Governor and Commanders knew that the assaults against women established conditions of war on the frontier and each invoked military discipline, including incarceration, to restrain the soldiers (Beilharz 1971, 73, 83, 161-62). Moreover, they prosecuted soldiers for major and minor crimes, including the rape and murder of Indian women, and issued numerous edicts to curb the soldier's abuse of Amerindians in general and women in particular (Thomas 1941, 16-57, 230-46; Moorhead 1975 27-160; Brinckerhoff and Faulk 1965, 7; Beilharz 1971, 27-30, 64-84, 160-62; Fages 1774, 2: pt. 1; Cook 1976b, 106; Archives of California 7: 256, 23: 421-22, 54: 175). The edicts had little effect.

In California, as throughout the Spanish empire, civil-military and ecclesiastical officials responded to the sex-gender issues with sex-gender policies defined and implemented in earlier colonization ventures. The response to both specific native-military problems and the more general need to populate the region was a dual strategy involving women.[3]

First, drawing upon a colonial tradition of promoting intermarriage with Amerindian noblewomen in order to advance particular political, military, religious, or social interests, colonial authorities sought to induce single soldiers to remain in California by awarding the use of land in perpetuity to those who married neophyte Indian women (Serra 1955, 1: 325, 379, 422, n. 140, 2: 29, 31, 149, 151, 153). Junípero Serra was an early and avid proponent of this policy that used intermarriage as an instrument of pacification and conquest. In his memorial to Viceroy Bucareli for improving conditions in the California establishments, Serra suggested that the viceroy reward men who married newly Christianized "daughters of the land," with three kinds of bounty: an animal for his own use the moment he married; two cows and a mule from the royal herd after he had worked on the mission farms for at least a year; and finally, a piece of land (Serra 1955, 1: 325, 341, 2: 149, 151, 153; Morner 1967, 35-37; Castañeda 1990, Chapt. 5).

The second part of the strategy, the plan for colonization, involved major efforts to populate California with three groups of families recruited from other parts of New Spain's northern frontier: soldier, artisan, and *poblador* (settler) families. The idea was that soldier families would establish and reside at the new presidios planned for San Francisco and Santa Bárbara, thereby strengthening military defenses and increasing the population base (Serra 1955, 1: 309; Echeveste regalmento; de Neve reglamento, Title 11, Sec. 23-27, Title 14; Bancroft 1884, 1: 215, 217; Beilharz 1971, 95-109).

The artisan group, husband and wife, would instruct the neophyte mission population in smithery, carpentry, herding, cooking, sewing, and all other manual and domestic arts essential to the self-sufficiency of the missions. Agrarian *poblador* families would establish and reside in the three projected *pueblos* (towns): San José de Guadalupe, Los Angeles, and La Villa de Branciforte. They would grow crops to feed themselves and to supply the presidios (Serra 1955, 1: 309; Echeveste reglamento; de Neve reglamento, Title 11, Sec. 23-27, Title 14; Bancroft 1884, 1: 215, 217; Beilharz 1971, 95-109).

Women were essential to these strategies. According to Serra, for example, the work of pacifying and Christianizing—or "reducing"—native people required that Indian women be taught and disciplined in the rudiments of "civilized" life that pertained to women, particularly the domestic arts and womanly virtues. The crown sought industrious Spanish women to instruct neophyte Indian women in cooking, cleaning, sewing, soap making, small husbandry, and sundry womanly duties (Serra 1955, 2: 203). Their task was to make frugal, moral Spanish wives and mothers out of these "uncivilized females whose shameless nudity was an offense to God and an untoward provocation to man" (Bolton 1930, 1: 97-104; Fages 1937, 66; Richman 1911, 398, n. 14).

Serra thought that the presence of women and families in the missions would immeasurably advance both the spiritual and the temporal conquest of the new California. By their example, Amerindians would learn the rudiments of Catholic family life, including the subservience of women to men, the sanctity and permanence of holy matrimony, the respect for authority, and the saving grace of baptism (Serra 1955, 2: 143, 203, 3: 199; Liss 17). Moreover, their example would reinforce the clerics' efforts to "uproot the immoral practice of polygamy among some of the Amerindian groups, and the unspeakable crimes of abortion and infanticide among others" (Fages 1937, 21, 22, 47; Lasuén 2: 210; Cook 1976b, 108-113).

The presence of women was further intended to convince Amerindians that Spanish soldiers would cease to depredate native women. Single women were encouraged to find husbands among the soldiers who were starved for women of their own kind (Bancroft 1884, 1: 340). The crown hoped that as marriage quelled their lustful behavior, the soldiers would choose to settle in the frontier once their military duty was completed. Thus the colony would prosper and be populated increasingly by *gente de razón* (people of reason), meaning Christians.

Thus, when Ana María Hurtado's family and the other families arrived, there was much rejoicing. However, this group, who constituted the first artisan, administrative, and professional classes recruited on six-year contracts to serve in the missions and the presidios of this remote colony, did not remain or settle in Alta California.

The artisans refused to stay because military officials here failed to meet the terms of their contracts. Neither the full rations allotted to wives, nor the families' clothing and other essentials were forthcoming (Serra 1955, 2: 109, 131, 137). Moreover, California offered little to artisans who could earn a comparable wage in a more populated area without having to buy goods at inflated prices in a military store (up to 150% inflation), risk starvation if the supply ships failed to arrive for a year or two, and live in danger of Amerindian rebellions (Serra 1955, 3: 145; Beilharz 1971, 34-44; Archives of California 7: 203, 270-74, 8: 133, 16 :22; Bancroft 1884, 1: 615-18, n. 29 and n. 30; Archibald 1978, 146-47; Culleton 1950, 129).

Artisan wives, or women from what may be considered the middle strata of eighteenth-century colonial Mexican society, did not settle in California. The women who came to stay belonged instead to the lower socioeconomic classes of New Spain (Bolton 1930, 3: 4; Hennessy 1978, 45-46; Moorhead 1974, 85-105; Campbell 1974, 106-118). They were the mothers, wives, daughters, and kinswomen of leather-jacket soldiers who staffed the frontier presidios of New Spain, of impoverished settlers who lived in the adjoining civilian pueblos, and of convicts from Mexico and Guadalajara sentenced to Alta California in lieu of other punishment. The women who settled Alta California were army wives and townswomen already living in the frontier presidios and pueblos of northern New Spain (Jones 1979, 208-10; Campbell 1974). They came with the two colonizing expeditions led by Commandant Fernando Rivera y Moncada in 1774 and 1781, and in the expedition led by Juan Bautista de Anza in the winter of 1775-76.

Presidarias y Pobladoras: The Journey North

Acting on the viceroy's instructions to recruit married soldiers with families for duty at the missions, Rivera y Moncada recruited soldier-settler families in Sinaloa during the late winter of

1774 (Escheveste reglamento; Palóu 1926, 3: 129-30; Serra 1955, 2: 103, 195; Bancroft 1884, 1: 217-19; Chapman 1930, 291). In order to encourage and attract "sturdy Spanish families" as soldier colonists to Alta California, Viceroy Bucareli authorized the Commandant to make land grants and to designate common lands for the use and benefit of the people in general (Hittell 1897, 1: 516-18; Serra 1955, 1: 309).

Little information has survived about the women who came with the Rivera y Moncada soldier-colonist recruits in 1774, but documents exist which chronicle the Juan Bautista de Anza expedition of 1775-76 that colonized San Francisco with women and their families from Sinaloa and Sonora. Although the personal views of the women who made that overland journey and their individual motives for migrating are not recorded, the documents make three facts abundantly clear. As a group the women were hardy and uncomplaining; they persevered on the trail; and their families were migrating to improve their lot (Bolton 1930, 3: 4, 13-14, 20, 29, 35, 56-57, 64-65, 73, 74, 97, 111, 118, 154-55).

In fact, Captain de Anza used the depressed state of the economy of Sinaloa and Sonora to recruit permanent colonists for the new military colony. The people he considered best suited to help occupy the River of San Francisco, de Anza wrote Bucareli, "are those of the *alcaldías* (towns with mayors) of Culiacán, Sinaloa, and Fuerte, in the Province of Sonora. Most of their inhabitants I have just seen submerged in the direst poverty and misery, and so I have no doubt they would most willingly and gladly embrace the advantages which your Excellency may deign to afford them" (Bolton 1930, 5: 209). To induce entire families to sign up for the California expedition, de Anza recommended that the royal treasury totally subsidize each family by providing clothing, rations, mounts, and all necessary items plus an advance on each soldier's annual salary.

Once Bucareli approved this plan to recruit and fully outfit forty soldier-settler families, de Anza set up a recruiting station in San Felipe de Sinaloa and began signing up recruits (Bolton 1930, 4: 428; Palóu 1926, 3: 68, 82, 4: 1-3; Chapman 1930, 290). In May 1775, de Anza and the twenty soldier-setter families began the four hundred-mile march from Culiacán in Sinaloa to San Miguel de Horcasitas in Sonora, which they reached in early August. Data on the age of the married women and their husbands who came with de Anza, on how long they had been married, and on the size of their families reveal that in general, these were not young or new families (Bolton 1930, 4: 426-31; Northrop 1984-87). Rather, they were in the middle of their familial life. The average age was twenty-eight years for the women and thirty-five years for the men. The twenty couples for whom data are available had been married an average of twelve years, and their families averaged four children, whose median age was eight years (Castañeda 1990, 147-50).

While the women's daily routine on the journey was not recorded, their primary responsibilities, including child care and laundry, appear to have differed little from their standard familial and household work (Bolton 1930, 3: 28). Women probably relied heavily on their daughters who were over the age of eleven for help with younger children and other responsibilities. Since girls married and started families as young as twelve years of age, pubescent females were expected to assume adult responsibilities.[1] Although the average family traveling to California was in mid-cycle, women's young age at marriage and long years of child-bearing meant that mothers brought both young and old children, as Martina Botiller and Juana Gaona exemplify.

Martina Botiller had eight children, her eldest was twenty years old, her youngest was three (Northrop 1984, 1: 105-6). Her daughters, Ana Josefa and María Encarnación, eighteen and sixteen years old, respectively, assumed a great deal of the responsibility for child care, meals, laundry, and other tasks. Juana Gaona, whose family included five children, had a twenty-year-old son and an infant daughter (Northrop 1984, 1: 35-37). In this family, nineteen-year-old María Josefa was expected to help her mother a great deal.

Younger women with infants and toddlers, however, did not have help from older daughters, sisters, or mothers. These women, nineteen years and younger, were themselves the mothers of young families. María Josefa Acuña, for example, had been married five years and had four children, ages one to four, when she and her family joined the expedition in 1775 (Northrop 1984, 1: 164-65).

The intrepid women who rode, walked, and sometimes staggered across desert sands and through snow-capped mountain passes shared their living space and their lives intensely on the trek from Culiacán to San Francisco. Thirty families shared ten tents, which they put up and took down daily. Within the confines of this space, as well as on the open trail, the women confronted the vicissitudes, the joys, and the sorrows of daily life, including becoming pregnant and giving birth. Within a single week they witnessed three marriages and buried a woman who had died in childbirth.

On 26 October, the third day out of Tubac during the stopover at Mission San Xavier del Bac, Father Font performed a marriage ceremony for three couples—the brides were all between twelve and sixteen years old (Bolton 1930, 4: 27-28; Northrop 1984-87, 1: 37, 81, 2: 37). These three young women who married en route to California, María Ana Bojórquez, her sister María Micaela, and Rosalía Zamora all reached their destination, where each bore children, but not all lived to raise them (Bolton 1930, 4: 428).

Whether migrating by land or by sea, women were equally vulnerable to the perils of pregnancy and childbirth, if not on the actual journey, then certainly in their frontier destination (Myres 1982; Schlissel 1982; Faragher 1979). Pregnancy, miscarriage, and childbirth on the trail from Culiacán to California during the de Anza colonizing expedition were well documented (Bolton 1930, 3: 6-8, 21, 23-25, 33, 35-37, 69-70, 4: 26-27, 47-48, 53, 62, 66, 147-51).[5] Eight persons, or twenty-five percent, of the thirty-two married women journeying north were pregnant at the start of the journey (Bolton 1930, 3: 69-70). Of the eight pregnant women, five had miscarriages, and three gave birth to children who survived the journey.

Births, of course, delayed the expedition. Normally women could not ride horseback for four to five days after giving birth, so after resting a day or two, they walked (Bolton 1930, 3: 44, 69-70, 5: 301). Time was of the essence as supplies were limited and the animals were giving out. The expedition needed to move on as quickly as possible.

On 4 January 1776, at eleven in the morning, the colonizing expedition arrived at Mission San Gabriel to the peals of bells, volleys of gunfire from the mission guard, and much rejoicing (Bolton 1930, 4: 176). After five weeks at this mission, the expedition resumed its northward march on the morning of 21 February and reached the northern presidio of Monterey on 10 March 1776

(Bancroft 1884, 1: 286-87; Bolton 1930, 3: 104-118). The women knew they were in Monterey only temporarily. They still had to march another one hundred and twenty miles north to the harbor of Saint Francis. After three months in Monterey, the women picked up again and with their families set out along Portolá's old route. After a ten-day march they reached their final destination. On 27 June 1776, the families of the de Anza colonizing expedition arrived at *La Laguna de los Dolores* (the Pond of Sorrows), the site of the mission dedicated to St. Francis of Assisi (Bolton 1930, 1: 458-72).

Since leaving Culiacán in May 1775, their migration from the tierra caliente (hot country) of Sinaloa over two thousand miles to the foggy, bone-chilling lands of the Pacific Coast had taken them thirteen months. Manuela Ygnacia Pinuelas, who died in childbirth the first night out of Tubac, was the only fatality of the entire journey (Bolton 1930, 3). Her children and the other *pobladoras* (women settlers) arrived safely and became the first *presidarias* and *pobladoras* of northern California above Monterey. As such, they extended Spanish colonialism to the northernmost tip of the empire.

Women's Lives and Society in Frontier California

Creating new homes and families exacted a heavy toll on the time and energy of women. They had to manage limited resources and maintain households with rations sent from San Blas. The supply ships, if they came at all, were often late and delivered food that was spoiled and clothing that was inadequate for their families' needs (Serra 1955, 3: 145; Beilharz 1971, 34-44, 67-84).

Little information exists on how women dealt with the hardships of inadequate housing, crowded conditions in the presidios, and scarcity of clothing and essential supplies.[6] In their oral histories, Apolinaria Lorenzana, Dorotea Valdéz, and Eulalia Pérez describe the life of women who worked in the households of presidial officers or in the mission system.[7] They relate how they supported themselves with the work of their hands by sewing, cooking, cleaning, nursing, midwifing, and working as *maestras* (teachers), *enfermeras* (nurses), and *llaveras* (keepers of the keys or matrons) in the missions.

While historians have focused on the lack of formal educational institutions in colonial California, they have missed the value the people placed on learning and knowledge. Women were not indifferent to literacy and education, and went to great lengths under the most difficult circumstances to learn to read and write and to pass that knowledge on to others. They taught their own, and in some cases other children, to read and write. Some also learned to speak and understand Amerindian languages and dialects. Finally, women memorized lengthy verses of poetry and songs, which they recited and sang. They also learned the hymns and dialogue from the Pastorela (the shepherd's play) and taught them to several generations of children for the annual Christmas celebration (Lorenzana 1878, 46).

Clearly, oral history and literature were important forms of knowledge and learning. People recognized the difference between formal education and knowledge, and valued both. Apolinaria Lorenzana describes how she taught herself to write:

> I had learned to read and recite the catechism as a child in Mexico. And then when I was a young girl, already in California, I taught myself to write, relying—in order to do so—on whatever books I saw. I copied the letters on whatever paper I was able to get ahold of—such as empty packets of cigars or whatever blank piece of paper I found that had been thrown away. In that way I was able to learn enough to make myself understood in writing whenever I needed anything. (Lorenzana 1878, 44)

In fact, Lorenzana, who appears to have been indentured by her mother at thirteen years of age, earned part of her living by teaching.[8] She taught reading, sewing, and the Catechism to young girls in San Diego and taught reading at the Mission to children of both sexes (Lorenzana 1878, 48).

Llaveras instructed Amerindian women in the domestic arts of Spanish-Mexican society and supervised the work of neophyte women, which included sewing, needlework, grinding corn, and all preparations for feeding and clothing the mission population (Pérez 1877, 16-17). As keeper of the keys the llavera was responsible for specific portions of the mission's stores and supplies such as foodstuffs, yardage, and dry goods. As matron of the *monjerío* (literally, the nunnery, as the neophyte women's dormitory was called) she was in charge of the unmarried neophyte girls and women. These girls were separated from their parents and families between the ages of seven and nine and remained within the mission compound until they were married (Lorenzana 1878, 7; Pérez 1877, 16).

Each night, after supper and evening prayers, the *llavera* escorted the girls to the *monjero*, took roll as they entered the structure in single file, accounted for everyone, locked the door, and took the key to the missionary. She unlocked the doors each morning at dawn (Pérez 1877, 16-17). Both as keeper of the keys and as matron, the *llavera* managed and supervised the domestic arrangements of the mission system. She performed all the domestic duties and supervised the work commonly associated with women's unpaid labor in the home.

Eulalia Pérez became the *llavera* at the Mission San Gabriel in 1821, three years after she was widowed. A practicing *partera*, she was, by her own admission, "the best midwife around" (Pérez 1877, 3-5). Fifty-four years old when she began to work at the mission, Sra. Pérez had given birth to twelve children, eight of whom were alive and between the ages of five and fifteen (Northrop 1987, 2: 116-18). As *llavera* she distributed the daily rations for the *pozolera* (communal cooking and eating area) and accounted for all the single neophyte women and men, the farm hands, and the cowboys (Pérez 1877, 10-13). She also managed the priest's kitchen and supervised the women who sewed clothing for everyone in the mission. Finally, she supervised the production of soap, the production of olive oil, and oversaw the delivery of leather goods used to make saddles and shoes (Archibald 1978, 146, 151).

The harshness of life in Alta California did not preclude sociability and celebration. People gathered to celebrate births, marriages, and religious and national holidays with food, merriment, song, and dance. They also celebrated the beginning and end of the harvest season. In Monterey women and girls sang and danced at *Los Aguajitos*, where they washed clothes in the canyon's numerous hot springs.

Dance was especially important as a medium of individual and group expression and allowed both men and women to demonstrate their skill, talent, and grace (Pérez 1877, 28; Czarnowski 1950, 21). Special dances were performed by children and adults, groups and couples, and married and single people alike. Women and men danced both together and separately. In the colonial period most of the dances were accompanied by songs with folk or peasant themes.

Eulalia Pérez was an excellent singer and dancer, who outdanced Chepa Rodríguez and another woman of renown in Santa Bárbara. Her fame was so great that no one took up the challenge to compete against her in a dance contest encompassing all of California (Pérez 1877, 29).

Both Apolinaria Lorenzana and Eulalia Pérez spoke about the importance of women in the social network that wove the community together. Lorenzana, in particular, spoke about being a madrina and the many children entrusted to her care by their parents. Being a godmother of baptism and marriage and a comadre was, in Lorenzana's view, an honor and a measure of the esteem in which she was held by the community. Thus, she states, "I had the satisfaction of knowing that everyone—young and old, rich and poor—thought well of me" (Lorenzana 1878, 44-45).

Woman's Consciousness, Man's World[9]

Histories of California and the Spanish borderlands do not discuss the experiences of Spanish-speaking women in the northern frontier. They do, however, focus on the distinct, open, and more flexible culture that was fostered by the frontier's isolation and distance from the central government and by that government's neglect of its needs. These elements created, if not a more egalitarian society, at least a distinct culture throughout the region (Jones 1979, xi, 252-53; Campbell 1974, 106-118; Moorhead 1974). These scholars, however, have defined that distinct culture exclusively in terms of the life and work of frontier soldiers and male settlers. The literature does not examine the experiences of women or their contributions to the distinct culture of the frontier (Jones 1979, xi, 252-53).

Until recently, historians have used standard concepts of politics which center on the development and operation of governmental bodies and structures from which women were expressly excluded. Thus, they failed to examine what women responded and reacted to as they lived the political events of their times, as they nursed the wounded and put food on the soldiers' tables, and as they farmed *ranchos*, supplied soldiers with horses, and slaughtered cows to feed them. Moreover, historians have not interpreted sex-gender, and women's presence on the frontier, in political terms. Yet, as the discussion of the policy of domestic unity and the examination of sexual violence against Amerindian women has demonstrated, sex-gender was a central political issue in the imposition of Spanish hegemony in Alta California.

Moreover, an examination of the lives and experiences of Spanish-mestiza women is necessary in order to establish a balanced description and analysis of society in colonial California. Women experienced the privations of frontier life differently, but no less harshly, than men. Women shared their experiences and spent much time in the company of one another. Women were midwife to one another, nursed each other through life-threatening and minor illnesses, celebrated together, served as godmothers to each other's children, taught their daughters to read and write, and served the Church and the state in the mission system. They were knowledgeable of the politics of the day and conscious that their participation was circumscribed by the fact of their sex. Dorotea Valdéz expressed that consciousness most clearly when she told her interviewer, "I was born in 1793, and I have witnessed every event which has transpired since that time, but being a woman, was denied the privilege of mixing in politics or in business" (Valdéz 1874).

Despite the structures that sustained gender hierarchies and circumscribed their lives, even on this remote frontier, women acted in their own behalf and empowered themselves in ways we are only now beginning to examine. They turned notions about women inside out and used their alleged "weakness" for purposes they deemed important (Adorno 1990; González).

One prime example of this is Eulalia Callis' 1785 suit for divorce from her husband, Governor Pedro Fages, whom she publicly accused of infidelity; and with whom, she publicly proclaimed, she would never again sleep—in order to get him to resign his post in California and return the family to Mexico City (Ynstancia 1785, Vol. 120, 66-81).

In her petition for a legal separation Callis stated that she had been arrested when she, against the advice of her priest and others, continued publicly to accuse her husband of infidelity. Although ill, she was taken to Mission San Carlos and kept incommunicado in a locked and guarded room, which she could only leave to attend daily Mass in the chapel. She remained at the mission two or three months. While at the mission, Father de Noriega excoriated her from the pulpit, threatening her with shackles, flogging, and excommunication. She stated that the forces arrayed against her would not "close the doors of my own honor and birth, which swing open in natural defense and protection" (Ynstancia 1785, Vol. 120, 67-68).

Eulalia Callis' actions directly challenged the political concepts and structures that were pivotal to the conquest, and as such, could not be tolerated. Her actions subverted the value system that required women to be subservient, meek, and powerless: she publicly accused Fages of infidelity; refused him sexual access to her body; refused to acquiesce to the priest and military officers who counseled her to forgive Fages' transgressions; she refused to be *depositada* or *recogida* (deposited or sheltered) in the mission and had to be arrested and taken by force; she sued for divorce; and she defended her honor and birthright.

Historians have dubbed Eulalia Callis the "notorious governadora" (Bancroft 1884, 1: 430-49). They have written with tongue-in-cheek about Fage's "domestic problems" and cast the governadora Callis as a fiery, tempestuous Catalan woman (Bancroft 1884, 1: 389-93). Historians of early California have not, however, examined the lives of women on the frontier, and thus cannot accurately interpret Callis' language or her actions.

Pregnancy, childbirth, miscarriage, and infection all too often spelled death for women. Callis, who was pregnant four times in six years, was all too familiar with the precariousness of life. She gave birth to Pedrito in 1781, had a miscarriage at Arispe in 1782, traveled to California while pregnant and was ill after the birth of María del Carmen in 1784; and buried an infant daughter eight days after her birth in 1786 (Archives of California 3: 49; Palóu 1926, 1: 67, n. 2; Bancroft 1884, 1: 390, n. 5; Culleton 1950, 108-9, 116-17). Thus, her "ploy" to get home appears to be an effort to save her own life and those of her children. She used contemporary gender ideology of women as weak and defenseless as a pivotal element in a strategy to save herself and her children from the high probability of early death on the frontier. A central part of that strategy was to take her situation of a "woman who has been wronged" from home to the streets—she made private matters public. According to Fages, Callis fabricated the story of his infidelity (Archives of California 22: 111). Callis, however, never publicly retracted her accusations or admitted to any fabrication.

Conclusion

This examination of Spanish-mestiza women in colonial California revealed the centrality of sex-gender to the politics and policies of colonization and the establishment of Spanish hegemony on this frontier. Spanish authorities in California, like their predecessors in the early conquest of Mexico some two and a half centuries earlier, were acutely aware that the biological and social reproductive power of Spanish-Mexican women was absolutely critical to the establishment and survival of Spanish society on the frontier. Placing gender and its intersections with race and class at the center of historical inquiry about frontier expansion forces us to pose entirely new questions and to define new categories of research and analysis. As we examine and define the nature of the politics of gender, we perforce must reexamine the politics of race, class, culture and sexuality.

The arrival of Spanish-mestiza women in the expeditions of 1774-1776 and 1781 had very specific political, economic, and social consequences. As wives and, if single, as marriage partners—and consequently as sexual partners—the presence and availability of Spanish-mestiza women diffused the political and military problems that resulted from the soldier's sexual abuse of Indian women. Women produced and reproduced the Spanish-Mexican population, which in California was the mainstay of population growth; they founded pueblos; and they fortified the economy. As *maestras*, *enfermeras*, *parteras*, and *llaveras* in the mission system, Spanish-mestiza women not only instructed Amerindian women in Hispanic women's domestic work, but they inculcated Spanish-Catholic religious, social, political, and economic values. Women also taught Spanish-Mexican children of both sexes and as midwives, godmothers, and nurses were central to the social networks that sustained the presidios and pueblos on this distant frontier.

However, the elasticity and relative freedom from some social constraints on the frontier did not fundamentally alter the struc-

tures or ideology of male domination nor male control. Neither
the scarcity of Spanish-mestiza women of marriageable age, nor,
in the case of Eulalia Callis, the possession of wealth and social position exempted women from male-defined, male controlled
norms of socio-economic, political, or sexual control. Women's
lives were conditioned by gender and racial hierarchies and patriarchal structures rooted in civil and canon laws that vested authority over a woman's sexuality, as well as over her economic, social and political being, in the male members of her family.

The historical record reveals, however, that women in Alta California did not meekly accept or adhere to male defined norms of
sexuality or passively accept male domination. Instead, as Eulalia
Callis' suit for divorce clearly reveals, women used multiple strategies to resist and to assert their own prerogatives and power. In
some cases women used the gender ideology which deemed
women to be weak and in need of protection to subvert the structures of male domination and to create the space they needed to
meet their desired objective. In other cases, they outrightly defied
civil and cannon laws regulating their social and sexual behavior.

We still know very little about the lives and realities of Spanish-
mestiza women during the eighteenth and nineteenth centuries in
Alta California and the northern Spanish-Mexican frontier that
became the core of the Chicana/o homeland. However, what becomes abundantly clear when we approach court, mission, civil,
military, and other documents with gender-specific questions, is
the conflictive, contestatory nature of life and society on the frontiers of expansion, including California. The "unique northern
culture" that social historians have been so wont to write about, if
not to extol, was rife with conflict centering on sex-gender and racial issues in the eighteenth century; and on these plus class issues
as society became more socially stratified and hierarchical in the
nineteenth century. We have yet not only to examine the nature of
these conflicts and the relations of power between women of different races and classes, but also to examine the multiple contradictions of women's lives under the conditions and structures of
colonialism. In brief, we have yet to describe and analyze both the
hegemonic and counterhegemonic strategies, roles, and activities
that women, depending on their position in society, employed in
California as this region changed from Spanish to Mexican to
Euro-American rule.

This examination of the generation of Spanish-mestiza women who settled Alta California has focused on some of the critical sex-gender issues in the research and writing of eighteenth century Chicana history. It forms part of the larger body of work in which Chicana/Latina feminist scholars are engaged as we actively define and refine conceptual and theoretical approaches to research, analyze, and interpret Chicana history.

Notes

1. I use the terms Spanish-speaking mestiza and Spanish-mestiza interchangeably to refer to Spanish-speaking women in Alta California during the Spanish colonial period, 1769-1821.

2. Since the earliest conquests, Spanish policy directed that Amerindian families from locations already missionized or colonized accompany the otherwise all-male expeditionary forces sent to establish new colonies. These families were to serve as "role models" and thereby help acculturate Amerindians in the new locale. Thus, Amerindian women from the missions of Baja California, who came as part of these families, arrived in Alta California with the expedition of 1769 (Bancroft 1884, vol. 1; Bannon 1970; Chapman 1916).

3. The discussion about the centrality of women and the family to consolidating Spanish power in California is based on my analysis and interpretation of correspondence and other documents from ecclesiastical, military, and civil government sources and the official regulations for the California establishments: Instrucción que debe observar el comandante nombrado para los establecimientos de San Diego y Monterey, 23 de Julio de 1773; and Reglamento para el gobierno de la provincia de Californias, 24 October 1781, Manuscript Collection, Bancroft Library, Berkeley, Calif. Hereafter cited as Echeveste reglamento and Neve reglamento, respectively.

4. The average age of first marriage for the women with the de Anza expedition of 1775-76 was sixteen years. Eleven women (32 percent) married prior to their sixteenth birthday: three at age twelve, two at thirteen, four at fourteen, and two at fifteen. These figures do not include the three girls who married at Mission San Xavier del Bac on 26 October 1775, during the journey north.

5. Bancroft, *History of California*, (1: 259), erroneously states that eight infants were born during de Anza's 1775-76 expedition to San Francisco. According to de Anza's translated and published diary, only three infants were born on the journey north and five women suffered miscarriages.

One of the miscarriages resulted in a still-birth. See Bolton, Anza's *California Expeditions*, (4: 69-70). Historians who rely primarily on Bancroft's discussion have perpetuated the same error.

6. Few details exist about how married women were able to make ends meet or how they survived the lean years. Spanish censuses do not list the occupations of women. The names of women who took in laundry or exchanged domestic or other services for goods, supplies, or services in the subsidized, subsistence economy of colonial California are generally not part of the official record.

7. In the late 1870s, Hubert Howe Bancroft commissioned the collection of oral histories and reminiscences from Californianas and Californianos and from Euro-American pioneers to California, see: Apolinaria Lorenzana, Memorias de Apolinarina Lorenana, Mayo de 1878, Santa Barbara, Manuscript Collection, Bancroft Library, Berkeley, California; Eulalia Pérez, Una Vieja y Sus Recuerdos, 1877, Mission San Gabriel, Manuscript Collection, Bancroft Library; Dorotea Valdéz, Reminiscences of Dorotea Valdéz, Monterey California, 27 June 1874, Manuscript Collection, Bancroft Library.

8. Apolinaria Lorenzana, in her Memorias 2, states that she and her mother came to California with the group of orphans sent from the Lorenzana orphanage in Mexico City in 1800. Her mother married an artilleryman in California and left with him when his tour of duty was up. She further states that her mother " . . . .handed me over to Don Reymundo" ("me entregó ella a Don Reymundo [Carrillo]")—translation mine. The narrative goes on to describe her work in the Carrillo and other households as well as in the mission.

9. Sheila Rowbotham. 1973. *Woman's Consciousness, Man's World* New York: Penguin Books.

There Is No Going Back: Chicanas and Feminism

Beatriz M. Pesquera
Denise A. Segura

American feminism has inspired a tremendous amount of research, little of which attends to feminist expressions among Chicanas, or women of Mexican descent, who form the second largest racial-ethnic group in the United States. This inattention is disturbing inasmuch as feminism purports to explain the nature of women's oppression and develop strategies for social change. Without sustained analysis of the diverse feminisms among women and the conditions that motivate them, theoretical formulations and strategies for change will continue to veer away from historically subordinate groups.

The paucity of knowledge about Chicana feminism, as well as the range of their political activities, results in researchers relegating Chicanas to the margins of social inquiry (Moraga and Anzaldúa 1981; Chabram and Fregoso 1990). Intellectual marginalization of Chicanas leads to an uncritical acceptance of the discourse of the late 1960s that situated Chicanas three paces behind Chicano men in the movement to overturn race-ethnic and class systems of oppression but silent on the question of patriarchy (Longeaux y Vásquez 1970; Lopez 1977; García 1989). Positioned thusly, Chicanas were largely excluded from the feminist debates of the time—a dilemma yet to be systematically reversed (Lizárraga 1977; Sandoval 1982; Alarcón 1990).

This article[1] explores feminism among two groups of Chicanas; 101 members of a group of Chicanas in higher education (MALCS) and 152 Chicana white collar workers. We analyze how Chicanas' social locations—their race-ethnicity, gender, and class—shape their political consciousness and orientation toward feminist politics. This analysis inquires into the contradictions posed by these simultaneous social memberships. We begin our investigation by presenting three scenarios based in the late 1960s to capture symbolically the dialectical tension between women's lives and the ideological configurations of the Chicano Movement, which privileged a Chicano subject, and the American Women's Movement which posited a universal woman.[2] We follow this with a brief critique of American feminism and the Chicano Movement advanced by leading Chicana activists of the late 1960s and early 1970s.[3] Then, using a 1988-89 survey of 101 Chicanas in higher education we discuss their appraisals of American feminism and the contours of Chicana feminisms. Finally, we examine attitudes toward feminism expressed by 152 Chicana white collar workers from a study conducted in 1989-90. Our research is grounded in a feminist historical-social constructionism that analyzes structural conditions, Chicanas' interpretations of their social locations and life options, and how these interpretations shape their consciousness.

On Feminist Consciousness

What is feminist consciousness? Tolleson Rinehart (1988) argues that feminist consciousness is a specific type of gender consciousness anchored in a commitment to egalitarian relations between the sexes. Klein (1984) and Cook (1989), on the other hand, assert feminist consciousness includes not only advocacy of gender equality but a sense of subjective unity with women and a desire to change existing institutional arrangements that maintain the status quo as well. Klein (1984) proposes three prerequisites to feminist consciousness. First, members must recognize their membership in the group and that they share interests with the group (or group identification). Second, members must reject the rationale for the situation of the group. Third, they must recognize the need for group solutions. "Only women who reached this third stage, where they believed that they deserved equal treatment but were denied opportunities because of sex discrimination, had a feminist consciousness" (Klein 1984, 3). According to Cook (1989, 84-85), people with "politicized feminist consciousness are significantly more likely to assign blame to societal factors than are those who are not feminists." Moreover, one must embrace a political stance that moves away from individualistic goals and action to a collectivist orientation to achieve group goals.

These formulations imply a unidimensional source of group identification based on gender when in fact, women experience gender, racial-ethnic, and class statuses concurrently. We argue that analyses of feminist consciousness should attend to the dynamics of each social location in framing women's experiences. It is theoretically possible and likely that Chicanas' multiple sources of group identification conflict at times with one another, rendering the development of a group consciousness based on the privileging of one social location over the others ahistorical and untenable. The interplay of the multiple axes of class, race-ethnicity, and gender informs a unique Chicana perspective or world view that guides their assessment of the relevancy of feminism. This cross-positioning motivates a distinct Chicana feminism grounded in the experience of being female and Mexican from largely working-class backgrounds. This experience is not monolithic, however, but one that highly educated Chicanas interpret somewhat differently than white collar Chicana workers. These differences reflect Chicanas' varied social locations, networks, and experiences.

Three Scenarios

Scenario 1: *". . .the Chicana woman does not want to be liberated"*
On 19 February 1990, we interviewed Martha Cotera, a prominent Chicana feminist and activist from Texas. In her interview, she recounted her involvement with alternative Chicano politics (specifically the rise of the "third" party in Texas, La Raza Unida), feminism, and civil rights. When we asked her to elaborate on the social context of Chicana feminism in the late 1960s, she related several accounts of the tension between male-defined Chicano political discourse and gender. One narrative centered on Enriqueta Longeaux y Vásquez, a Chicana activist and one of the editors of *El Grito del Norte*, a Chicano Movement newspaper published in New Mexico. Cotera related that twenty years ago, Longeaux y Vásquez had telephoned her to discuss the March 1969 First National Chicano Youth Conference held in Denver, attended by several thousand people from across the United States.[1] Cotera recalled that Longeaux y Vásquez was extremely upset—

to the point of tears—that the Chicana Caucus at this conference
had adopted the position that "...the Chicana woman does not
want to be liberated." Longeaux y Vásquez (1970) chronicled the
Chicana Caucus position in an article in the best-selling book *Sisterhood is Powerful*, edited by Robin Morgan. Albeit unintention-
ally, this article reinforces stereotypes of Chicanas as submissive
and passive and uninterested in feminism.

Scenario 2: *"El Plan Espiritual de Aztlan," March 1969*
One of the major conferences of the Chicano Movement was the
First National Chicano Youth Conference hosted by the Crusade
for Justice, a Denver-based, militant grassroots Chicano Movement organization. This Conference gave birth to "El Plan Espiritual de Aztlan," also known as "The Chicano Movement
Manifesto." The "Plan" provided an ideological framework and
concrete political program for the Chicano Movement emphasizing nationalism and self-determination. The "Plan" stated: "Cultural values of our people strengthen our identity and are the
moral backbone of the movement. Our culture unites and edu-
cates the family of La Raza towards liberation with one heart and
one mind.... Our cultural values of life, family, and home will
serve as the powerful weapon to defeat the gringo dollar value system and encourage the process of love and brotherhood" (Anaya
and Lomeli 1989).

The symbolic representation of familism (or family solidarity)
and political cultural nationalism occurred with the marriage of
Rodolfo "Corky" Gonzalez's daughter and a militant member of
the Crusade for Justice. Corky Gonzalez, an ex-boxer and writer,
headed the Crusade for Justice.

Scenario 3: *"The Redstockings Manifesto"*
A few months after the March 1969 Denver Conference, in New
York, the "Redstockings Manifesto" appeared in *Notes from the Second Year: Women's Liberation, Major Writings of the Radical Feminists*
(Firestone and Koedt 1970). Section III reads: "We identify the
agents of our oppression as men. Male supremacy is the oldest,
most basic form of domination. All other forms of exploitation
and oppression (racism, capitalism, imperialism, etc.) are extensions of male supremacy: men dominate women, a few men dominate the rest.... *All men* have oppressed women" (Firestone and

Koedt 1970, 113).

In August, 1969, *The Feminists*, another radical women's liberation group, implemented a membership quota: "That no more than one-third of our membership can be participants in either a formal (with legal contract) or informal (e.g., living with a man) instance of the institution of marriage. (Firestone and Koedt 1970, 117). This membership quota grew out of their critique of marriage as a primary locus of female subordination and oppression.

On 22 November 1969, the Congress to Unite Women held workshops in New York on "What Women Want." One of the workshops was titled: "How Women are Divided: Class, Racial, Sexual, and Religious Differences." Evelyn Leo who participated in this workshop reported, "The first exchange that took place is worth noting. A black woman said she had been at a workshop that morning and went on to complain about what a waste it had been because everyone was talking around the subject and not at it, etc. A white woman responded and said, 'It was not as black as you are painting it.' Need I say more?" (Leo in Tanner 1970, 127-128)

These scenarios highlight the polarized nature of insurgent politics during this period. Each position articulated an analysis of oppression based on race-ethnicity or gender. The Chicano Movement exalted marriage and reproduction as integral to the politics of cultural reaffirmation. A fundamental feminist position, on the other hand, indicted marriage and reproduction within the traditional patriarchal family as a primary source of all women's subordination. Although Chicanas recognized the need to struggle against male privilege in the Chicano community, they were reluctant to embrace a feminist position that appeared anti-family (Orozco 1986; García 1989). Caught between two incompatible ideological positions, Chicanas developed their own discourse reflecting their multidimensional sources of oppression and validation (Alarcón 1990; Apodaca 1986; Moraga and Anzaldúa 1983).

Chicanas and the American Women's Movement

The writings of Chicana feminists of the late 1960s and early 1970s demonstrate considerable ambivalence toward American feminism. Chicanas, both those who called themselves feminists and those who eschewed this label, characterized the Movement as predominantly white and middle-class with interests distinct from their own (Cotera 1977, 1980; Del Castillo 1974; Hernández 1971; Nieto-Gómez 1973, 1974; Vidal 1971). With few exceptions, Chicanas did not distinguish between the "women's rights" branch and the "women's liberation" or "left" branch.[5] The women's rights branch concentrated on programs to integrate women into the mainstream of American society (Freeman 1984; Jaggar 1983). The women's liberation branch called for a radical restructuring of society to eliminate patriarchy, or the system of male control and domination of women (Andersen 1988; Jaggar 1983). Although both branches of the Women's Movement advocated for women, the issues of women of Color[6] were often overlooked (Davis 1981; Garcia 1989; hooks 1981, 1984; Hull, Bell Scott, and Smith 1982; Moraga and Anzaldúa, 1983).

Chicanas questioned the feminist call to "sisterhood" because it assumed unity based on one set of shared interests (gender oppression) and overlooked the historical class, race-ethnic, and cultural antagonisms between women. Chicana activists contended that the American Women's Movement and feminism could not be relevant to Chicanas until race-ethnic and class concerns became integrated into their political and theoretical formulations (Flores 1973; Moraga and Anzaldúa 1983; Nieto-Gómez 1973, and 1974; Sosa-Riddell 1974). Chicanas doubted, however, that such an integrative approach would emerge in light of the racism and what Anna Nieto-Gómez (1973) referred to as "maternal chauvinism" in the Women's Movement. With this term, Nieto-Gómez directed attention to Chicanas' virtual exclusion from feminist agendas and writings as well as the condescending attitudes among some Movement activists toward Chicanas.[7] In the rare instances Chicanas were included, their experiences tended to be cast in ways that reinforced cultural stereotypes of them as women who did not "want to be liberated" (Longeaux y Vásquez 1970). Most often, however, Chicanas have been silent objects within feminist discourse because they are neither included or excluded by name. Thus, Chicanas in this period concluded they were not "equal" sisters in the struggle against sexual oppression (Cotera 1980; Moraga and Anzaldúa 1983).

Chicana feminists also criticized what they interpreted as an individualistic upward mobility ethos within the American Women's Movement (Sutherland 1970). They posited an alternative view; one rooted in the collective struggle for liberation of the entire Chicano community.

Chicanas and Cultural Nationalism

Chicanas' critique of American feminism and the Women's Movement resonate with a strong collective orientation formed during the heyday of Chicano cultural nationalism. Ideologically, this perspective identified the primary source of Chicano oppression in the colonial domination of Mexican Americans following the annexation of Northern Mexico by the United States after the U.S.-Mexico War of 1846-48 (Acuña 1981; Almaguer 1971; Barrera, Muñoz, and Ornelas 1972; Blauner 1972). As part of the process of colonial domination, Chicanos were limited in their access to education, employment, and political participation. Thus, race-ethnicity defined the life chances of Mexican Americans rather than individual merit. Cultural differences between Anglos and Mexicans became the ideological basis that legitimized the unequal treatment and status of Mexicans in the United States (Blauner 1972; Montejano 1987; Takaki 1979). Ideologically, Mexicans were viewed as intellectually and culturally inferior.

Cultural nationalist ideology countered this pejorative perspective by celebrating the cultural heritage of Mexico in particular, indigenous roots, la familia, and political insurgency (Macías 1974; Mirandé 1985). The term, "Chicano," arose as the symbolic representation of self-determination (Chicano Coordinating Committee on Higher Education 1969; Alvarez 1971; Acuña 1981). It conveys a commitment to politically struggle for the betterment of the Chicano community. Cultural nationalism idealized certain patterns associated with Mexican culture. For example, Chicano Movement groups often organized around the ideal of la familia.[8] Any critique of unequal gender relations within the structure of the family was discouraged. Cynthia Orozco's historical research on Chicanas in the Chicano Movement and the Chicana Movement speaks to the dilemma of raising a critique of gender inequality: "When Chicanas raised the issue of male domination, both the community and its intellectual arm, Chicano Studies, put down the ideology of feminism and put feminists in their place" (1986, 12).

Chicanas who deviated from a nationalist political stance were subjected to negative sanctions including being labelled *vendidas* (sell-outs), or *agabachadas* (white identified) (López 1977; Nieto Gómez 1973, 1974). Once labeled thus, they became subject to marginalization within Chicano Movement organizations. Martha Cotera points out how even the label "feminist" was a social control mechanism: "We didn't say we were feminist. It was the men who said that. They said, 'Aha! Feminista!' and that was a good enough reason for not listening to some of the most active women in the community" (1977, 31). Such social and political sanctions discouraged women from articulating feminist issues.

The ideological hegemony of cultural nationalism was exemplified in the first official position taken by the Chicana Caucus at the 1969 National Chicano Youth Conference. While the motives behind caucus participants' decision to take the position that Chicanas are not interested in women's liberation have not been documented, the hostile climate to feminism within the Chicano Movement undoubtedly played a role in their decision.

Chicana writings and organizational activities of this period resounded with frustration over patriarchy in the Chicano Movement and a "maternal chauvinism" in the Women's Movement. Time and time again Chicanas argued that ending race-class oppression would not automatically eliminate sexual oppression (Del Castillo 1974; Flores 1973; Martínez 1972). Similarly, freedom from sexual oppression would not end oppression on the basis of race-ethnicity and class. They sought various ways to reconcile the tension between cultural nationalism and feminism. Chicana feminism reverberates with the dialectical tension between their lives and the ideological configurations that dichotomize their experiences and exploit their political loyalties. We now consider the extent to which this tension exists today among two groups of Chicana women.

The Women of MALCS

To explore the context of Chicanas attitudes toward feminism and their feminist consciousness, we analyze the relationship between the Chicano Movement, the American Women's Movement, and Chicana feminism based on a questionnaire administered to women on the mailing list of MALCS (Mujeres Activas en Letras y Cambio Social). This organization of Chicana/Latina women in higher education was founded in 1983 at the University of California, Berkeley. MALCS's charter and activities demonstrate familiarity with Chicana concerns, a feminist orientation, and sensitivity to cultural concerns. Each year MALCS organizes a four-day summer institute which includes panels on Chicana research and workshops on Chicana empowerment.

In our questionnaire, we asked women to answer a series of largely open-ended questions (with some closed-ended questions) on the Chicano Movement, the American Women's Movement, the Chicana Movement and feminism. In 1988, we mailed the questionnaire to all 178 women on the MALCS mailing list; 101 were completed and returned for a response rate of 57 percent.

Nearly all of the women who answered our questionnaire are associated with colleges and universities: 38.6 percent of them are faculty; 25.7 percent are graduate students; 8.9 percent are undergraduates; and 8.9 percent are professional staff at a college or university campus. Eleven women said they were employed outside of a university setting, and seven did not provide us with information on their employment or education.

The women were between 22 to 65 years old with a median age of 35 years, and a mean age of 38.1 years. This age distribution means that a majority of the women were college-age (17-22) during the heyday of the Women's Movement (1967-77). Moreover most of the women have activist backgrounds. Over three-fourths (78.2 percent) of the women either belong to, or have previously been involved in women's organizations. Women overwhelmingly (84.2 percent) self-identified as a "Chicana feminist."

The women of MALCS shared certain perceptions about their current and past experiences. They have varied work, family, community and political backgrounds and attitudes. Thus, it is impossible to characterize one single type of Chicana feminism. Hence, we offer a typology of Chicana feminism to try and capture the broad range of their critical interpretations of their feminisms. We hope this not only counters stereotypical views of Chicanas as non-feminists, or even anti-feminists, but presents them as women whose self-reflections demonstrate resistance, accom-

modation, and change—sometimes in contradictory ways—
rooted in simultaneously privileged and marginalized social locations. This analysis contributes to research on feminist consciousness by giving life and an historical base to the multidimensional
social contexts that frame Chicana feminism.

We emphasize that this group of Chicanas is not a representative sample of U.S. women of Mexican descent. But, as academicians or highly educated women, the women of MALCS inform
the public discourse on feminism and Chicana issues. While their
perceptions offer considerable insight on possible formulations of
Chicana feminism, they may not be generalizable to other Chicana women—an issue we explore later in this paper among a
group of Chicana white collar workers.

The Women's Movement and Chicana Concerns

Nearly all MALCS survey informants criticize the American
Women's Movement for failing to "adequately" address Chicana
concerns. MALCS Chicanas argue that the American Women's
Movement largely articulates issues best relevant to relatively
privileged, well-educated middle-and upper-class white women.
They object to what they perceive as a marked tendency within
the American Women's Movement to present itself in global
terms (e.g., *The* Women's Movement). Women feel this obscures
important racial-ethnic and class differences among women. As
one twenty-four-year-old graduate student writes:

> The "movement" has failed to adequately address classism and rac-
> ism and how it impacts on women as a class and in dealing with our
> areas of common concern (i.e. women and the family). I think we
> have been used to present a collective voice on behalf of women but
> have not been extended the same degree of importance to areas that
> concern us differently, i.e., class and race issues. In other words—
> white women also have to overcome their own prejudices as they try
> to overcome prejudice altogether.

Most of the women also object to any analysis of oppression that
puts gender first. They argue that overreliance on a gender critique inhibits the development of a more inclusive perspective sensitive to the ways race-ethnicity, class, *as well as* gender, shape the

Chicana experience. Although informants rarely distinguished between the different segments of the American Women's Movement, those that did (make this distinction) tended to have similar
criticisms. This suggests that informants feel Chicana concerns
are neglected across all the political or ideological groupings
within the American Women's Movement.

Despite their criticisms of the American Women's Movement,
nearly all of the informants endorse its key maxim—that ending
female subordination is essential. Many women credit the Movement for developing a critique of patriarchy—something that influenced their own development of Chicana feminism. Yet, while
they acknowledge that Chicanas can benefit from the struggle to
overthrow male privilege, most feel that any gains netted from
this particular struggle will be inadequate and largely incidental.
Moreover, since white, middle-class women tend to define the direction of the struggle against patriarchy, they are likely to benefit
the most.

A few informants credit feminists for beginning to move the
concerns of working-class and racial-ethnic women from, what
bell hooks (1984) terms, "margin to center." Many women feel,
however, this action has come from the *critiques* and *demands* of
women of Color. Not all women share this view however, as the
following twenty-seven-year-old graduate student indicates:
"Women of Color, particularly Chicanas themselves, have struggled as a group since the late '60s, early '70s to raise their/our
own issues as women from an oppressed nationality group in the
U.S. Our fight within the predominantly white, middle-class
'women's movement' has been to address the issues of class and
race, as *inextricable* [her emphasis] to our gender issues." This
woman's words speak to the need for white feminists to acknowledge Chicanas active resistance to patriarchy *as well as* race-ethnic
and class oppression.

Chicana Feminism

Nearly all of the informants (85 percent) self-identify as Chicana
feminists—only sixteen do not. Sixty-two women discussed the
meaning of Chicana feminism.[9] From their descriptions of Chicana feminism, we developed the following typology: *Chicana Lib-*

eral Feminism (n = 28), *Chicana Insurgent Feminism* (n = 21), and *Chicana Cultural Nationalist Feminism* (n = 13). Each category is grounded in the material condition of the Chicano people and highlights different aspects of Chicana feminism. Each encompasses diverse ways of interpreting oppression and advocating strategies for social change.

Chicana Liberal Feminism centers on women's desires to enhance the well-being of the Chicano community, with a special emphasis on improving the status of women. This perspective advocates change within a liberal tradition emphasizing access to social institutions, employment and equal treatment in all areas of life. Women in this category endorse political strategies to improve the status of the Chicano community through education, employment, health care services, and political involvement. As one twenty-six-year-old graduate student said: "[The] term 'Chicana' in itself represents a certain degree of feminism. She strives to understand the political, social, and economic state her people are in and actively seeks to make change that will advance her *raza* [people]." This perspective affirms Chicanas' desires to develop a personal awareness of women's needs and espouses an active commitment to improve the social and economic condition of the Chicano community-at-large.

Chicana Insurgent Feminism, on the other hand, emanates from a political tradition that contests the social relations of production and reproduction. Women who articulate these sentiments call for Chicana self-determination which encompasses a struggle against both personal and institutional manifestations of racial discrimination, patriarchy, and class exploitation. For example, the following fifty-year-old Chicana faculty member advocates revolutionary change to end oppression:

I believe that the impact of sexism, racism and elitism, when combined, results in a more intensely exploitative, oppressive and controlling situation than when these conditions exist independently of one another. The status and quality of life of the Chicano community as a whole can only improve/change when that of women within that community changes/improves. Any revolutionary change must include a change in relationships between men and women.

This woman argues that the cumulative effects of oppression are particularly pronounced for Chicanas. Similar to the previous informant, she links the liberation of Chicanas to the overall struggle of the Chicano community. Her words, however, contain a more strident and uncompromising tenor. For her, Chicana feminism ties liberation of the Chicano community to the struggle against patriarchy. Politically, she espouses a radical praxis advocating revolutionary change.

Other informants discussed the need for feminism to incorporate oppression based on sexual orientation and international solidarity with other oppressed peoples. One forty-year-old Chicana faculty member said, "I am active and critical with respect to political, social and cultural manifestations of sexism, racism, hispanophobia, heterosexism, and class oppression, and committed to working with others to create a more just society. It also means that I am moved by a sense of ethnic solidarity with Chicano, Mexican and other Latino people." This informant and a small, but vocal group of women advocate recognizing oppression on the basis of sexual orientation as central to Chicana feminism. Resonating the sentiments of the majority, this woman views political activism as a critical component of Chicana feminism. In general, *Insurgent Feminism* engages in a critique that calls for the radical restructuring of society.

Finally, *Chicana Cultural Nationalist Feminism* includes a small group of women that identify as feminists but are committed to a cultural nationalist ideology. They believe that change in gender relations should be accomplished without annihilating traditional cultural values. For example, one forty-one-year-old Chicana graduate student wrote: "I want for myself and for other women the opportunities to grow, and develop in any area I choose. I want to do this while upholding the values (cultural, moral) that come from my being a part of the great family of Chicanos."

Reminiscent of the slogan popularized within the Chicano Movement (that all Chicanos are members of the same family—*la gran familia de la raza*), *Chicana Cultural Nationalism* articulates a feminist vision anchored in the ideology of *la familia*. While advocating feminism this perspective retains allegiance to cultural nationalism which glorifies Chicano culture. *Chicana Cultural Nationalism* overlooks the possibility that these cultural traditions often uphold patriarchy. This speaks to the difficulty of reconciling a critique of gender relations within the Chicano community while calling for the preservation of Chicano culture.

Despite their different interpretations of oppression and strategies for social change, MALCS Chicanas articulate a feminist consciousness. They demonstrate a subjective identification with multiple groups each reflecting an affinity with women's unequal access to power vis-a-vis men, their membership in a socially subordinate racial-ethnic group, and a symbolic attachment to their working-class origins. Moreover, they reject the ideological and structural configurations that maintain Chicanas in a socially subordinate position. By and large they consider themselves Chicana feminists with interests that both intersect and diverge from those of Chicano men and white women. Both their sense of belonging to socially subordinate groups and their awareness of their social locations in society contribute to the high level of feminist consciousness within this group of women. MALCS Chicanas advocate social change—reformist in nature for some, revolutionary in nature for others. Chicana feminism then, exhibits what Cook refers to as a politicized feminist consciousness.

The attitudes of MALCS Chicanas towards feminism led us to consider whether their views are shared by other Chicana workers. In the following section we discuss white collar women's attitudes toward the Women's Movement and feminism. We also offer a preliminary view related to feminist consciousness. We explore the extent to which the strong sense of group consciousness we found among MALCS members resonates among the Chicana/Latina white collar workers.

Chicana White Collar Workers

The Chicana white collar workers selected for this study work at a major public university in Northern California.[10] We chose this site because it allowed us to access Chicana workers who work in an academic setting (like MALCS women) but are outside the relatively privileged research and teaching sector. We feel that exploring attitudes toward feminism among a group closer in income, working conditions, and status to the MALCS Chicanas is the next logical step in an inquiry on feminism that begins with academic Chicanas. Moreover, it provides us with a sense of the extent to which Chicana academics actually represent views beyond their relatively privileged realm.

For this study, we designed a mail survey containing a series of closed-ended questions on work, issues of race and ethnicity, the Women's Movement, and feminism. The actual questions were based on the views of the MALCS respondents as well as selected questions from other studies on American feminism.

In 1989, we mailed the questionnaire to all 312 self-identified "Hispanic" women workers at the research site; 152 women (48.7 percent) returned the questionnaire. The women's ages ranged from twenty to sixty-one years, with an average age of 36.5 years. They are well-educated: all but three women have high school diplomas; 65 percent have post-high school educations short of a bachelor's degree; and 15 percent have B.A.'s or above. About one-third of the informants belong to an Hispanic workers advocacy group on the campus. Nearly half have been involved in organizations aimed at promoting the needs of their racial-ethnic group and community. Relatively few women (20 percent) indicated they had been members of a group to promote women's needs or interests.

Chicana White Collar Workers and Feminism

Women in the study are familiar with the Women's Movement. Most of the informants (72.2 percent) feel the Women's Movement tries to empower all women.[11] About half of the Chicana/Latina workers believe that all women have benefited from the Women's Movement. When asked whether or not the Women's Movement advocates specifically for Chicana/Latina women, however, few respondents agree (20.3 percent). It is important to note that a relatively high number of women (37 percent) did not express an opinion on this particular question. Moreover, about one-quarter of the respondents feel the Women's Movement is not comprised of women from diverse racial backgrounds. This suggests that the Chicana/Latina workers are either unsure about the relevancy of the Women's Movement to their group, or are ambivalent about it. They do, however, appreciate its beneficial aspects.

Most of the women express opinions compatible with feminist

positions on key issues including a high level of concern with women's rights (94.7 percent) and agreement that women's roles should continue to change (93.2 percent). With respect to the controversial issue of women's right to a legal abortion, the respondents lean toward a pro-choice position with 43.4 percent favoring women's right to a legal abortion under "any" circumstances and another 48.7 percent favoring this right under "certain" circumstances. Only 5.9 percent denounce abortion under all circumstances. Concurrently many of the respondents would feel comfortable calling themselves "feminists" (52 percent), but most would not join a feminist organization (66.9 percent).

Some of the sentiments expressed by Chicana/Latina white collar workers complement those of the MALCS study. That is, both groups of women recognize the contributions of the Women's Movement to improve the status of women in our society. They are ambivalent however, with respect to the lack of a specific focus on Chicana/Latina issues. In general, the Chicana/Latina workers are more positive about the Women's Movement and American feminisms. Unlike the MALCS respondents, the white collar workers do *not* believe that the Women's Movement is primarily a white, middle-class movement. When presented with a "feeling thermometer" designed to gauge their feelings toward feminists, most Chicana/Latina workers indicated they felt warm or hot toward feminists.[12] Perhaps most surprising is the high number of women (52 percent) who feel they would feel comfortable calling themselves "feminists." There is a high degree of support for issues commonly associated with feminists, including the opinion that women's roles need to continue changing, and support for abortion rights. These findings are significant in that they counter commonly-held assumptions that Chicana/Latina women sustain more traditional gender values and are less likely to embrace feminist attitudes.

Chicana/Latina white collar workers demonstrate considerable attachment to key features of Mexican/Chicano cultural identity including Spanish/English bilingualism (60 percent) and Catholicism (67.8 percent). They also reveal a high degree of race-ethnic consciousness. Specifically, they are aware of the unequal location of their group in U.S. society—85 percent believe that "Mexicans do not share equally in the good life." By and large, women reject individualistic explanations for the persistent, low social status of

Mexicans in society. Rather, over half cite institutional discrimination in education and employment. Further, they recognize the need for group solutions (e.g., 70 percent advocate bilingual education; and 70 percent support teaching Mexican history and culture to all students).

Women also demonstrate high awareness of the ways gender construction intersects with Chicano/Mexican culture to constrain Chicana/Latina workers. When we asked women why Chicanas/Latinas are not employed in high-paying jobs, a majority cited both institutional and familial circumstances. That is, Chicanas are limited both by inadequate access to good jobs as well as "traditional" familial roles and gender expectations of women embedded in the ethnic community.

Women in this study affirm the need to formulate group solutions to eradicate gender inequality, often in support of key feminist positions (e.g., equal pay for comparable work). Their awareness of the unique social location of their group suggests elements of a combined race-ethnic and feminist consciousness.[13] In sum, Chicana/Latina white collar workers recognize and affirm their membership in a subordinate group and endorse group solutions to redress inequality.

Conclusion

The Chicanas in this study express feminist consciousness. For Klein, constituent features of feminist consciousness include the recognition of shared membership and shared sets of interests with the group, rejection of the rationale for the situation of the group, and affirmation of the need for collective solutions.

Using this criteria, MALCS survey informants express a feminist consciousness along all three dimensions. They identify themselves as Chicana feminists with a set of interests separate from both Chicano men and white feminists. Moreover, MALCS informants articulate an understanding of the ways that social, economic, and political forces maintain their subordinate status. Finally, this group of women calls for social change—reformist in nature for some; revolutionary in nature for others. Irrespective of the specific form their feminism takes, MALCS Chicanas affirm their struggle as integrally bound to the social and political struggles of the Chicano/Latino community-at-large.

Chicana white collar workers also demonstrate a feminist con-sciousness. A majority would feel comfortable calling themselves "feminists." They believe women's roles need to continue to change and uphold a pro-choice stance. They also articulate an awareness of the unique social vulnerability of Mexicans in the U.S., and advocate structural changes. Although the majority do not belong to organizations that focus specifically on women's is-sues, most of the women are or have been involved in organiza-tions that address community and/or ethnic concerns.

MALCS and Chicana white-collar workers share a strong group consciousness and espouse collective solutions to inequality. They differ however, with regard to their evaluation of the Wom-en's Movement—a movement aimed at redressing gender in-equality. MALCS informants express more negative criticisms of the Movement's efficacy to address Chicana concerns. This cri-tique is influenced by their perception that the Women's Move-ment primarily constitutes middle-to upper-class white women whose concerns reflect their class status. They assert that the bene-fits netted by Chicanas result from a "trickle-down effect" as op-posed to advocacy of working class, racial-ethnic women grounded in a direct understanding of their distinct material con-ditions.

The majority of the Chicana white-collar workers in this study do not perceive the Women's Movement as primarily comprised of white middle-class women. They express more positive evalua-tions of the gains to Chicana women resulting from the Move-ment's struggle to eradicate gender inequality. Similar to the MALCS informants, however, Chicana white collar workers do not believe the Women's Movement addresses the *specific* concerns of Chicana women.

How can we account for the differences in attitudes toward feminism between Chicana academics and Chicana white collar workers? Convergence in the mean ages of both groups of women places them in a similar political generation. That is, they repre-sent a cohort that has experienced the emergence of the "second wave" of American feminism and has been exposed to potential benefits from this Movement's activities.

Although both groups of women constitute a political genera-tion, they differ in their social locations, networks, and experiences. MALCS members have direct experience in both the Chicano Movement and the American Women's Movement; therefore they form a "politicized generation." With few exceptions, the white collar informants have not been involved in either social movement. The MALCS women work in close proximity to white feminist academics; most are also involved in Women's Studies programs. Moreover, their place within the university situates them to engage in the debate over the production of ideologies and agendas that comprise modern-day feminism. One result of this contestation across race-ethnic and class lines is a more critical or negative evaluation of American feminism and white feminists. This negative evaluation is compounded by the relatively greater access to opportunity in the academia of white women vis-a-vis Chicana faculty and graduate students (Baca Zinn, Cannon, Higginbotham, and Dill 1986).

The warmer attitudes toward feminism among Chicana/Latina workers may reflect their employment in situations where reforms advocated by the Women's Movement can benefit them (e.g. training opportunities, equal pay, affirmative action). Lewis (1983) observes that women do, in fact, articulate greater support for feminism when they perceived immediate benefits. Although Chicana/Latina white-collar workers are critical of race or class barriers, they do not always see feminist issues in class or racial-ethnic terms. Because the overwhelming majority of Chicana white-collar workers have not participated in the Chicano Movement or the Women's Movement, they do not have the same sense of the contradictions and contestations within these movements experienced first-hand by the MALCS women. These differences in social location, networks, and experiences between MALCS women and white-collar workers shape each woman's evaluation of feminism. Irrespective of these differences, both the MALCS women and the Chicana white collar workers affirm the significance of the struggle to eradicate all forms of social inequality. Their feminist consciousness flows from their group status as Mexican women in the United States.

Notes

1. The authors would like to acknowledge that the first part of our article

title is the final line from Ana Castillo's poem, "We Would Like You To Know," in *My Father Was a Toltec* (1988). Our research was supported, in part, by research grants from the Academic Senates of U.C. Davis and U.C. Santa Barbara as well as the University of California Consortium on U.S.-Mexico Relations (U.C. Mexus). Authors' names are randomly ordered.

2. We recognize that there are various branches of the American Women's Movement and numerous types of feminisms that are currently the subject of intense analysis. We use these larger terms because we are not interested in entering the debate of what American feminisms are, but rather discuss the shape and forms of Chicana feminisms.

3. In the late 1960s and early 1970s there were numerous Chicana activists that identified themselves as feminists. The constraints of space do not allow us to include all of them in our analysis. The Chicanas highlighted in this paper are among the most prolific writers of the time period under review.

4. One of the co-authors of this paper, Beatriz M. Pesquera, also attended this conference while an undergraduate student at Merritt College, Oakland, California. Her recollections inform Scenarios 1 and 2.

5. One notable exception is Anna Nieto-Gómez (1974, 4-5) who stated: "What is the Anglo women's movement? First, you have to understand that it is not a unified movement. There are at least three positions. There are the liberal feminists who say, 'I want access to power. I want access to whatever men have . . .' Then there are radical feminists, who say that men have the power, and that men are responsible for the oppression of women. A third position is that of women's liberationists which says that women's oppression is one of the many oppressions in the economic system of this country. . . "

6. We capitalize the word, "Color" as in women of Color since it refers to specific racial-ethnic groups. See Hurtado (1989).

7. Anna Nieto-Gómez (1973, 43) stated: "The women's movement seems to perpetrate a sense of maternalism by treating the Chicana in a childlike manner. During the 1972 National Women's Political Caucus Convention, the lack of Chicana representation, negative attitudes towards the Chicana caucus structure and the actions taken in respect to the Women's Education Act of 1972 seem to demonstrate this kind of *maternal chauvinism* [our emphasis] as an extension of racism."

8. For example, the Denver-based Chicano Movement organization, the Crusade for Justice stressed the concept of family unity as one of the central principles for self-and community-development (Lopez 1977). The national student organization, MEChA (Movimento Estudiantil Chicano de Aztlan) called upon students to recreate a feeling of *familia*, and "promote brotherhood" among Chicano students (Chicano Coordinating Committee on Higher Education 1969).

9. Thirteen women provided non-specific answers that did not fall into any discernable pattern; seven women did not elaborate on the meaning of Chicana feminism.

10. One shortcoming of this study is that we do not distinguish native-born Chicanas from foreign-born Mexican women. There is little published work on women of Mexican descent that makes this distinction. Also, relatively few of the informants in both studies indicated they were foreign-born Mexicans or Latinas. For readers interested in the differences between native-born and foreign-born Mexican women, see Tienda and Guhleman (1985).

11. We should note that we are in the process of interviewing one-third of this group of informants (n = 50). Thus far we have spoken with forty women. All of these women assert they are "fairly familiar" with the American Women's Movement. They indicate that their main source of information is the media. Few have taken women's studies courses; few have good friends they consider "strong" feminists.

12. Feeling thermometers were introduced in the 1964 American National Election Study. Wilcox, Sigelman and Cook (1989, 246) observe they are "standard tools in survey-based political research. Respondents use feeling thermometers to locate attitude objects on an imaginary scale ranging from 0 (very cold) to 100 (very warm)."

13. Inasmuch as our questionnaire did not have open-ended questions, the white collar respondents could not elaborate on this issue. Follow-up interviews (in progress) should shed additional insight on this important question.

Chicana Lesbians: Fear and Loathing in the Chicano Community

Carla Trujillo

The vast majority of Chicano heterosexuals perceive Chicana lesbians as a threat to the community. Homophobia, that is, irrational fear of gay or lesbian people and/or behaviors, accounts for part of the heterosexist response to the lesbian community. However, I argue that Chicana lesbians are perceived as a greater threat to the Chicano community because their existence disrupts the established order of male dominance, and raises the consciousness of many Chicana women regarding their own independence and control. Some writers have addressed these topics (Moraga 1983, 103, 105, 111, 112, 117), however an analysis of the complexities of lesbian existence alongside this perceived threat has not been undertaken. While this essay is by no means complete, it attempts to elucidate the underlying basis of these fears which, in the very act of the lesbian existence, disrupt the established norm of patriarchal oppression.

Sexuality

As lesbians, our sexuality becomes the focal issue of dissent. The majority of Chicanas, both lesbian and heterosexual, are taught that our sexuality must conform to certain modes of behavior. Our culture voices shame upon us if we go beyond the criteria of passivity and repression, or doubts in our virtue if we refuse (Castillo 1991; Alarcón, Castillo, and Moraga 1989). We, as women, are taught to suppress our sexual desires and needs by conceding all pleasure to the male. As Chicanas, we are commonly led to believe that even talking about our participation and satisfaction in sex is taboo. Moreover, we (as well as most women in the United States) learn to hate our bodies, and usually possess little knowledge of them. Lourdes Argüelles (1990) did a survey on the sexuality of 373 immigrant Latina women and found that over half of the women possessed little knowledge of their reproductive systems or their own physiology. Most remarked they "just didn't look down there."

Not loving our bodies affects how we perceive ourselves as sexual beings. As lesbians, however, we have no choice but to confront our sexuality before we can confront our lesbianism. Thus the commonly held viewpoint among heterosexuals that we are "defined by our sexuality" is, in a way, partially true. If we did not bring our sexuality into consciousness, we would not be able to confront ourselves and come out.

After confronting and then acknowledging our attraction, we must, in turn, learn to reclaim that what we're told is bad, wrong, dirty, and taboo—namely our bodies, and our freedom to express ourselves in them. Too often we internalize the homophobia and sexism of the larger society, as well as that of our own culture, which attempts to keep us from loving ourselves. As Norma Alarcón states, "[Chicana lesbians] must act to negate the negation."[1] A Chicana lesbian must learn to love herself, both as a woman and a sexual being, before she can love another. Loving another woman not only validates one's own sexuality, but also that of the other woman, by the very act of loving. Understanding this, a student in a workshop Cherríe Moraga and I conducted on lesbian sexuality stated, "Now I get it. Not only do you have to learn to love your own vagina, but someone else's too."[2] It is only then that the subsequent experiences of love and commitment, passion and remorse can also become our dilemmas, much like those of everyone else. The effort to consciously reclaim our sexual selves forces Chicanas to either confront their own sexuality or, in refusing, castigate lesbians as *vendidas* to the race, blasphemers to the church, atrocities against nature, or some combination.

Identification

For many Chicanas, our identification as women, that is, as complete women, comes from the belief that we need to be connected to a man (Flores-Ortiz 1990). Ridding ourselves of this parasitic identification is not always easy, for we grow up, as my Chicana students have pointed out, defined in a male context: daddy's girl, some guy's girlfriend, wife, or mother. Vying for a man's attention compromises our own personal and intellectual development. We exist in a patriarchal society that undervalues women.[3] We are socialized to undervalue ourselves, as well as anything associated with the concept of self. Our voice is considered less significant, our needs and desires secondary. As the Chicanas in the MALCS workshop indicated (Flores-Ortiz 1990), our toleration of unjust behavior from men, the church, the established order, is considered an attribute. How much pain can we bear in the here-and-now so that we may be better served in the afterlife? Martyrdom, the cloth of denial, transposes itself into a gown of cultural beauty.

Yet, an alliance with a man grants a woman heterosexual privleges, many of which are reified by the law, the church, our families and, of course, "la causa." Women who partake in the privleges of male sexual alliance may often do so at the cost of their own sense of self, since they must often subvert their needs, voice, intellect, and personal development in these alliances. These are the conditional contradictions commonly prescribed for women by the patriarchy in our culture and in the larger society. Historically, women have been viewed as property (Sanday 1974). Though some laws may have changed, ideologically little else has. Upon marriage, a father feels he can relinquish "ownership" and "responsibility" of his daughter to her husband. The Chicana feminist who confronts this subversion, and critiques the sexism of the Chicano community, will be called *vendida* if she finds the "male defined and often anti-feminist" values of the community difficult to accept (Moraga 1983, 113).

The behaviors necessary in the "act of pursuing a man" often generate competition among women, leading to betrayal of one another (Castillo 1991; Moraga 1983, 136). When a woman's sense of identity is tied to that of a man, she is dependent on this relationship for her own self-worth. Thus, she must compete with other women for his attention. When the attention is then acknowledged and returned, she must work to ensure that it is maintained. Ensuring the protection of this precious commodity generates suspicion among women, particularly single, unattached women. Since we're all taught to vie for a man's attention, we become, in a sense, sexual suspects to one another. The responsibility is placed entirely upon the woman with little thought given to the suspected infidelity of the man.

We should ask what role the man places himself in regarding his support of these behaviors. After all, the woman is commonly viewed as his possession. Hence, in the typical heterosexual relationship both parties are abetting the other, each in a quest that does not improve the status of the woman (nor, in my view, that of the man), nor the consciousness of either of them.

How does the Chicana lesbian fit into this picture? Realistically, she doesn't. As a lesbian she does many things simultaneously: she rejects "compulsory heterosexuality" (Rich 1980); she refuses to partake in the "game" of competition for men; she confronts her own sexuality; and she challenges the norms placed upon her by culture and society, whose desire is to subvert her into proper roles and places. This is done, whether consciously or unconsciously, by the very aspect of her existence. In the course of conducting many workshops on lesbian sexuality, Chicana heterosexuals have often indicated to me that they do not associate with lesbians, since it could be assumed that either (1) they too, must be lesbians, or (2) if they're not, they must be selling out to Anglo culture, since it is implied that Chicana lesbians do and thus any association with lesbians implicates them as well. This equivocation of sexual practice and cultural alliance is a retrograde ideology, quite possibly originating from the point of view that the only way to uplift the species is to propagate it. Thus, homosexuality is seen as "counter-revolutionary."

Heterosexual Chicanas need not be passive victims of the cultural onslaught of social control. If anything, Chicanas are usually the backbone of every familia, for it is their strength and self-sacrifice which often keeps the family going. While heterosexual Chicanas have a choice about how they want to live their lives (read: how they choose to form their identities[4]), Chicana lesbians have very little choice, because their quest for self-identification comes with the territory. This is why "coming out" can be a major source of pain for Chicana lesbians, since the basic fear of rejection by family and community is paramount.[5] For our own survival, Chicana lesbians must continually embark on the creation or modification of our own familia, since this institution, as traditionally constructed, may be non-supportive of the Chicana lesbian existence (Moraga 1986, 58).

Motherhood

The point of view that we are not complete human beings unless we are attached to a male is further promoted by the attitude that we are incomplete as women unless we become mothers. Many Chicanas are socialized to believe that our chief purpose in life is raising children (Moraga 1983, 113). Not denying the fact that motherhood can be a beautiful experience, it becomes rather, one of the few experiences not only supported, but expected in a traditional Chicano community. Historically, in dual-headed households, Chicanas (as well as other women) were relegated to the tasks of home care and child rearing, while the men took on the task of earning the family's income (Sacks 1974). Economic need, rather than feminist consciousness, has been the primary reason for the change to two-income households. Nevertheless, for many Chicanas, motherhood is still seen by our culture as the final act in establishing our "womanhood."

Motherhood among Chicana lesbians does exist. Many lesbians are mothers as by-products of divorce or earlier liaisons with men. Anectodal evidence I have obtained from many Chicana lesbians in the community indicates that lesbians who choose to become mothers in our culture are seen as aberrations of the traditional concept of motherhood, which stresses male-female partnership. Choosing to become a mother via alternative methods of insemination, or even adopting children, radically departs from society's view that lesbians and gay men cannot "successfully" raise children. Therefore, this poses another threat to the Chicano community, since Chicana lesbians are perceived as failing to partake in one of their chief obligations in life.

Religion

Religion, based on the tradition of patriarchal control and sexual, emotional, and psychological repression, has historically been a dual means of hope for a better afterlife and social control in the present one. Personified by the Virgen de Guadalupe, the concept of motherhood and martyrdom go hand in hand in the Catholic religion. Nevertheless, as we are all aware, religion powerfully affects our belief systems concerning life and living. Since the Pope does not advocate a homosexual lifestyle,[6] lesbians and gay men are not given sanction by the largely Catholic Chicano community—hence, fulfilling our final threat to the established order. Chicana lesbians who confront their homosexuality must, in turn, confront (for those raised in religious households) religion, bringing to resolution some compromise of religious doctrine and personal lifestyle. Many choose to alter, modify, or abandon religion, since it is difficult to advocate something which condemns our existence. This exacerbates a sense of alienation for Chicana lesbians who feel they cannot wholly participate in a traditional religion.

In sum, Chicana lesbians pose a threat to the Chicano community for a variety of reasons, primarily because they threaten the established social hierarchy of patriarchal control. In order to "come-out," Chicana lesbians must confront their sexuality, therefore bringing a taboo subject to consciousness. By necessity, they must learn to love their bodies, for it is also another woman's body which becomes the object of love. Their identities as people alter and become independent of men, hence there is no need to submit to, or perform the necessary behaviors that cater to wooing the male ego. Lesbians (and other feminist women) would expect to treat and be treated by men as equals. Men who have traditionally interacted with women on the basis of their gender (read femininity) first, and their brains second, are commonly left confused when the lesbian (or feminist) fails to respond to the established pecking order.

Motherhood, seen as exemplifying the final act of our existence as women, is practiced by lesbians, but usually without societal or cultural permission. Not only is it believed that lesbians cannot become mothers (hence, not fulfilling our established purpose as women), but if we do, we morally threaten the concept of motherhood as a sanctified entity, since lesbianism doesn't fit into its religious or cultural confines. Lastly, religion, which does not support the homosexual lifestyle, seeks to repudiate us as sinners if we are "practicing," and only tolerable if not. For her personal and psychological survival, the Chicana lesbian must confront and bring to resolution these established cultural and societal conflicts. These "confrontations" go against many of the values of the Chicano community, since they pose a threat to the established order of male control. Our very existence challenges this order, and in

some cases challenges the oftentimes ideologically oppressive attitudes toward women.

It is widely assumed that lesbians and heterosexual women are
in two completely different enclaves in regard to the type and
manner of the oppression they must contend with. As illustrated
earlier in this essay, this indeed, may be true. There do exist,
however, different levels of patriarchal oppression which affect all
of us as women, and when combined inhibit our collective liberation. If we, as lesbian and heterosexual Chicana women, can open
our eyes and look at all that we share as women, we might find
commonalities even among our differences. First and foremost
among them is the status of *woman*. Uttered under any breath, it
implies subservience; cast to a lower position not only in society,
but in our own culture as well.

Secondly, the universal of the body. We are all female and subject to the same violations as any woman in society. We must contend with the daily threat of rape, molestation, and harrassment—
violations which affect all of us as women, lesbian or not.

As indicated earlier, our sexuality is suppressed by our culture
—relegated to secrecy or embarrassment, implicating us as
wrongful women if we profess to fulfill ourselves sexually. Most of
us still grow up inculcated with the dichotomy of the "good girl-
bad girl" syndrome. With virtue considered as the most admira-
ble quality, it's easy to understand which we choose to partake.
This generates a cloud of secrecy around any sexual activity, and
leads, I am convinced, to our extremely high teenage pregnancy
rate, simply because our families refuse to acknowledge the possibility that young women may be sexually active before marriage.

We are taught to undervalue our needs and voices. Our opinions, viewpoints, and expertise are considered secondary to those
of males—even if we are more highly trained. Time and again, I
have seen otherwise sensible men insult the character of a woman
when they are unable to belittle her intellectual capacities.[7] Character assassinations are commonly disguised in the familiar "*vendida* to the race" format. Common it seems, because it functions
as the ultimate insult to any conscientious *política*. Because many
of us are taught that our opinions matter little, we have difficulty
at times, raising them. We don't trust what we think, or believe in
our merits. Unless we are encouraged to do so, we have difficulty
thinking independently of male opinion. Chicanas must be con-

stantly encouraged to speak up, to voice their opinions, particularly in areas where no encouragement has ever been provided.

As Chicanas (and Chicanos), most of us are subject to the effects of growing up in a culture besieged by poverty and all the consequences of it: lack of education, insufficient political power and health care, disease and drugs. We are all subject to the effects of a society that is racist, classist and homophobic, as well as sexist, and patriarchally dominant. Colonization has imposed itself and affected the disbursement of status and the collective rights of us as individuals. Chicana women are placed in this order at a lower position, ensconced within a tight boundary which limits our voices, our bodies, and our brains. In classic dissonant fashion, many of us become complicit in this (since our survival often depends on it) and end up rationalizing our very own limitations.

The collective liberation of people begins with the collective liberation of half its constituency—namely women. The view that our hierarchical society places Chicanos at a lower point, and they in turn must place Chicanas lower still, is outmoded and politically destructive. Women can no longer be relegated to supporting roles. Assuaging delicate male egos as a means of establishing our identities is retrograde and subversive to our own identities as women. Chicanas, both lesbian and heterosexual, have a dual purpose ahead of us. We must fight for our own voices as women, since this will ultimately serve to uplift us as a people.

Notes

1. Personal communication with the author at MALCS (Mujeres Activas en Letras y Cambio Social) Summer Research Institute, 3-6 August 1990, University of California, Los Angeles.
2. Chicana Leadership Conference, Workshop on Chicana lesbians, 8-10 February 1990, University of California, Berkeley.
3. There are multitudes of feminist books and periodicals which attest to the subordinate position of women in society. Listing them is beyond the scope of this essay.
4. As Moraga (1983, 103) states, "only the woman intent on the approval can be affected by the disapproval."
5. Rejection by family and community is also an issue for gay men, however their situation is muddied by the concomitant loss of power.
6. Joseph Cardinal Ratzinger, Prefect, and Alberto Bouone, Titular

Archbishop of Caesarea in Numedia, Secretary, "Letter to the Bishops of
the Catholic Church in the Pastoral Care of Homosexual Persons," 1 October 1986. Approved by Pope John Paul II, adopted in an ordinary session of the Congregation for the Doctrine of Faith and ordered published
(Grammick and Furey 1988, 1-10).
7. This occurred often to the women MEChA (Movimiento Estudiantil
Chicano de Aztlán) leaders who were on the Berkeley campus between
1985-1989. It also occurred to a Chicana panel member during a 1990
National Association for Chicano Studies presentation, when a Chicano
discussant disagreed with the recommendations based on her research.

The Politics of Race and Gender: Organizing Chicana Cannery Workers in Northern California

Patricia Zavella

Scholarship on women workers and labor history is beginning to show the complex issues involved in gender and labor organizing. Much of the literature focuses on the structural characteristics of the labor market, or on the gender ideology affecting women union members (Milkman 1985; Sacks and Remy 1984; Kessler-Harris 1982). This body of research clarifies the importance of gender in organizing women workers. But, as feminist scholars are aware, to understand fully the situations of women of color a multilayered analysis is needed. Women of color experience gender, class, and racial statuses concurrently, and a feminist analysis of labor organizing should focus on the totality of women's experience (Davis 1981; Swerdlow and Lessinger 1983; Nakano Glenn 1985; Joseph 1983; hooks 1983).

This article discusses the multiple issues involved as Chicanas, or Mexican-American women,[1] developed a critical consciousness and became participants in rank-and-file cannery labor organizing within the Teamsters union during 1977-78.[2] This study aims to bring out the complexity of gender, race, and class and their theoretical importance, as well as to aid activists in organizing Chicana workers in other industries. The issues involved in this research stem from the various approaches to organizing Chicana workers.

One possible approach is to organize Chicanas on the basis of their gender. Here organizers would have to contend with the presumption that women workers are more difficult to organize than male workers because women have domestic obligations and men do not. Thus organizers must recognize the division of labor within families, guided by the ideology that women should take responsibility for housework and child care, and that women's "place" should be in the home and does not involve the movement.[3] This popular ideology takes on a particular meaning when applied to Chicanas because of the commonly held notion that Chicano cultural values—deference to machismo and extreme dedication to home and family—prevent Chicanas from fully participating in labor organizing. This point of view ignores the history of Chicanas' participation in labor organizing.[4] Nevertheless, other problems of organizing Chicanas on the basis of gender remain.

Another approach would be to organize Chicanas on the basis of their ethnicity, making an appeal to Chicanas along with their Chicano cohorts and suggesting that the interests of women can be included within a Chicano ethnic perspective.

In 1977-78, two rank-and-file committees in the Teamsters cannery union—one in "Bay City" and the other in "Sun Valley," California—attempted to organize Chicana cannery workers by using these two radically different approaches.[5] As the following discussion emphasizes, the outcomes generated by the two perspectives were quite different.

One committee emphasized a women's separatist, although not explicitly feminist, strategy. This perspective assumes that female separatist organizing—the formation of women's culture and organizations—is an important organizing strategy for winning women's equality. Estelle Freedman's observation could be applied to the women's committee: "Any female-dominated activity that places a positive value on women's social contributions, provides personal support, and is not controlled by antifeminist leadership has feminist political potential" (Freedman 1979, 527).

The second committee set about organizing Chicana cannery workers primarily on the basis of ethnicity. Chicano nationalism was closely related to union politics in the canning industry. There had been a long-standing union jurisdictional conflict between the International Brotherhood of Teamsters, which represented cannery workers in northern California, and the United Farm Workers Union (UFW). Some Chicano cannery workers identified with the nationalist Chicano movement of the United Farm Workers, and affiliating with the UFW formed the core of their original organizing strategy.[6] Once the Teamsters and United Farm Workers unions signed a jurisdictional pact, Chicano Teamsters were forced to develop a new organizing strategy.[7]

The above-mentioned committees show how cannery activists had "contending ideologies" or approaches to women's participation in labor organizing. Sarah Eisenstein suggests that working women's attitudes and experiences as labor organizers grow out of the women's "active response both to new conditions of work and working-class life, and to the ideas that were available to them" (Eisenstein 1983, 5). This study suggests that the ideas and ideologies of the feminist movement and the Chicano movement were salient to Chicana cannery workers and to cannery worker organizers. Yet these two ideologies were not used exclusively, and there was an overlap when the "women's committee" and the "Chicano committee" formed an alliance with other cannery workers' committees and launched a successful suit against canning management and the Teamsters union on the basis of race *and* sex discrimination.

Making things more complicated still was the ultimate significance of grassroots organizing efforts aimed at race and sex discrimination. By the late 1970s, economic changes created a new context for organizing workers. Within an increasingly global economy, in which market and other constraints led to the demise of the canning industry in the Santa Clara Valley, the efforts at restructuring the internal labor market through a discrimination suit were ultimately of limited significance. This organizational dilemma reflected the convergence of several historical processes: the decline of the canning industry in which women (Mexican-Americans in particular) had become the predominant labor force, and the structure of the canning labor market in which women and men occupied very different structural positions.

Considering these issues, it becomes evident that women cannery workers' resistance needed to address two problems—women's daily struggles as working women, and the transformation of the world economy as experienced in the local labor market. This framework illustrates the strengths and limitations of two perspectives on organizing women that are exclusively gender-or ethnically-oriented. Theorist and organizers alike should pay simultaneous attention to Chicanas' experiences as well as to the structural and ideological context within which organizing takes place.

The Context of Organizing

The cannery labor force has long been segregated by race and sex, and more recently even by age. The perishable nature of the raw produce and the need for human judgment in handling it have imposed constraints on organizing production within canneries. These constraints have created a divided cannery labor market: mechanization of certain processes occurred in the late nineteenth century, while other processes continued to be performed by manual labor until quite recently. Further, most canning production is seasonal. Besides mechanization, management and union policies (after unionization by the Teamsters), as well as informal practices, contributed to the development of a bifurcated labor force. Men usually held the skilled jobs within canneries; women could get only unskilled, seasonal jobs, usually during summer months.

Mexican-Americans began settling in the Santa Clara Valley after World War II, when finding employment in the canning industry was relatively easy. Cannery employment in the Santa Clara Valley began declining in the late 1950s, however, so that only workers with high seniority could survive the layoffs. The result was that by the late 1960s the cannery labor force was extremely segregated by race and gender. Middle-aged women, especially Chicanas, formed a significant portion of the seasonal labor force (Zavella 1987). Chicano labor organizers sought to end what they perceived as institutional discrimination against Mexican-American women and men, who found barriers to job mobility.

There were several changes beginning in the late 1960s that influenced labor organizing by cannery workers. One of the most important was the repeal of lifting restrictions on certain cannery jobs. A 1971 court ruling, *Rosenberg v. So. Pacific*, struck down prior legislation restricting women from holding jobs that required lifting more than twenty-five pounds. The removal of this barrier meant that women could apply for what had been "men's jobs." Furthermore, the Equal Employment Opportunity Act (1972), which amended the 1964 Civil Rights Act, provided a legal basis for challenging race and sex discrimination in employment.

Other changes that influenced cannery organizing stemmed from the ideologies and resources of prior labor and social movements. In particular, the United Farm Workers Union, led by Cé-

sar Chavez, and the Teamsters union had a long-standing jurisdiction dispute over the representation of agricultural, packing-
shed, and cannery workers. Chavez delegated one of the UFW
lawyers to begin organizing cannery workers. Many Chicano cannery workers identified with the Chicano nationalist elements of
the United Farm Workers movement.[8] Many of them had been
farm workers themselves or still had relatives and friends who
were farm workers. Beginning in the early 1970s, there were de-
certification elections in some locals to remove the Teamsters and
to include "Teamsters for Chavez" in the UFW (Brown 1981,
246).

Organizing efforts within the canning industry were also affected by dissident Teamsters. Teamsters for a Democratic Union
(TDU) began organizing caucuses within many Teamsters locals,
and their newspaper, the *Fifth Wheel*, provided sympathetic coverage of Teamster struggles in different industries. The women's
movement, with its aim of challenging sex discrimination and advocating women's rights to equal treatment at work, was another
important influence. The example of feminist legal action was
particularly important to the suit filed by cannery organizers.

The Bay City Cannery Workers Committee

The Bay City Cannery Workers Committee was founded in the
late 1960s and was organized primarily by women. However, the
women organizers did not envision an explicitly feminist separatist women's group. Rather, they went through a gradual process
of establishing close relationships with female coworkers and later
became politicized. After years of working together in the "wom-
en's department," Connie García, one of the founders of the committee, and her friends had established a close "work-based network"—a network which included friends, acquaintances, and
even relatives from work whose members socialized at breaks and
lunchtime. There were a variety of these networks, but some of
the friendships that women established with coworkers became
"work-related networks." That is, coworkers became close friends
or even fictive kin of one another, and they socialized together
apart from the job. Work-related friends also provided important
emotional or social support for one another.[9]

The women who participated in these work-related networks slowly became aware of the discrimination against them. Connie García recalled how she became aware of it:

> I never noticed it [discrimination] too much. I wasn't very aware of discrimination per se. I had always known it was there; I had felt it all my life. But it was never clearly defined as discrimination. It wasn't until I got a little older and started looking around and wondering why all we Chicanas and Blacks used to work on the lines all the time, [while] the little Anglo girls got work in the lab. They got to work in the bottle lines where it was cleaner, and it wasn't so hard work, and you didn't have to be getting all dirty and wet and everything. And we started wondering why.

It is interesting that García (and apparently her coworkers) did not separate gender from race but saw a similarity of experience between Chicanas and Black women. Yet at the same time it was clear that white women workers were receiving better treatment. To García, the discrimination she and her coworkers experienced was based on race and gender: "We felt that not only were we being discriminated against because we were women, but because we were minority women. You know, there are Anglo women who work in the canning industry that have really good jobs, and they got the advancement where we didn't."

These Chicanas began developing a critical consciousness about their experiences through the discussions they had with one another. García said: "Then myself and several other women would talk about it, and we'd say, "Gee, how come those new [white] kids would go out and work the bottle line, and you know how it's nice and clean over there and it's not dirty like here.' So we started asking why we couldn't go over there." The women raised these questions with management, which did not respond to their concerns. García remembered being rebuffed by her supervisor when she inquired about the possibility of being moved to better jobs: "He said, "Oh no, no, no. You girls are awful good here.' You know, and 'It's the same pay, so why even go to a new job that you won't know?' And crap like that!" Another woman recalled her initial intimidation when she dared to apply for a promotion: "I did, a lot of times, put in bids, applications for better jobs, and never got them. Then you kind of just heard [things], and you just ignored it because you didn't want to really make a hassle about it. But I'm sure it wasn't because I wasn't qualified."

These problems inevitably came up when the women met to eat lunch or when they socialized together during the off-season. After much discussion, García and her friends decided to seek promotions to the better jobs that had usually been held by men:

> Well, in about 1972 with the weight restriction lifted, we started pushing for "men's" jobs. And we were told asinine reasons [by supervisors]: "No you can't do that because you have to crawl underneath things, you wouldn't want to get all dirty," and "It's too dangerous," or "This crank is too hard for you to turn," but they never gave us a chance to do it. They assumed that we could not. So when we first started, you know, we used to talk to each other and everything. We kind of got motivated to do something about it.

The women approached their union officials with complaints about how they were being discouraged from applying for better jobs, and they found little support. García said, "They'd [the union officials] give you some dumb excuse, like 'I don't know what you want me to do about it,' or 'Hey, I'll look into it, I'll see what I can do,' and you never heard from them again. So you never bothered calling them anymore. You realize that the union isn't going to do anything for you, so why bother?"

After receiving no response from the union, the women decided to try one more season of putting in bids for promotions. When they were not successful, they began organizing women workers: "That is why we got started, because we needed each other, because we had nobody else. And two heads are better than one. With a little bit of knowledge here and there, we were able to accumulate a greater knowledge of how to fight the company, how to fight the union, how to fight the smear of discrimination in the industry."

The original strategy was to serve as unofficial union officials, a process that continued for a long time: "To this day, I'm an unpaid shop stewardess, because people have confidence in me and because I am bilingual," García said. Elena Gómez, another founder of the committee, said:

> What I have been doing, and the rest of the girls in our group have been doing, it became common knowledge that we were just a bunch of "big-mouthed women," and we were hassling. There's a lot of

women who called me up and asked me, "What can I do? I want this job and they won't give it to me." And I'd say, "Well, what are your qualifications?" They'd tell me and I'd say, "Well I don't see why you can't have it. First call the union. Make the grievance to the union. I know what they are doing to tell you. But the minute they tell you they are going to look into it, call me, and I'll go to the company and hassle it for you." A lot of the girls got better jobs, jobs they had wanted for a long time.

The women in the group spent several years "hassling," which often included a frenzy of meetings. Garcia recalled:

> It [organizing] was a hell of a lot of work [laughs]!. . . There were days I'd come home just long enough to change clothes, and take off to some other town organizing, or go to a meeting. My phone would ring until eleven at night, people would call and say, "Hey, we're having this problem," and I'd go down and meet with them. . . . A lot of it was just relating to other cannery workers and trying to put this motivation into them, so that they wouldn't be so passive anymore, so that they would want to fight for their rights. . . . And that's all it was for the first two or three years.

Eventually the women organized a committee of Chicana cannery workers to address the discrimination against them.

Despite their success in organizing Chicanas, the leaders encountered several problems that they had not anticipated in organizing women, problems that stemmed from women's responsibilities in their families. Garcia believed that an obstacle to organizing women was the possible intimidation that arises when women have been socialized to defer to men:

> Women have never been very political, nor have they ever been allowed to speak their mind. We've always been mothers, housekeepers, nurses, maids, and that was our job. . . . We accepted it because that's the way we were taught, that we should accept it. And then they [women] were afraid because they just don't like to make waves, because the ones who have the power in the industry are men: Supervisors are all men—fore*men*, lead*men*,—and they're [women] afraid that if they caused any commotions, any problems, that they'd [men] make it harder on them. And they did! Hey, you'd better believe they did. But that doesn't mean that you can't fight them back on their own grounds.

Garcia found that husbands' and the women's own beliefs that
they should take primary responsibility for household tasks were
also a barrier to organizing women:

> I had a big problem when I first started doing this kind of work [orga-
> nizing women]. Their husbands won't let them do it. I never ne-
> glected my family, I came home and saw to them first, I saw that they
> were fed and clothed before I split. But my ex-husband is very fond of
> saying that if I had never joined the committee we'd still be married.
> Now our marriage was falling apart ten years ago, but he doesn't see
> that. And a lot of husbands use the same thing to intimidate their
> women.

During the canning season, workers often put in a lot of overtime
hours and sometimes worked six or seven days a week. Many
women had additional obligations to perform household duties at
home,[10] so their time was particularly limited during the work season. The organizers learned that they had to take women's home
responsibilities into account: "If I was going to have a meeting
here I had to schedule it so that husbands wouldn't be upset because their wives weren't home.... So I used to schedule the
meeting early so the wives could get home and cook dinner and
make sure their husband and the kids were fed before they could
come to the meetings."

The demands or desires of husbands also provided excuses for
women, excuses that wives did not provide for men: "I don't
know how many times girls would agree to go with me [to meet-
ings]," Garcia said, "and then in the morning they'd call and say,
'I can't go 'cause my husband wants to do this, my husband
wants that.' Yet the men in the committee never had that problem
.... It's real difficult to organize the women." Garcia found herself turning her frustration on the women: "I just get so mad for
them! I wish that they could feel the same anger that I feel! And
when they don't feel it I get angry at them."

These problems came to a head in a later organizing effort
when the women's committee decided to have one of the women
run for president. Although the candidate was narrowly defeated,
rumors suggested that it was her gender that had defeated her: "A
girl friend called me up before the election and she said, 'I was
talking with [some men], and they're so stupid, they said they
weren't going to vote for you because you're a woman.' I said,

'God love them if that's the worst thing God did for me [laughs].'"

Despite these difficulties, García, Gómez, and their cohorts persevered. The members of the committee then extended an invitation to a group of Black women who had organized their own committee, and the two groups occasionally had joint meetings. Elena Gómez believes that the feminist movement provided inspiration for organizing women cannery workers: "I think a lot of it has to do with the women's movement—it's so strong now. Women see all these other lawsuits going on and they realize [that] they have rights." This committee did not exclude men, though one member estimated that about ninety percent of the members were women. But García acknowledged that the Bay City committee was different: "The Cannery Workers' committees are run primarily by men; the members are men. Our chapter was unique because it was essentially all women."

Although they were not explicitly feminist in ideology or identification, these women were concerned with discrimination against minority women, and they took inspiration from the feminist movement. These women of color implicitly used a women's separatist strategy that included female leadership, women members supporting one another, and an overall concern with women's issues. By using this strategy, the organizers implicitly placed a priority on gender as the basis of their organizing. They encountered frustrating problems by using this model—the lack of support by male family members and women's family obligations—that could indicate problems in their approach. The success of their organizing efforts hinged on the support the women provided to one another and the instances when women overcame resistance by their husbands. It was difficult, however, to sustain a women's organization beyond the core group of dedicated organizers.

The Sun Valley Cannery Workers Committee

At the same time that women were organizing in Bay City, a group of cannery workers were forming the Mexican-American Workers Educational Committee in Sun Valley. The original membership was small and included primarily Chicano or *Mexicano* men. Like the initial meetings of the women, a Sun Valley member recalled, their early meetings were filled with discussion of their problems: "We would have general meetings at the church. There would be about twenty, twenty-five workers there, and we would have a bitch session." By learning about others' problems, members began to realize that they needed to change the union. Their goals were to educate cannery workers regarding their contractual rights and to advocate representation of Mexican-American workers within the Teamsters cannery union. Daniel Rodríguez, one of the founders of the Sun Valley Committee, recalled: "We formed the committee to pressure the union to defend the rights of workers, so they [management] would give more weight to the union." Since so many cannery workers spoke Spanish and could not understand the contract, which was written in English, the committee also sought bilingual meetings and the translation of union contracts into Spanish.

The Mexican-American Workers Education Committee soon changed its name to the Comité de Trabajadores de Canería, or Cannery Workers Committee (Comité or CWC). The members elected a president, vice-president, secretary, and treasurer, but the organization operated in an informal manner, with decisions arrived at through consensus. The Comité originally had no funding, and had to rely on donations and fund-raising to support its activities. It was strikingly heterogeneous in political ideology and in the organizing skills and experience of its members.

At one end of the political spectrum was Daniel Rodríguez, who had had a lot of experience in labor organizing. His father had been a socialist union official in Mexico, and Rodríguez had participated in union activities himself. He saw many similarities between the situation of corrupt union leaders in Mexico and Teamster officials in Sun Valley. When he was a young man, some corrupt union officials had tried to buy his loyalty, and Rodríguez angrily denounced them: "And my fighting spirit wouldn't let me participate in what for me were dirty activities. Because union leaders are like politicians. They are corrupt because they always gain benefits for themselves, not the worker." (This interview was conducted in Spanish.) Rodríguez believed that unions in the United States should be stronger: "Like in Mexico, unions are very strong, and besides being strong, are political. With the help of a union, one can make disputes locally or at the federal level, and with a lawyer or representative of the government, get support for the workers." Rodríguez recalled that his former union had its own building in Mexico that had served as a center for cultural activities: "There we would have meetings, afternoon get-togethers; [we would] celebrate birthdays, baptisms, dances, and holidays." He went on to explain how work was organized differently in the United States:

> Having a building where they could have meetings and social events, that was very different from the unions here in the United States. Here work and family life are very separated, but in Mexico it is not. There one's family can participate in the union; it was a more general thing. For example, on the sixteenth of September [Mexico's Independence Day] the whole family could come to the celebration. It was free, the employers donated money for drinks and food, the union paid for the orchestra. And everyone danced, they ate, they had a good time.

Rodríguez hoped that his activities in the committee would make the Teamsters union stronger, but for the benefit of the workers. He saw his former union in Mexico as a good model for the United States and hoped that the Comité could work toward a more family-oriented union where wives and children could participate in union social activities.

Another participant saw the struggle of the Cannery Workers Committee as part of a larger workers' movement for union democracy: "We are part of a broad historical process nationally, where union locals, caucuses, or committees are challenging entrenched union leaders, corruption, policies, lack of responsiveness to workers' needs, and lack of meeting the needs of special populations such as Chicanos or Chicanas as women. It is a general rank-and-file movement."

A third member believed that the purpose of the Comité was to build a city-wide coalition so as to influence city council elections and otherwise participate in city politics. A younger member, who had received some college education, characterized the group: "The focus ranges from communist world revolution, to leaving the Teamsters, to democratizing the Teamsters, to taking over this local, to getting a little relief for themselves." He believed that the lack of ideological unity was actually a strength of the group: "But that's good, there *should* be a range of ideologies."

The group's tolerance of divergent views also allowed outside organizers to join the Comité relatively easily. Some of these "outside" members often had extensive training and superior organizational skills, and they were able to influence the ideological direction of the Comité. More important, although Marxists were only a small part of the Comité's membership, Marxist literature was used to red-bait the whole group. Despite the ideological differences, nationalism was a core feature, as one member explained:

> Folks experience national oppression and respond to it better than the question of women. For example, Antonio is a shop steward, electrician who works year 'round, and is a seasonal foreman in the pear season. He studied to be an electrician in Mexico City but came here to work in the cannery because it pays more. He understands that he has reached his limit in the cannery; he has experienced racism in his daily life at work. Nationalism is an interest, it has always been the strongest appeal of the Comité.

In this case, nationalism meant the analysis of discrimination against Chicanos and *Mexicanos* on the basis of their racial status and the advocacy for their rights and needs as Chicano workers. Daniel Rodríguez had a different meaning of nationalism:

> The Mexicans from here [United States] and the Mexicans from Mexico, to me they come from the same root, they are the same [people]. I don't understand why the Mexicans from here can't get along as they should with the Mexicans from Mexico. To me, they are both Mexicans. And I care for the Mexicans from here in the United States as much as the Mexicans from Mexico. But today, in reality the Mexican youth from Mexico are better prepared, they understand more, they have more consciousness that we are the same people, that we come from the same root, and that we should be united.

Yet the racial homogeneity of the Comité's membership, and its nationalist platform made it difficult to attract other cannery workers to support them in the local elections.

These problems became apparent during the election of 1975. The Comité ran a slate of four members, only one of whom actually qualified to run for union office.[11] The Comité leadership realized that their candidates would not win, but they used the election as an educational campaign. There was some success. Normally elections were held during the off-season, and union of-

ficials could expect about four hundred members to vote. After
being threatened with an injunction on the election, the Teamsters
International president agreed to hold peak-season elections in the
future. The CWC was able to get about a thousand workers to
vote. Yet the Comité was very much a marginal organization, and
the membership decided to change strategies for the 1978 election.

One of the major problems in the Sun Valley Cannery Workers
Committee was the lack of participation by women. Of the original membership, only a few were women, and most of them left
because of pressure from their husbands. After these women left,
the remaining women were mostly the wives of the organizers.
Further, the original ideology did not include a focus on women's
issues per se. Rather, the perspective was one of racial discrimination—Chicano and Mexicano cannery workers were victims of
discrimination by canning managers and the Teamsters union.
This meant that women's issues were subsumed under ethnic interests. For example, when asked what issues were important to
women, one male member replied that the Comité did not know;
their orientation was toward *la raza* [Latino people]. In other
words, there was an assumption that the interests of Chicanas and
Chicanos were the same and that an "orientation" toward the interests of all Chicanos would include women's interests.

There were several reasons for the lack of participation by
women in the Sun Valley Comité. Most of the male members
were workers who had worked for many years in the industry and
had high seniority. Their problems were very different from the
problems of seasonal women workers. One member realized that
a major weakness of the CWC was the inability to recruit female
members: "The leadership is centered in men. They have dealt
with women's issues but haven't been able to accept women [lead-
ers]. The CWC leadership is year 'round, relatively privileged
men—Bracket I, IA, mechanics and foremen—who have a consciousness that that is as far as they are going to go because they
are Mexican. It is a privileged section of Chicanos and *Mexicanos*."

Another man with many years of experience as an organizer
was disturbed that there was not "significant participation" by
women in union or Comité activities:

> I tried to figure out how to organize women, and I can't. I think that
> to incorporate women into the union, first you have to organize sepa-

rately as women, and then incorporate them into other activities. Women should be organized in the kitchens, in the homes, at *tardeadas, lo que sea* [afternoon get-togethers, or wherever], not in union meetings. They don't attend meetings, they don't have the time to attend, to waste while people talk and start meetings late. The men can all get together, ride together, pick up a six-pack and go to the meeting. Women can't. Women also have children and need some place to leave them; child care at the meetings is not provided. Women also need to organize themselves. Any attempt by men to organize hasn't worked.

This man was inadvertently describing the women's separatist model used by women in the Bay City Committee. He was also willing to acknowledge that the Sun Valley Comité's stance on women's issues may have actually discouraged women's participation in the group: "The men in the CWC felt threatened by domineering women." Another male participant characterized the Cannery Workers Committee: "The Comité has a definite Mexican orientation, with males in control." The few women who had participated in the Sun Valley Comité were mostly middle-aged, without young children, and bilingual. These women were better able to communicate with union leaders and managers, as well as with women workers, and had fewer responsibilities at home than women with young children. One man explained: "It's hard to get women to participate, due to pressure from their husbands, pressure from [having to work] two shifts, doing all the home work. The CWC never responded well to that. The CWC recognizes that they need women on the committee, but in terms of practical tasks such as having child care, there is no need because there are no women in the CWC. But they recognize the contradictions."

It seemed that the solution would be to have women organizers who could recruit women members for the Comité. Yet the group was not able to attract a woman who would organize and remain a part of the Comité. Thus the committee implicitly focused its efforts on educating and advocating primarily for the rights of Chicano and Mexican men, even though it claimed to represent Chicanas as well.

The Regional Network

Rank-and-file committees were established at cannery locals in six cities in northern California, and representatives from these committees formed a regional network that met periodically between about 1970 and 1977. Connie Garcia described how the women from the Bay City Committee were invited to join the regional network, "We were approached by a group from [another city], the Cannery Workers Committee. And we decided that these people are having the same kinds of problems that we are, we should all work together and maybe we can learn from each other. Because none of us were really professional organizers. We didn't know how to fight the companies. So we just got together, we rapped, and pretty soon we just kind of organized our own chapters and went from there." The purpose of the regional meetings was to inform one another of the individual committee activities and to plan strategies so as to coordinate their actions.

Several workers from the regional committees filed complaints with the State Fair Employment Practices Commission. After hearings in Sacramento, their complaints were certified as evidence of discrimination on the basis of race and sex. The workers then filed suit (*Maria Alaniz et al. v. California Processors, Inc.*) in 1973, alleging race and sex discrimination on the part of California Processors, Inc., and the Teamsters California State Council of Cannery and Food Processing Unions.

After the suit was filed, one of the first activities of the regional network was to educate the members about the content of the collective bargaining agreement between the international Brotherhood of Teamsters, the Cannery Workers Council, and California Processors, Inc. The workers invited lawyers to translate and explain the contract in lay terms. One worker recalled, "We went through that contract and we examined it; we memorized it so that they couldn't say, 'Hey you don't know what the hell you're talking about.' This is something that cannery workers had never done before."

While they were waiting for the results of the suit, members of the regional network continued their organizing efforts by producing a newsletter. The *Cannery Worker* was distributed free between 1973 and 1976. Most of the articles were written by workers from all of the regions. The newsletter was a fairly sophisticated product, with well-written articles based on research among workers, and a professional layout. Some of the problems discussed included the inadequate pension plan, health and safety problems in the plants, and special assessments by the union.[12] The *Cannery Worker* served a critical function in educating cannery workers about the limitations of their contractual rights with the Teamsters union, and it openly criticized Teamster policies and leaders.

The regional network meetings became the place where the disparate concern with women's issues by the two committees was confronted. Connie García recalled that the women's "biggest problem" in participating in the regional network was "getting the men to take us seriously. . . . Sometimes the men freeze you out. I had to hassle in the Comité [about] this problem, in our own group I had to hassle it! Many times, we'd talk about things that we wanted to do to improve the industry, and it was all very male-oriented. I'd say, 'Hey I'm here, I'm here for a reason, 'cause I want to make it better for the women. How about a little input for the women?' "

The regional meetings often became a forum in which women confronted the male members about the inattention to women's issues and lack of women's leadership in the other committees. Gómez said: "Well, I'd hassle with them, because you know I don't give up. I'd say, 'Women have specific problems.' And we'd have some really screaming arguments, let me tell you, until they accepted me. Until they realized that I was not there to give them a bad time, I was there because I was very concerned. Then whenever I brought up something they'd say, 'You're right, Elena, yeah we were forgetting that,' you know?"

These and other struggles were going on[13] at the time that the discrimination suit reached settlement. In 1976, the San Francisco Federal District Court ordered the implementation of an affirmative action program that would provide access to promotions and better wages for women and minorities. The major change was the establishment of plant seniority—based on date of hiring whether in a seasonal or regular job—and the elimination of a rule that had allowed a worker "dibs" on his or her job the following season. The program also established preferential hiring, training programs, and monetary incentives so that women and minorities could qualify for and secure promotions. Affirmative action "parity"—the goal for hiring victims of discrimination—

was defined as women making up thirty percent of the high-paying jobs, and "parity" for minorities was to equal their proportion
of the county population. For Chicanos, this was 17.5 percent.[14]

The Teamsters union was ordered not to intentionally engage
in any discriminatory practice; to provide Spanish translations of
all bylaws and collective bargaining agreements, as well as to
make an annual determination of which minority groups constituted a significant percentage of its active membership; and to
provide translations of bylaws and contracts in the appropriate
language if necessary. The union locals were also ordered to record the number of grievances filed by women and minorities and
to report them to the State Council of Cannery and Food Processing Unions. Further, the Teamsters State Council was ordered to
hire minority and female employees in union staff positions in the
same proportion as their representation in the work force.[15]

The affirmative action program provided the possibility of promotions for members of minority groups much faster than for
women. By defining parity for minorities as their proportion of
the county population—which was relatively low—rather than
their proportion of the largely minority cannery labor force, the
canners could achieve compliance fairly quickly. Just two years after the settlement in 1978, fifty of sixty-four plants covered by the
Conciliation Agreement suit had achieved their goals for hiring
minority males in all of the higher-paying jobs, and thirty-six had
hired enough minorities as skilled mechanics. Only one plant had
achieved the goal for hiring women in high-bracket jobs, and only
four plants had hired enough women in the mechanics' jobs.
There were no separate parity goals set for minority women.[16]
Since these data are for the northern California canning industry
as a whole, it is impossible to figure out how many women in
Santa Clara Valley canneries were affected by the affirmative
action program. I would estimate there were very few.[17] Further,
the overwhelming majority of back-pay claims were eventually
denied because of insufficient evidence. The result, then, was that
the affirmative action program benefitted minority men and, to a
lesser extent, white women.

By the late 1970s the canning industry had begun a severe decline in northern California. Chicano women became rivals of
Chicano men and white female workers for the few promotions to
be had. Not surprisingly, the tension over this competition for jobs

was expressed in the regional committee meetings. Connie García said: "And I had a lot of the guys tell me 'Well, women are taking men's jobs, and that means that some of us aren't going to be able to work.' In the Comité! At general meetings! I had to explain, 'If the woman has more seniority than you, then she has the right to take that job.'"

The women organizers then, were forced into a situation where they had to "hassle" with their own allies. García found that confronting union officials was hard enough, but having to confront her fellow organizers was discouraging: "Sometimes I'd tell Elena, 'Sometimes I wonder if its really worth it. These people are so damn ignorant that they can't see beyond their noses!' And she'd go, 'Aw Con, you know, that's the way things are,' and pretty soon she'd get me out of my bad mood, you know [chuckles]? Everybody needs someone like that to calm them down."

Meanwhile, the Teamsters' and United Farm Workers' jurisdictional conflict escalated as both unions sought to represent farm workers. After violent incidents in the fields, in which one farm worker was killed, the two unions negotiated a truce in 1977. They agreed that for the next five years cannery workers would remain under the jurisdiction of the Teamsters, and farm workers would be organized exclusively by the United Farm Workers. Many Chicano cannery workers felt betrayed by this agreement, for it left them in a union that they believed did not meet their needs as workers.

The nationalist tone of the cannery workers' movement became problematic at this point, and the ideological perspective of the various committees was called into question. Some committee members wanted to exclude avowed Marxists or socialists and have only Chicanos or *Mexicanos* as committee members. Others were willing to tolerate different ideological perspectives and wanted a multiracial membership that focused on workers' issues. Eventually the regional network disbanded because this disagreement could not be resolved, and the different committees continued organizing at their union locals.

The Sun Valley Union Election Campaign

The Sun Valley Cannery Workers Committee began a strategy of infiltrating the teamsters local from within, and in the process altered its campaign ideology to appeal to all disgruntled cannery workers, especially women.

In the 1978 local union elections, the Cannery Workers Committee ran a slate of candidates for union office. This was notable because the slate was multiethnic-including an Italian-American man who ran for president and a Japanese-American woman who ran for trustee. The slate had the simple slogan: "Vote for a Change." The incumbent secretary-treasurer (the position with the real power) was college educated, and this added to the perception by members of the committee that he could not understand their problems as workers. The Comité sought to replace him with a Chicano worker who would provide leadership regarding the needs of all workers.

The overall message of the Cannery Workers Committee campaign included basic union issues: an end to "special assessments," better health and safety at the plants, worker input into contract negotiations, vigorous contract enforcement. The Comité called for an end to discrimination and for the education of cannery workers regarding their contractual rights and grievance procedures. The Comité issued a series of leaflets suggesting that the incumbents had neglected the concerns of workers and that the CWC slate should include candidates who would be sensitive to the needs of cannery workers, including Spanish-speakers. The Comité also demanded Spanish translations of the union contract and bilingual union meetings. The campaign slogan was bilingual —"*Justicia e Igualdad*/Justice and Equality"—as was all of the campaign material.

This was a local election in which the Teamsters were forced to campaign actively for the votes of the largely Mexican and Chicano labor force. The majority of the candidates on the Teamsters slate of sixteen were Spanish-surnamed. Both Teamsters and the Comité purchased spots on the local Spanish radio stations, with Mexican music and announcers exhorting cannery workers to vote, and ran advertisements in local community newspapers to get out their election message—"Experience and Leadership."

The election was a watershed for many reasons. This was the first time that many cannery workers would be present for peak-season union elections. The Cannery Workers Committee provided basic education on how to vote, including procedures and locations and the hours the polls would be open. This kind of education was crucial because many cannery workers could not read or write English and had difficulty understanding spoken English. The eventual turnout reflected the value of teaching workers how to vote: more than five thousand workers voted, some for the first time. The Comité won six out of the ten positions it sought, a victory that symbolized its potential strength to change the Teamsters union from within.

When asked what were the important issues of this campaign, Tony Divencenzo, who had run for president on the Comité slate, said: "The past regime was consistently lax—they weren't taking care of issues people were bringing up." He described the meaning of the election results: "It was a breakthrough for the people: People finally realized that they [union officials] weren't doing the job. Finally they [the people] can beat a machine that has been there a long time; [so] any type of machine can be broken. . . ."

By September 1978, with funds from the Catholic Church's Campaign for Human Development, these efforts at union democracy were given institutional support with the opening of the Cannery Workers Service Center (CWSC) in Sun Valley. The center held bilingual classes offering shop steward training, produced a newsletter, and provided legal counseling and referrals to social services. This service center in many ways was modeled on the United Farm Workers' service center. Several members of the Cannery Workers Committee served as board members for the CWSC. With support from its legal consultants, the service center was able to get the union to provide contracts in Spanish after a two-year effort.

Despite the victories in the race and sex discrimination suit, and in the Sun Valley local election campaign, workers from several committees realized the limitations of their organizing activities. They were quite literally outside agitators in the sense that they were not allowed to participate in union activities except in the capacity of union officials. For example, even though Comité members could influence other workers to file grievances, neither they nor workers' lawyers were allowed to attend the arbitration hearings. One Comité member found this to be a problem: "Once you join the union, you give up the right to challenge, other than through the union procedure. You give up the right to self-representation." Thus, they realized that the Comité had a limited role in the highly bureaucratized arbitration procedure and other union activities: "All the Comité can do is agitate, raise workers' consciousness, raise issues." Connie García from the Bay City Committee had similar views about organizing women: "Our main job is education. If somebody comes to us [with a problem], we try to solve it for them. [But] we make them do it [file a grievance] themselves, because we cannot really go and hassle for them because we get locked out of personnel offices, we get thrown out of union halls. We have to push this person."

Soon after the 1987 elections, the decline of canning in the Santa Clara Valley began in earnest. By 1984, eight canneries had closed and almost nine thousand cannery workers had lost their jobs (Zavella 1987, chap. 6). At the time, several people experienced this period as a "calm before the storm," although most did not realize what was in store for the industry. Connie García said:

> I have a feeling that what's happening now is they think we're running scared: "The X plant closed, this one might not be there too much longer, now we can push the people around. We'll stop using the seniority list for advancement, we'll go back to the old slave tactics that we used before." I see it coming. . . . I get very upset! Because I can see the whole thing starting all over again, 'cause for a while there the company was going primarily by seniority and qualifications. Now they're going back to qualifications [only] . . . that we had them throw out in court.

The members of the regional network created a "parallel central labor union" (Lynd 1979) that duplicated the union structure but operated informally, and pushed aggressively for the needs of the rank-and-file membership. The Cannery Workers Service Center functioned as a "shadow" union hall (Brown 1981) for the alternative labor union, providing the services and advocacy that the CWC membership believed the Teamsters union should have provided. Yet, as outsiders, they had little recourse to internal resources. When the industry eventually began relocating to California's Central Valley, the "outside" labor union was left behind.

Conclusion

In reflecting about the two approaches to organizing Chicana cannery workers, it is apparent that both models were successful in some senses but needed to modify and expand their approach in others. Both committees built their organizational membership on relationships that had been firmly established, either in the workplace or in the community or in both. The "women's committee" in particular was formed by women who had intense work-related networks that were continued and deepened in the off-season outside work. For the most part the women had not been prior organizers. They politicized one another in the course of social activities and informal discussions and "motivated" each other to begin more formal organizing. The "men's committee" also was formed by men who had worked, socialized, and "bitched" together. Yet it appears that some of the male members had had a history of participation in labor organizing in other situations.

With the benefit of hindsight, we can criticize the Chicano committee with its ethnic, nationalist approach that did not appeal fully to Chicana workers. Some members of that group were well aware of the need for a gender approach in their organizing efforts, especially in attracting women organizers and somehow modifying what seemed like male dominance within the group. Others assumed that women's interests should be included in an "orientation" based on race. Though this group eventually abandoned its focus on race and sought to recruit all dissatisfied Teamsters, especially women, it had established a tradition of male leadership. The group was successful in securing institutional support in the form of the Cannery Workers Service Center and gained important union elected positions—all of which benefitted women cannery workers. Nevertheless, this committee did not create a significant appeal to women workers or develop women's leadership.

The women's committee, on the other hand, developed out of women's critical consciousness about their experiences on the job. The focus of their political activity was job discrimination. Women's family responsibilities were seen as barriers to their full participation in organizing and were the sources of great frustration. It would have been more helpful to focus on organizing support mechanisms—particularly child care—rather than on frustration. Additionally, the women might have found ways to include husbands in their activities to convince reluctant spouses of the value of the committee's work. Although the women's committee took inspiration from the feminist movement and aimed at changing the institution that supported discrimination on the basis of race and sex, the concerns of women's daily lives were not addressed.

Both of these committees, then, can be seen as products of their context of origin—the Chicano movement and the women's movement—which had an exclusionary appeal. It is only recently that feminists are beginning to articulate a public discourse that goes beyond the critique of women's oppression within families and recognizes how women's work and family roles are related. Chicano activists, on the other hand, have begun forming coalitions with other community and workers' organizations and criticizing the fact that Chicanas' interests are not fully included within a Chicano perspective. As we examine the limitations of these movements, it becomes apparent that a separatist politics, whether based on race or on gender, is problematic when organizing women of color.

Further, the experience of these two rank-and-file workers' committees suggests the importance of the changing structure of the labor market for organizing workers. The U.S. economy has become a global system in which the competitive pressures of production costs and other factors have "de-industrialized" several manufacturing locations, as occurred with canning in northern California. Labor organizers, then, will have to pay close attention to the ways in which capital constantly adapts and restructures to accommodate the changing conditions of production in order to develop appropriate strategies for organizing women workers.

Acknowledgments

The research for this article includes participant-observation— I was an organizer for one of the committees discussed herein. I would like to thank the workers and labor organizers who educated me about the cannery workers' movement, and I regret that they must remain anonymous. Felipe Gonzales made many useful comments on successive drafts of this article. Bill Friedland, Lupe Friaz, and Jaime Gallardo also made helpful comments on this chapter. Ann Bookman and Sandra Morgen deserve special acknowledgments for their patience and enthusiastic support, as well as their helpful suggestions for revisions.

Notes

1. "Chicana/o" refers here to persons of Mexican heritage who were born or reared in the United States; "Mexicans" or "*Mexicanos*" refers to those who migrated as adults to the United States form Mexico. The terms that my informants used to identify themselves varied, depending on the context, and sometimes different terms were used interchangeably. For a discussion of the context and complexity of Mexican-American ethnic identification, see García (1981); Limón (1981); Gonzales (1986); Miller (1976).

2. Cannery workers were represented by the California State Council of Cannery and Food Processing Unions, International Brotherhood of Teamsters, Chauffeurs, Warehousemen, and Helpers.

3. Reyna Rapp (1978) analyzes the facets and pervasiveness of family ideology in American culture. See also Collier, Rosaldo, and Yanagisako (1982); Milkman (1976). For a critique of how culture determinism has been used to explain Chicana's labor force participation rates, see Ruiz (1984); Segura (1984); Zavella (1984).

4. Coyle, Hershatter, and Wong (1980), and Clementina Duron (1984) address the stereotypes of Chicana traditionalism directly, showing the ways Chicanas have established alliances with other labor activists and how Chicanas had to challenge traditional notions within their own communities. For other works on Chicana's participation in labor organizing, see Almaguer and Camarillo (1983); Cantarow, O'Malley, and Strom (1980); M.T. García (1980); Mirande and Enriquez (1979); Mora (1981); Wilson and Rosenfelt (1978).

5. There were thirteen Teamster cannery union areas in northern California, stretching from Salinas in the South to Watsonville near the Central Coast, Vacaville in the North, and Modesto in the west Central Valley, and there were several within the Santa Clara Valley itself. "Bay City and "Sun Valley" are pseudonyms.

6. For discussions of the struggle for unionization by farm workers in California, see Friedland and Thomas (1974); Galarza (1964, 1977); Kushner (1975); Levy (1975); Nelson (1966); Matthiessen (1969); Taylor (1975); Thomas and Friedland (1982).

7. I did participant-observation with this group in 1977-78, including helping to coordinate a union election campaign. I made my status as anthropologist clear to the organizers, and the members developed organizational ideology and strategies. All of the informants cited here have fictional names.

8. The United Farm Workers organizing drive, which began in 1965, was an important impetus for the Chicano Movement—or *La Causa Chicana*—which was a political and cultural florescence seeking change in higher education and education generally (for example, the Los Angeles student walkouts), an end to the Vietnam War, and the creation of new cultural expressions in the theater (with the expansion of Chicano *Teátros*), the arts, and literature. See Acuña (1981); García (1974); Rosaldo, Seligmann, and Calvert (1974).

9. See Zavella (1985). I argue that work-based and work-related networks are important expressions of women's cannery work culture. Also see Zavella (1987), esp. chap. 4; Benson (1978, 1983); Costello (1985); Lamphere (1985); Melosh (1982).

10. See Zavella (1987), esp. chap. 5, for discussion of women's household responsibilities. I argue that the segregation of women into seasonal jobs, with unemployment during the off-season, influenced many women to remain homemakers. These women saw themselves as housewives who happened to work seasonally and took responsibility for the majority of household tasks during the work season.

11. To qualify to run for union office, one had to be a union member in good standing, which meant one had to have attended all meetings except two within the previous two-year period. This provision of the bylaws excluded the participation of seasonal workers, who often did not attend union meetings during the off-season. See Zavella (1987), chap. 2.

12. *Cannery Worker*, all issues, 1973-1976.

13. The whole question of participation by "outsiders" (noncannery workers), especially those affiliated with political organizations, was hotly debated. Also, a group of workers intervened in the suit because they found the initial Conciliation Agreement inadequate.

14. This figure was for the "Spanish-origin" population in Santa Clara County-a category that includes greater numbers of people than does the "Mexican-origin" category. So although the cannery labor force was made up of mainly Mexican-American workers, the broader Spanish-origin category was used to represent the class of discriminated-against workers.

15. The intervening workers had been dissatisfied because the goal of thirty percent of new promotions for women did not equal the proportion of women (approximately fifty percent) in the cannery labor force. The true extent of discrimination against Mexican-American women as distinct from Mexican-American men was denied; there was inadequate compensation for the discrimination suffered by minority men; and there were no fines levied on the Teamsters union. The intervenors' motions for reversal were denied. See Zavella (1987), esp. chap. 2.

16. Unpublished Status Report, Cannery Industry Affirmative Action Trust, Walnut Creek, September 21, 1979, 2.

17. A Department of Labor study estimated that to gain proportional representation for women, more than half of all promotions would have to be given to females. When the María Alaniz suit was filed (in 1973), a pilot training program had been established to provide the necessary training to women and minorities. An evaluation of the three-year program showed that only thirty-five percent of promotions had gone to women. See U.S. Department of Labor (1978).

Psychoethics, Bioethics
and Policies of
Identity and Difference

Las Tres Marías
Catalina Govea

Key Issues in Latina Health: Voicing Latina Concerns in the Health Financing Debate

Adela de la Torre

Demographic Trends: Implications for Latina Health

Latinos in the United States represent a rapidly growing and diverse population. According to the recent census, there are over twenty-two million Latinos comprised of several subgroups: Mexican-origin/Chicano, Puerto Rican, Cuban, and other Central and South American groups. As a result of geographic proximity, as well as political and economic forces, the Mexican-origin population comprises the bulk of the Latino population in the United States. Over sixty percent of Latinos in the U.S. are of Mexican-origin, twelve percent are Puerto Rican, and about five percent Cuban (Gantz McKay 1991). Latinos are the fastest growing group in the United States due to both relatively higher fertility rates and their high rates of immigration.

Concentrations of Latinos in various states, i.e., Mexican origin in the Southwest, Cubans in Florida, and Puerto Ricans in New York, reflect not only patterns of network migration, but also magnify the problems and concerns facing these various groups. For example, in states such as California and Texas, where about one-quarter of the residents are of Mexican origin, inequities in health or education affecting Mexicanos/Chicanos will be of greater significance in policy deliberations and formation. Another critical component in the demographic Latino profile is the increased feminization of poverty. The breakdown of the two-parent household, as well as the legacy of the Reagan administration's attack on social welfare programs targeted for the poor and working poor, has disproportionately affected minority groups, particularly Latinas. According to one study: "In the Southwest, more women became head of households between 1970 and 1980. Over forty percent of all Chicana and Black female headed families were poor in 1980, whereas only eighteen percent of White female headed households in the Southwest were poor" (de la Torre and Rochin 1990, 8).

Although poverty measures generally focus on income and earning, "it is also a social condition apparent by such indicators as housing, schooling, nutrition, and medical care" (Gordon-Bradshaw 1988, 247-48). In the United States, no social indicator is more sensitive to economic status than access to health care. As private health insurance is largely determined by employment status, workers who work part-time, are self-employed, are in sectors such as agriculture, personal services, sales or who work for small businesses are the least likely to have health insurance coverage (General Accounting Office 1991a). Unfortunately, many Latinas/Chicanas fall within this status, thus limiting their access to private health insurance, and subsequently, influencing the observed health status problems. Access to health care for Latinas is not only a problem of financial constraints, but also, reflects limited access to regular and routine medical care (Council of Scientific Affairs 1991). Thus, both financing as well as the delivery of care play pivotal roles in describing the access problems facing Latinas. It is only within the context of access to care can the significance of the health status problems facing Latinas be understood and strategies to ameliorate their specific health problems can be appropriately developed and delivered.

Latina Health Status Issues: An Overview

In general, the Latino population is relatively youthful. Whereas the general population exhibits an aging pattern with fertility levels below a steady state of reproduction, the Latino population exhibits a relatively high fertility rate: for the United States general population the fertility rate is about 65/1000 live births, compared to 97/1000 live births for Hispanics. A typical pattern observed of Latinas is that they give birth at younger ages and have on average more children than the general population (Ginzberg 1992). Given the relatively higher fertility rates for Latinas an obvious need is access to prenatal and postpartum care, as well as to family planning information.

Several studies that focus on health behaviors and access to care of Latinas observe that these women underutilize such services. According to one study: "Excluding Cubans, sixty percent of Hispanics initiate prenatal care in the first trimester, compared with eighty percent of Whites. Hispanics are three times as likely as non-Hispanics to receive no prenatal care. Among the subgroups, Puerto Ricans received prenatal care later and less often." (Council of Scientific Affairs 1991, 249).

Underutilization of health services by Latinas, particularly those services such as prenatal care, that are comparatively better financed by the public sector than other outpatient services, is a major concern for many public health advocates because of the increased risk associated with insufficient prenatal care for low income women (Braverman, Oliva, Miller, Reitter and Egerter). Although Latinas underutilize prenatal care, birth outcomes for specific subpopulations, such as Mexican-Americans, are relatively good. It has been suggested that surprisingly positive birth outcomes for certain Latina subpopulations can be attributed to low levels of acculturation and recent immigrant status (Furine and Munoz 1991). Despite their lower social class, the positive health behaviors of recently immigrated Latinas with respect to alcohol, drug and cigarette use influence the observed birth outcomes. That is, studies of recent immigrant Latinas, particularly Mexican-origin Latinas, suggest relatively low levels of alcohol, tobacco, and drug abuse during pregnancy. However, there are no guarantees that such behaviors will be replicated over time, particularly as these women become more incorporated into the dominant culture and greater economic pressures are placed on their families.

Although low-risk health behaviors are critical in reducing maternal and infant morbidity and mortality, without appropriate health screening increased adverse health outcomes are possible. Early detection of disease and appropriate diagnosis and treatment result not only in cost savings, but also, generally more successful outcomes. It is within this context of health screening and high risk health behaviors that Latinas become a highly vulnerable population.

Recent epidimiological studies on cancer have indicated that Hispanic women have twice the rate of invasive cervical cancer as compared to White non-Hispanic women (Ginzberg 1992). Early detection through relatively low cost Pap smears and intervention require Latinas to be adequately screened and to maintain continuity of care. Both criteria, although necessary for low-cost prevention and treatment, are lacking due to limited access to care and inadequate knowledge and/or perception of the danger of the disease (Ginzberg 1992). Other diseases of which Latinas are at higher risk, and that could benefit from better access to regular and continuous care are type II diabetes (there is a higher incidence for both Puerto Rican and Mexican-American origin women) and obesity. Approximately one-third of Mexican-American and Puerto Rican women are obese (Ginzberg 1992). The occurance of type II diabetes is approximately two to three times that of the non-Hispanic population. Moreover this often strikes a younger age group and leads to complications if not immediately treated. Obesity has long been associated with increased risk of cardio-vascular disease and other health problems. Early intervention with proper nutritional counseling and improved diet and exercise greatly reduce the risk from this disease.

A final area that has become of increasing concern to the public has been the increase in AIDS transmission within the Latino population. This particular problem is of increasing concern when examining the transmission of pediatric AIDS. A recent study in New York City concluded that forty percent of all AIDS patients under thirteen were Latino (Ginzberg 1992). Although over fifty percent of the AIDS transmission can be traced to intravenous drug abuse in New York City, sexual transmission of the disease within the Latino population cannot be dismissed as a critical factor. Unfortunately, AIDS transmission within Latino subgroups has been viewed disproportionately as a problem of the Puerto Rican community due to a high rate of IV drug abuse and limited research on other Latino subgroups. However, a recent study by Gonzalez-Block and Hayes-Bautista suggest that the incidence of AIDS among Latinos in the United States may increase due to Mexican nationals who enter the migrant stream to the United States and who are at risk for the disease. According to their study of AIDS in Mexico: "It is among the blue collar workers and the non-specialized urban service employees where AIDS is growing at the fastest rate, thus propagating more rapidly precisely among the social groups that are most likely to migrate the the U.S."

(Gonzalez-Block and Hayes-Bautista 1990, 6).

The major transmission category of the disease for the Mexican-origin population can be attributed to homosexual and bisexual contact among men. However, a recent study of Los Angeles County concluded that the largest percentage of pediatric AIDS cases in the county are Latino children. Thus Latinas, although not highlighted statistically as the major problem in the AIDS epidemic, become central in their role as pregnant mothers at risk, transmitting the disease to their infants in utero (Latino Community Project 1990).

Many of the aforementioned health problems of Latinas become problematic and costly if not diagnosed early, and promptly treated and monitored. In particular, as this population is primarily young and of childbearing age, health programs targeted at family planning, prenatal and postpartum care, and gynecological screening for sexually transmitted diseases and cervical cancer merit consideration so as to reduce morbidity and mortality rates. Early treatment, periodic screening, and continuity of care for Latinas will shift the delivery of services from the more difficult and costly end stages of a disease to a more cost effective and managed care solution.

Access to Care: Employment Limits to Health Insurance

The health problems faced by Latinas are less symptomatic of unique biological features of these women, rather they reflect their class and occupational position. With the exception of AIDS, early intervention and treatment should rapidly reduce morbidity and mortality rates associated to the diseases that are problematic for Latinas. Thus, improved access to health care is critical in improving health outcomes and maintaining preventative health care measures.

Access to health care can be broadly defined by the factors that facilitate the use of medical services. Health insurance or financing for health care, maintenance of continuity of care at a regular site of health care delivery, and type of delivery site all are critical factors in enabling individuals to seek and obtain health care. For Latinos, issues such as level of acculturation have also been factored into studies addressing use of health care services (Solis,

Marks, Garcia, and Shelton 1990).

Given the poverty status of Latinas and their occupational location in the labor force, lack of health insurance has become the key factor in limiting their access to care. Although it has been argued that the employment and occupational position of Latinas mirrors their level of educational attainment and immigrant status, they also fill a critical void as a low-skilled, low-cost labor force for small industrial enterprises in ethnic communities, particularly in the Southwest (Torres and de la Torre 1991). For Latinas, who are often concentrated within the small business labor markets, health insurance is virtually nonexistent, or at best insignificant, for maintaining preventative health care practices. Unfortunately, the relatively high costs for small businesses to provide affordable health insurance to their employees provide little incentive for these employers to seek employee health insurance. There is little likelihood of this situation changing as small employers must compete in a relatively unfavorable small-group health insurance market where employee premiums are higher. Bias toward employing low risk employees by small businesses and insurers results in the overall lower health care costs of these employees. A recent study by the U.S. General Accounting Office suggests that the small insurance market premiums for small companies often times are based on age, sex and health status of employees. "The average premium costs for women in their twenties can be nearly twice as high as those for men of the same age, partly because of the costs associated with pregnancy and partly because of generally higher use of services" (General Accounting Office 1991b, 8). Given the relatively youthful age profile of Latinas and their higher fertility rates, small businesses are faced with a potentially higher fringe benefit package for the employees if they choose to provide health insurance to these women. Forcing these employers to provide employee health insurance in the current small insurance market is tantamount to providing them with a license to discriminate against Latinas in employment in order to reduce their health care premium costs. Finally, given the low rate of unionization in the small business sector and the inability of the Federal government to successfully jumpstart the economy and stimulate growth in states such as California, employee initiated demands for health care insurance coverage is unlikely in the short run, since jobs, rather than health insurance, become the more critical issue. Therefore, under the current voluntary health insurance market system there is little impetus for reform in the small business sector.

Policy Alternatives: Viable Financing Options

Clearly, the health insurance problems facing Latinas are symptomatic of the greater malaise facing the health care sector. Latinas are among the over thirty-seven million Americans who are uninsured due to the lack of adequate and viable financing mechanisms for the care of the poor and the working poor (Kern and Bresch 1990). However, not all states share the burden of the uninsured in equal numbers, nor do all ethnic/racial groups proportionately share the same levels of uninsured status. Most of the uninsured in the United States live in approximately twelve states. "One third of the uninsured are in three states—Florida, Texas, and California—representing almost twelve million people. A huge percentage of these are not just illegal aliens (or "undocumented workers"), but simply poor people" (Employee Benefits Research Institute 1991). The three states with the largest number of uninsured in the United States, also have significant Latina/o populations. Not surprising, then, is the ethnic/racial breakdown of the United States uninsured population. The largest proportion of uninsured of any group is Latinos: one-third of all Latinos are uninsured; followed by Blacks, one-fifth of all Blacks: and Whites, one-seventh of all Whites (General Accounting Office 1991b).

Given the disproportionate representation of Latinas in the ranks of the uninsured, it is incumbent that they enter the health policy debates targeted to reform the current financing system. Reforms of the present financing system are currently being debated at both Federal and state levels. Strategies developed by various constituency groups, for example, insurance companies, physicians, employers, etc., are molding the future financing reform programs, yet with the exception of a few Hispanic public health interest groups, the Latina voice is not present. (An example of such a group would be COSSMHo, National Coalition of Hispanic Health and Human Services Organization in Washington, D.C.) Yet, input into what is financed and how it is financed will directly affect both the health and employment status of these women.

It is within the context of the current health policy debates that two reform mechanisms will be assessed. Although this discussion does not exhaust the array of suggestions for financing reform, these two policy recommendations, Medicaid expansion, and state-level financing reform, are the most "popular" mechanisms to tackle the problem of the uninsured. In the former case, i.e., Medicaid expansion, specific suggestions concerning reform of the Medicaid law that would address the special needs of the Latina population will be developed. In the latter case, state reform, while not explicitly focusing on the unique needs of Latinas, will focus on the common ground they share with other uninsured groups and examine one proposed state solution, the Universal New York Health Care (UNY-Care) model.

Without question, in our pluralistic health care delivery system, the key to access to services is adequate financing for services rendered. Policy recommendations to improve access and delivery of services have little relevance without recommendations for current and future financing. In the short run a micro-incremental approach may prove to be the most effective in addressing this specific problem (Schlesinger and Kronebusch 1990). At the Federal level, Medicaid expansion, which allows for subsidizing individual and employer "buy-ins" may assist in reducing the number of uninsured working poor (Schlesinger and Kronebusch 1990). However, for Latinas a speedier and useful alternative to the "buy-in" approach would be an expansion of eligibility and reimbursement policies targeted to working poor and poor women. In the short run, this could assist in addressing the inadequate financing issue for needed preventative and screening services that do not result from pregnancy, but may affect future gynecological and obstetric needs of these clients.

In 1988, OBRA expansion of Medicaid increased the availability of pregnancy related health services for working poor pregnant women (Barber-Madden and Kotch 1990). Unfortunately, many Latinas do not seek care or use their entitled services until they become aware of the services, their pregnancy is verified, and their eligibility is determined (Solis, Marks, Garcia, and Shelton 1990). Prenatal care is therefore unnecessarily delayed during the critical first trimester of pregnancy. A solution to this problem is to expand eligibility to include working poor women of child-bearing age for obstetrical and gynecological services, to encourage continuous use of low cost preventative and diagnostic services, and to ensure early entry into prenatal programs. Using the same eligibility criteria developed under the OBRA expansion of 1988, women at risk of pregnancy or of child-bearing age would be entitled to yearly gynecological screening. This would include not only Pap smears, screening for diabetes and AIDS, but also include pregnancy screening. Using the existing EPSDT Program (Early Screening and Detection and Treatment Program), targeted to children up to eighteen years of age and required by all Medicaid programs for preventive care (well-care as opposed to sick-care), and expanding the availability of care for working poor women, i.e., using 185% of poverty level as a basis for determining eligibility for this Medicaid screening program, would be a policy alternative that would allow for building or augmenting an existing Medicaid program. Given that EPSDT is required for all Medicaid programs, all states would be required to provide the augmented benefits for working poor women under the more inclusive eligibility requirements. Currently, Medicaid programs for non-pregnant women and medically-indigent programs vary across states with varying eligibility criteria. Although states such as New York are relatively generous in providing health services for the poor, states such as Texas are not, and require more rigorous poverty standards for eligibility to their Medicaid program. Therefore, given the disparity in eligibility requirements across states, a federally mandated program will ensure greater access in those states that are less generous with their Medicaid benefits (National Coalition of Hispanic Health and Human Services Organization 1990).

A second alternative to expanding Medicaid benefits, which is often criticized as a costly alternative for states due to the Federal-state cost sharing nature of the program, is to examine a state mandated program that will deal directly with the uninsured and underinsured individuals in the state. This alternative, although a more radical and macro-incremental approach to transforming the financing of health care at the state level, may provide states with greater control over containing costs and delivering services (Schlesinger and Kronebusch 1990). For states such as California and New York, where Medicaid cost-sharing with the Federal government is relatively high, federally imposed expansion is not as attractive , given the current state deficit crises in these states. For Latinas, as well as for other poor and working poor groups, such an approach should increase the array of primary and preventative low-cost health services and minimize the need to develop piecemeal strategies from various state and Federal funding sources to obtain adequate access to care. Clearly, in the states with large numbers of uninsured the political climate is ripe for state reform proposals that provide cost effective coverage and provide needed services to the uninsured. Specific models that address universal financing and/or develop subsidies and risk pools for small businesses at the state level may be the most practical mechanism of tackling the uninsured problem in these states, and, if successful, may serve as a blueprint for future Federal financing models.

The New York model, Universal New York Health Care (UNY-Care) would develop a single-payer framework, while combining and retaining existing payers. Ultimately, a major goal would be to reduce the waste from the considerable transaction costs resulting from the current multiple-payer system through the creation of an independent public-benefit corporation with a board of governors selected jointly by the governor and the legislature. By standardizing accounts, insuring speedy reimbursement and simplifying billing for hospitals and physicians, costs should be substantially reduced. Combined with enhancing the efficiency of the current multiple-payer system, is the ultimate goal of expanding employment-based insurance, subsidizing insurance for the working poor, children, minorities and the unemployed, and providing a system that will promote universal access to care for all New York residents. Approximately twelve and one-half percent of the state's population is uninsured. In order to significantly reduce this number UNY-Care would do the following: (1) streamline and expand job-based insurance; (2) purchase publicly-subsidized health insurance for unemployed individuals; and (3) subsidize insurance for those whose income falls 200% below the poverty level on a sliding scale basis. Financing for these benefits would require reliance on a payroll tax for those employers who could not meet UNY-Care standards for health insurance. Employers offering coverage for the first time would be privy to substantial subsidies for the first four years and could avoid offering coverage to part-time employees by payment of the payroll tax. In addition to setting up a universal financing system for all New York residents, as the single buyer for care, UNY-Care will be able to use its monopoly power to control costs and budgets. This will allow for better long-run planning, given the availability of all sources of revenue, and assist in curtailing the current double-digit inflation rates evident in the medical sector (Beauchamp and Rouse 1990).

There is no doubt that the UNY-Care model will be closely scrutinized by other states with large numbers of uninsured and underinsured. From an access perspective, this model, in the long run, will provide comprehensive care to Latinas, the poor and other working poor. From a broader health policy perspective, it provides the beginning of a broader blueprint for structural reform of the health care system, with the subsequent risks of altering other arenas of the economy, such as employment in small enterprises. A critical element in the viability of this proposal will be to balance the competing interests, i.e., private insurers, small businesses, physicians, hospital providers, and workers, to insure that the trade-offs for universal entitlement to health care truly merit such a reform.

Conclusion

Currently, at both state and Federal levels the crisis of the uninsured and underinsured is being debated. This issue is of immediate relevance to the Latina population as they are disproportionately represented within the ranks of the uninsured and underinsured and will certainly slide through any cracks in the new health safety net. The health status problems they face reflect both the demographic and occupational location of many of these women that could easily benefit from micro and/or macro incremental change in the financing of health care. Although an array of health policy proposals are currently being debated in major states, such as California and Texas, there is a glaring lack of the Latina voice in setting this critical agenda. Two policy recommendations, one using the existing Federal Medicaid policy and the latter, introducing an innovative state single-payer financing system to ensure universal access, are assessed in light of the health needs of Latinas. Expansion of the Medicaid entitlement program, EPSTD, is one example of a short run strategy that would allow for selective diagnostic screening and early treatment of Latinas of childbearing age. Indeed, any attempt to introduce these women to early and continuous care will in the long run net lower health care costs associated with decreased morbidity and mortality rates from specific "Latina" health problems and complications from unmonitored pregnancies.

The second macro approach, the UNY-Care model, offers a more comprehensive approach to health care reform, tackling the areas of universal access and cost containment. Here a synthesis of concerns that affect Latinas, the poor and working poor, and actors of the health arena, unify to minimize the zero-sum nature of this proposal. A critical caveat here is to recognize that the employment effects of such reform may disproportionately impact Latinas and that safeguards to ensure their employment stability be considered in the final development and implementation of small business subsidies. No doubt the time is right for such reform, so is the time for Latinas to voice their concern and their agenda.

La Mujer y La Violencia:
A Culturally Based Model for the
Understanding and Treatment of Domestic
Violence in Chicana/Latina Communities

Yvette Flores-Ortiz

Introduction

The incidence of domestic violence has risen sharply in the last decade (Strauss and Gelles 1989). Between two and six million women are battered each year; of these, between two and four thousand are killed (Family Violence Project 1989). While specific figures for family violence among Chicanos and Latinos are not available, clinical and anecdotal data do suggest a serious violence problem in Raza communities (Flores-Ortiz and Carrillo 1989).

This paper offers a model of analysis and treatment for Raza families with a problem of violence which incorporates an understanding of gender, cultural, historical, and political processes.

The Context of Family Violence

Definitions
Family violence includes the physical, emotional, psychological, sexual and moral abuse of any family member. Family violence is a cyclical process which begins with a build up of stress that the individual is unable to release in more appropriate ways. When the level of stress is not tolerable, the pent-up anxiety is released through an act of aggression. This is followed by a period of remorse, acts of repentance and in couples, by a honeymoon phase where the perpetrator promises never to hurt the victim again. When stress and tension build up again, the cycle is repeated. Over time, the honeymoon phase no longer is present. The cycle

then runs quickly from tension build up to violent release.

Domestic violence includes the use of anger and intimidation, threats and humiliation, isolation and restriction of freedom, abuse of male privilege, use of children to control the actions of women, sexual, economic, emotional and moral abuse (Roberts 1984; Walker 1979). At the root of this exploitation is the man's need for power and control (Roberts 1984).

Etiological Explanations

The interpersonal dynamics of abusive families and the psychological characteristics of batterers and victims have been explained from a number of theoretical perspectives, including psychoanalytic, social learning, family systems and most recently, feminist theory. While they differ in the explanation of the causes of violence, these theories concur on the description of the victim and perpetrator. The victim is described as lacking self-esteem, experiencing difficulty in expressing her own needs, demonstrating a long suffering, martyrlike endurance of frustration, depressive and/or hysterical symptoms, stress disorders and psychosomatic complaints.

The batterer is described as a man lacking self-esteem and appropriate avenues for expressing his rage. He has poor impulse control and his insatiable ego needs are derived from childhood deprivation. His interpersonal relationships are characterized by mistrust, insecurity, and jealousy. As a child, the batterer is believed to have suffered abuse and neglect form both parents, or to have witnessed domestic violence. His own childhood victimization is believed to culminate in an insatiable need to control others, particularly women, through force, intimidation and violence. In general, batterers learn to be violent because their aggression has been reinforced and they have not learned more effective and appropriate ways of problem solving or coping. Furthermore, gender role socialization encourages male aggression and female passivity. Thus, societies and cultures that emphasize rigid sex role differentiation are believed to produce a familial context ripe for spousal and child abuse.

The psychoanalytic and social learning theories fail to provide an analysis of the larger social context in which violence occurs (Flores-Ortiz et al. 1991). Family systems theories begin to offer a more comprehensive analysis of the context of violence by viewing it as a family problem, grounded in dysfunctional patterns; specifically, imbalances of power (Madanes 1990), rigid boundaries (Minuchin 1974), rigid sex roles, and rigid efforts to maintain family cohesion.

Feminist theorists, however, (Luepnitz 1989; McGoldrick 1989) critique both individual and systemic theories for their disregard of the gender issues inherent in the problem of violence against women. Domestic violence is rooted in patriarchal systems and values which objectify women and dehumanize men. Thus solutions to the problem of family violence are viewed as resting partly on the empowerment of women and in radical change within social institutions, including marriage and parenthood.

Existing etiological explanations, however, continue to lack a class and race analysis, thus ignoring the impact of colonization and neo-colonization on the psychological development of women and men. Furthermore, a failure to consider the impact of social, cultural, and political variables affecting families has resulted in theories and programs that blame Latino cultures solely for the victimization of women. Moreover, while increased feminist consciousness has permeated the understanding and treatment of domestic violence, an understanding of the cultural context in which violence takes place continues to be largely ignored. This is evident in research, theory, and practice.

La mujer en la familia:
Socio-cultural correlates of domestic violence

Latino families must deal with a complex interaction of experiences that can contribute to family violence (Bernal and Flores-Ortiz 1982; Flores-Ortiz 1982; Falicov 1982) including: migration, acculturation, under-employment, under-education, and economic stress. Furthermore, the long term impact of colonization in their countries of origin and neo-colonization in the United States often creates a "victim system" (Pinderhughes 1982) which can be summarized as an expectation of suffering and exploitation. This expectation is often reinforced by patriarchal and religious influences.

Dysfunctional Latino families demonstrate a number of characteristics which contribute to the development of family violence

(Bernal et al. 1989; Flores-Ortiz and Bernal 1989; Flores-Ortiz et al. 1991). Among these are: (a) frozen cultural patterns; (b) parentification of children; (c) indirect or intrusive patterns of communication; (d) intergenerational problems.

Culture Freezing

This refers to the development of rigid, stereotyped values and behaviors as a result of a difficult migration process (Sluzki 1979) in which cut-offs from family of origin or culture of origin occur. The immigrant family attempts to recreate, in a new context, their ideal of what a Latino family is. This ideal may be based on distorted and rigid notions of Latino culture. However, to maintain family unity and to protect the family from external threat, many Latinos develop rigid boundaries around their family, minimizing contact with the "Anglo World." This pattern often is facilitated by social discrimination and racism which prevents many Latinos from participating fully in Anglo society. The excessive protection of the family eventually results in social isolation, lack of trust in the new culture and in fears for the safety of women and children.

In families where cultural freezing has occurred, a pattern of rigid sex role expectations typically develops. The man perceives his primary role as provider and negotiator with the outside world; he expects the woman to create for him a safe haven to which he can retreat. Stereotypic cultural patterns of machismo prevail, where the man feels entitled to all freedoms and the woman to none.

At an individual psychology level, cultural freezing can result in the internalization of negative cultural stereotypes of machismo. This pattern can be seen in Latino men who fit the psychological profile of batterers already described; they tend to have little trust in women other than their mothers. They view women as treacherous, thus in need of being controlled, protected, guided.

The experience of colonization and neo-colonization also impacts the self-esteem of Latino men. Batterers often describe themselves as burros, beasts of burden, surplus people. The psychological impact of such self-perception typically is overwhelming anger and hostility which cannot be expressed directly towards the aggressor, but which can be vented on those perceived as weaker (typically women and children). The men who exhibit excessive machismo tend to mask their vulnerability with a veneer of stoicism. In addition, they attempt to control their emotions and narcotize their pain through the use of substances. In turn, the abuse of alcohol or other drugs allows them to feel the pain and often act aggressively. However, when the man becomes violent under the influence, he tends to blame the substance and not himself for his actions. Furthermore, a frozen cultural view that all Latinos drink supports inappropriate drinking patterns that can exacerbate the problem of violence.

Women in battering relationships also have been impacted by cultural freezing, the colonial legacy, and the racism of the new social context. Among the major cultural variables that contribute to the cycle of domestic violence is the myth of martyrdom (Bernal and Alvarez 1983). Through religious and cultural images (the virgin, Malinche, Mary Magdalene, etc.) women are seen as self-sacrificing, self-effacing, long-suffering martyrs or as treacherous whores. These cultural stereotypes have been reified by social scientists (i.e. Diaz-Guerrero 1954) and become then not cultural stereotypes but cultural mandates and ideals that, when frozen, translate into "this is how a 'good' Latina is, or ought to be". Guided by these cultural "mandates" women often feel that it is their lot in life to suffer. They are to be defined by their family roles and their primary obligation is to preserve the family at all costs, under any circumstances.

Furthermore, the socialization process in dysfunctional families tends to make women feel primarily responsible for the psychological, emotional, and physical well being of the men. They will attempt to make the home a haven from stress. They may even assume the role of primary parent, so the men do not have to deal with the stress of parenting. Over time, the wife's efforts to protect the man further imbalance the family relationships; she is overburdened and he eventually will resent (and blame her) for the emotional distance between himself and his children. If he beats her, she is made to feel responsible for her own victimization. From a cultural perspective, machismo without control and excessive martyrdom create a perfect context for family violence.

Thus, in a context of cultural freezing, particularly when economic and social victimization also occur, violence may begin as a result of external stress and eventually be maintained for generations.

Parentification of Children

The psychological make-up of people who grow up in violent families differs. Not all children of batterers grow up to be violent men or victimized women. Family theorists explain these differences on the basis of the concepts of parentification (Minuchin 1974; Bernal 1980) and family loyalty (Boszormenyi-Nagy and Spark 1984). Certain children in dysfunctional families are consciously or unconsciously picked by the parents to fulfill the role of assistant parents and to become responsible for meeting the previously unmet psychological needs of the adults. It becomes the child's responsibility to parent the parents. The parents are unable to provide for the child the basic love, nurturance, and security all human beings need to develop: psychological integrity and emotional security. The child instead is expected to provide these for the parent. Since the child will fail, the parent is usually excessively punitive as he continues to feel that the world fails him. Thus the child and the parent become bound in an exploitative relationship wherein the child must sacrifice him or herself for the parent.

In violent Latino families, parentification is exemplified by over reliance on one child, usually the eldest, to help raise the other children, to become mother's confidant, or father's ally, or to mediate family disputes. Parentified children typically do not feel entitled to ask for any emotional, spiritual, or physical support. Rather, they expect to have to take care of everyone at the expense of their independence, well being, and emotional health. They tend to suppress their feelings of outrage at the injustice in their life; women can only express their rage in indirect ways. Men, however, have the cultural and social sanction to express their anger in violent ways, although typically they do not see the relationship between their actions and their own victimization.

In families where substances also are abused, the children are victimized further, often through physical abuse or incest. Because children are fundamentally loyal and depend on their parents for their very existence (Boszormenyi-Nagy and Spark 1984), efforts to change learned patterns of abuse invoke feelings of disloyalty. Thus parentified and exploited children are very likely to enter dysfunctional marriages where continuing victimization may occur. In this way, family dysfunction is perpetuated generation after generation.

Family Communication

Family communication refers to the overt and covert rules under which a family operates. These rules include the expectations of sex role behavior, child-rearing patterns, and conflict resolution strategies people learned in their own families of origin. Violent families are characterized by indirect communication, mind-reading, difficulty expressing feelings, emotional withdrawal, fear, and violent displays of anger.

Latino batterers often are unable to display feelings other than anger; they order, command, yell, and offend verbally. The spouse is afraid of his moods and their unpredictability, of his outbursts and his drinking; she is afraid of him. She often attempts to shield the children from his violence by interfering with *any* direct communication between them and the father. She often interprets (or excuses) the father's behavior to the children.

It is also in this area of family communication where the other types of violence are visible. Psychological, emotional, moral abuse leave no physical scars or bruises that can call attention to the problem. Emotional withholding, expressions of excessive jealousy, verbal expressions of rage assault the individual's own sense of self and integrity (Walker 1979).

Intergenerational and Cultural Value Conflicts

In immigrant families one of the major post-migration crisis is the acculturation of the children and the subsequent value change away from parental expectations. This change poses a threat to family unity. In families where cultural freezing is occurring, and where the conditions for family violence exist, conflicts between the parents and children may escalate to violence. Invariably, the wife will be blamed; since she is the one responsible for raising the children. The man may exercise greater control, further restricting the freedom of the wife and children in order to prevent further acculturation. Inevitably this fails; he may feel more frustrated and powerless, and respond with physical violence.

A variant of this crisis occurs when an immigrant male becomes involved with a second generation Latina or with a woman from a different ethnic or cultural group. Often the value differences are profound, particularly with regards to the role of women. If the man believes that women should be controlled and if she resists, he may respond with violence, to "get her in line."

In summary, Latino families with a problem of violence are characterized by rigidity, isolation, cultural value differences, dysfunctional communication, and a repetition of learned patterns of communication, problem-solving, and childrearing that maintain the problem of violence. As with most other cultural groups, Latinas who are battered are typically blamed for their own situation by the batterer, the larger cultural system and the social institutions that exist to help her.

Latinas who are battered tend not to leave their partners or husbands for very long. They may temporarily use shelters, social service resources, but eventually return home. An understanding of why this happens requires an analysis of socioeconomic, cultural, and psychological factors. The battered woman may lack financial resources, she may be so beaten down and depressed she is unable to see alternatives. If she was victimized as a child, she may accept this life as her lot. Furthermore, the cultural pull to return, give him another chance, and preserve the family is very strong for Latinas. If she has financial, social, legal resources to separate and seek safety, she will still need to contend with the feelings of cultural and familial disloyalty that will come as a result of her actions, since she may have been raised to put herself and her needs last. Thinking of her safety and her need to leave the husband may elicit feelings of selfishness, disloyalty, of being a "bad Latina." Often, social service workers become frustrated at the seeming inability of the Latina to leave the batterer. Unwittingly, the woman and her culture are blamed for the abuse and for the inability to stop it. To end the violence, Latinos must confront and understand the historical and cultural roots of their oppression and seek cultural solutions to the problems of abuse.

Guidelines for Evaluating and Treating Domestic Violence in Latino Families

The goal of family treatment for Latinos is to seek in the culture of the family resources and solutions to end the violence, the exploitation, and the pain.

The key to treating the problem of domestic violence in a culturally integrated way is to offer services for the family. Regardless of the specific interventions available, the agency must have a commitment to address the needs of the entire family (Carrillo 1982, and 1989; Flores-Ortiz et al, 1991). The first step in the treatment of domestic violence is assessment of lethality, the likelihood that a homicide may occur. In such cases, it will be in everyone's best interests if the couple temporarily separates. Presented as an effort to save the family and protect everyone, such recommendations even when enforced legally are more likely to be accepted and followed through by the family.

Following an assessment of lethality, the evaluation needs to focus on the socio-economic and cultural context of the family, including the woman's economic viability and everyone's level of acculturation, cultural connection, and familial (including extended family) resources. Part of an integrated case management includes the identification of social and cultural needs. Psychological evaluations of the children and the adults can be helpful in determining the need for individual psychotherapy as well as the assessment of child abuse or neglect.

With regards to cultural needs, the national origins of the clients, their history of migration, reasons for migration, and post migration experiences is also needed. Many recent immigrants from Central America are suffering from war related trauma; such experiences may predispose individuals to family violence.

In addition to information regarding their migration and current living status, a detailed family history and history of violence is essential. On the basis of this detailed history, determinations are then made on the best method of treatment. If the man is living with his family, the involvement of the family in treatment is essential. It facilitates the continued assessment of lethality and the protection of the woman and children. In summary, a thorough evaluation of domestic violence must include an assessment of the entire family, with a focus on facts concerning the migration history, level of acculturation and biculturality of family members. In addition, psychosocial needs, cultural expectations and resources need to be identified so that appropriate treatment recommendations can be made.

Treatment Recommendations

The following recommendations are made based on experience in the treatment of domestic violence with Latino families in the Bay

Area of San Francisco, Calif. (Carrillo 1989; Flores-Ortiz et al. 1991).

The underlying assumption of therapy with violent men and women is that they are individuals out of balance, experiencing cultural freezing, and suffering the impact of parentification and neo-colonization. The therapeutic goals then, are (1) to stop the violence and victimization, (2) learn new ways of problem solving, and (3) to examine critically the cultural, social, and political roots of their violence.

Separate group treatment of batterers and spouses is most effective as a first intervention. For Latinos, the treatment must emphasize cultural metaphors and rituals which are familiar to the men. For example, understanding how they learned violence in the home and in the culture through the songs, the "dichos," the examples of the other men. Often, the problem of violence is redefined as a lack of control (estar desenfrenado), the therapeutic goal for the group then becomes to learn how to put on the brakes and how to attain physical, emotional, and spiritual balance (see Carrillo 1989).

The overarching goal for the group treatment is the redefinition of culture. That is, the men and women separately come to analyze, critique, and modify the cultural rules and roles they learned as children. The purpose of this analysis is to "unfreeze" the culture. Thus didactic information is presented and cultural stereotypes are directly challenged in respectful ways. The goal of these interventions is neither to blame nor idealize Latino cultures, but to identify frozen and stereotypic cultural beliefs in order to modify these and to seek resources for healing within the culture. In some instances a correlate of domestic violence is a cut-off or disconnection from the culture of origin. This process often leads to feelings of marginality, particularly when the individual makes efforts to acculturate to Anglo society and fails. In such cases, a focus on cultural reconnection is useful.

The treatment of domestic violence is in part a political process. Before behavior changes can occur, both men and women need to learn the role that patriarchy, colonization, and their own history of gender oppression have played on the development of violence in their current families. In this manner, men and women come to understand their own victimization and the larger social context in which it occurred.

With such understanding, the men and women begin to examine their own victimization in their families or origin. Here the goal is not to blame the parents, or the culture, or themselves. Rather through an empathetic understanding of the context of previous generations, batterers and their families can begin to see the multigenerational pattern of abuse and start to forgive their families and themselves. This understanding is facilitated by the use of the genogram or family tree, redefined as *el espejo*. Additional interventions, include the use of the group support to redefine *carnalismo* and *compañerismo* through the use of the other men as *tu eres mi otro yo*. Each man is a mirror and reflection of the other; through the process of dialogue in the group, each can learn from the other and redefine the type of man each wants to be.

Through an understanding of how and why they became violent, the men are exonerated from guilt, however, they remain responsible for stopping the violence now. The group aims to identify fair and just ways to relate to others and to live without the use of substances as an escape. Sobriety is a requirement of treatment and appropriate treatment referrals are made. The men are required to attend AA or NA. The women are encouraged to attend ALANON, ACA, or related groups. In addition, referrals are made to parenting classes for families where child abuse or neglect is present or a risk. Such classes are recommended to all families, however, in order to expand their knowledge of what appropriate parenting is.

Group therapy for women focuses on examining their own internalized cultural stereotypes of "la sufrida," "la matir." In addition, in the supportive context of a woman's group, each studies her own history and family of origin to identify dysfunctional patterns as well as cultural resources. The role of patriarchy and unfair child rearing practices which differentially empower males and females are examined in order to change parenting styles which may contribute to future imbalances in their children.

Phase 1
The first phase of treatment lasts four to six months. The work is primarily psycho-educational. The men and women gain a great deal of cognitive understanding of the roots of violence. Women also learn about resources in the community, how to develop a safety plan, how to protect their children. A major goal of the

woman's groups is to help the women attain power—social, political, and economic power—and to develop a sense of entitlement. They deserve better, they have the human right to safety and happiness. But first a lot of healing must occur.

An assessment of the adults, children, and family is made at the end of the first phase of treatment. If the violence has ended, if sobriety has been maintained, then the men may proceed to an advanced group. At this juncture determinations also are made regarding the need for ancillary individual or family therapy. If sufficient progress has not been made (as determined by the counselors, staff, and the family members themselves) the men and women may repeat phase 1 of treatment.

Phase 2

The next step of treatment centers on group or individual psychotherapy with the aim of connecting the information learned didactically with their own experiences at a feeling level. Both men and women are helped to mourn past loses, including their own victimization in childhood, their country, their dreams, their past. Through ritual, sacrifice, and other culturally congruent methods, the clients are helped to let go of their past so they can start a new life.

These groups run approximately 12 weeks and are followed by another assessment of the family members. At this point determinations are made regarding the next step of treatment; if the spouses are living together family or couple therapy is indicated.

Phase 3

Family or couple therapy is offered in a brief (10 session model) (Flores-Ortiz et al. 1991) and is based on two premises: (1) once the violence and the substance abuse stops the family must learn new ways to problem solve, parent, and form a family. However, before this can occur the relational injustices and imbalances in the family must be addressed and (2) to stop the generational cycle of violence, the family must understand their own family of origin relationships, attempt to develop new ways of relating to them, and initiate efforts to prevent the legacy of abuse in future generations.

The model of treatment utilized is based in the intergenerational family therapy of Ivan Boszomenyi-Nagy (Boszomenyi-

Nagy, and Spark 1984) and modified to work with Latinos by Bernal and associates (Bernal et al. 1983; Bernal 1982; and Flores-Ortiz, Flores-Ortiz and Bernal 1989). This treatment model is resource based and attempts to foster a dialogue in the family where issues of trust, loyalty, respect, and justice can be addressed. This approach is useful with Latino batterers and their families because of its focus on relational ethics and rebalancing of accounts. This method of work allows for the couple to discuss directly and openly the hurt and resentment they carry, to openly address the ways in which the husband is indebted to his wife for the years of abuse and what he needs to do to repay her in an ethical way. The specific treatment interventions address the systemic and hierarchical imbalances that are present in violent families (i.e. the necessary over involvement of the mother in parenting and domestic affairs, the emotional distance between father and children) and identifies ways to change them. Thus the treatment includes systemic interventions (Haley and Madanes 1988; Minuchin 1981) and address problems in communication, power relationships and takes steps to prevent further parentification of the children.

This model of treatment continues to address the cultural freezing and the need to redefine culture which was initiated in the group treatments. Furthermore, through a reconstructive dialogue (Boszormenyi-Nagy, and Spark 1984) the family continues to make the emotional and cognitive connections between their own victimization and the violence in their current family.

The focus on fairness and ethics in relationships facilitates a discussion of gender issues and imbalances. The couple must now determine what kind of marriage they wish to have, what kind of parents they wish to be, and in so doing, confronts directly the loyalty conflicts that may arise from being different types of spouses and parents than their own parents were. In the course of therapy, the couple explores their own gender oppression and seeks avenues to foster mutual respect. Ultimately, the man must come to recognize and respect the fundamental right of his partner and daughters.

The couple is helped to identify which cultural patterns and legacies they wish to discard in order to prevent further injustices in their families. In this context intergenerational conflicts, value differences between the parents and children, and the need to accept the bicultural reality of the U.S. born offspring are discussed and negotiated.

As a result of the family treatment, couples often develop more flexible marital arrangements; they may begin to develop a couple relationship where issues of power, sexuality, and roles can be negotiated without conflict. They often develop extrafamilial friendships and relationships which replace the isolation previously experienced. Women who were previously prisoners in their own homes may return to school, seek work, or learn to drive. The goal here is to foster both economic and emotional inter-dependence in a context of compañerismo.

This model of treatment aims to address the emotional, psychological, social, cultural, and gender issues of violent families. Its emphasis on the ethics of relations facilitates the discussion of moral, psychological and emotional abuse that other treatment approaches tend to ignore. A treatment program that helps families balance relationships without ascribing blame and which respects the cultural values of its members and the rights of women can have profound success with violent families who wish to keep the family together.

This paper has offered a model of treatment of violent Latino families. Its clinical usefulness has been demonstrated, (Flores-Ortiz et al. 1991). Furthermore, unlike other family therapy approaches, this model directly addresses gender, class, and cultural issues.

The problem of violence in Latino communities presents a challenge to all social scientists. We need to better understand and change the larger social context that fosters violence and the abuse of women. We need to strengthen our communities and foster health in our families. Latina scholars need to develop an integrated, culturally based theoretical model that explains and addresses the complexity of abuse in Latino families. We need to address the issues of gender, politics and family without polemics. Fundamentally, we need to look inside our own homes and struggle with our respective legacies of colonialism, race and gender oppression so that we, each in our own unique way, can begin to stop the cycle of violence in our Raza communities.

The Bioethics of
Reproductive Technologies:
Impacts and Implications for Latinas

Adaljiza Sosa Riddell

Introduction

Reproductive control and reproductive technologies are two areas in women's health that have been the focus of political as well as medical and ethical debates. Many of the unresolved issues raised by these technologies have become increasingly subject to public scrutiny as demonstrators take to the streets and impede the operation of women's health clinics, and as the legal system attempts to codify the "grey area" of medical science. Challenges to women's rights to terminate unwanted pregnancies, issues of surrogate motherhood, and debates on individual property rights of frozen embryos, are examples of the array of ideas surfacing for public and legal scrutiny.

Women of color, specifically Chicanas/Latinas, have been largely excluded from these struggles over women's minds, hearts, and bodies. Newspaper and magazine articles note the visible absence of women of color in the struggles between the anti-abortionists, pro-life groups, and the pro-abortion, pro-choice groups. A recent conference on abortion in Sacramento, California, included a panel on "women of color," but this was evidently the first time such an event had featured voices of women of color (Sacramento Bee, September 15, 1990). While Chicanas/Latinas have had little voice in political battles over birth control and abortion, they are also largely excluded from legal and ethical discussions involving the latest reproductive technologies. Critical feminists have been discussing and writing about their concerns over reproductive technologies for at least a decade. "Critical feminists are exploring three major areas: a) the link between genetic

engineering and reproductive technologies; b) the different meaning of the new reproductive technologies for Third and First
World women, within and between countries; and c) what the application of reproductive and genetic engineering will mean for
women in the future, as well as women here and now" (Spallone
and Steinberg 1987). Chicanas/Latinas have been the subjects but
not the participants of those discussions. Furthermore, they have
not been immune to the effects of reproductive technologies on
their lives. We need to ask ourselves why this condition of silence
and exclusion exists. Continued absence from these debates en-
sures that Chicanas/Latinas will, after all, continue to be absent
from the decision-making.

This essay intends to open the debates on reproductive technologies to the concerns of Chicanas/Latinas, to inform Chicanas/
Latinas as well as other women about the major issues involved,
to encourage Chicana/Latina scholars to contribute to the debates
on reproductive technologies through intensive research, and to
encourage all Chicanas/Latinas to engage constructively in current debates over the development of new technologies. In this essay, the author does not advocate for or against the further development of reproductive technologies, nor for any specific form of
regulation of those technologies. To paraphrase Genoveffa Corea
in her piece entitled "Egg Snatchers" (Arditti, Klein, and Minden, 1984, 47-51), this is a scream of warning to Chicanas/
Latinas, a warning to those who have not yet heard it and to those
who have heard the warning but may not have enough information to make informed decisions, to become informed, indignant,
and involved.

Defining Reproductive Technologies in a Sociocultural Context

How do we define reproductive technologies? One basic definition
is that reproductive technologies are "all forms of biomedical interventions and help a woman may encounter when she considers
having or not having a child." (Arditti, et al. 1984, 1). Reproductive technologies have several thrusts: control of fertility, control of
infertility, and intervention with fetal development. The availability and impact of such interventions and assistance must, however, be considered within the cultural and societal context in

which Chicanas/Latinas operate, paying close attention to the details of their past experience with reproductive technologies.

For Chicanas/Latinas, the development and potential widespread utilization of reproductive technologies simply augment and intensify the dilemmas of an already extremely complex scenario. What may be deemed reproductive "freedom" (the freedom to avoid or terminate a pregnancy) for most women may become societally or governmentally controlled fertility for women of color, practices which, taken to their extreme, can result in genocide. Poverty and the economic realities of single female-headed households, limited access to health care services, and the serious health risks resulting from their occupational stratification render freedom of reproductive choice for Chicanas/Latinas a mockery. Their rights as women often come into conflict with both dominant and internal cultural values that are patriarchally imposed in either case. For Chicanas/Latinas, reproductive technologies have historically equalled reproductive control of their fertility and infertility within a dual patriarchal system, rarely increasing their reproductive choices.

Chicanas/Latinas are caught in a double bind because of the patriarchal structures they face within their families and within the larger society. The one mirrors and manipulates the other. Patriarchal structures within the cultures of Chicanos and Latinos benefit the larger society, and patriarchy within the larger society benefits Chicano/Latino males. Chicanas/Latinas may not want to deny their culture and yet they are often constrained by it. There is no clear cut evidence that Chicanas/Latinas oppose abortion, yet they are often controlled by the stereotype of the "sainted mother." They have their own internal struggles over the role motherhood plays in their lives, yet very few Chicanas/Latinas readily forego motherhood. Mexicanas, Chicanas, and Latinas may want to view their children as their greatest treasure but socio-economic conditions contribute to inter-family stresses. While fertility is extremely important to Chicana/Latina identity (Vélez-Ibáñez 1980), the desire to improve the quality of their own lives is equally important.

The unfortunate reality about the role of fertility in Chicana/Latina identity, however, is that any statement on its importance may be based solely on assumptions and speculation. These assumptions and speculations about the centrality of "motherhood" to Chicanas/Latinas result from various ideas. One idea is that the focus on motherhood is derived from strong religious and/or cultural beliefs. An opposing concept is the theoretical analysis that the Chicana/Latina's role as the producer of laborers within the family unit serves the capitalist economy. Still other concepts include the model of the family unit as necessary for economic survival, or simply the idea that Chicanas/Latinas believe fervently in their motherhood role.

Historically, the Chicana/Latina's experience with reproductive technologies has been that of having their fertility controlled. If they are also denied access to those reproductive technologies which are used to solve infertility problems, then their infertility as well as their fertility is beyond their control. The ability of Chicanas/Latinas to reproduce has been both highly valued and utilized as an instrument of control. These negative encounters with reproductive technologies are reasons why new reproductive technologies that enhance fertility are even more problematic for Chicanas/Latinas than for women in general, and more painful to address, contemplate or assess.

The Impact of Older Reproductive Technologies on Chicanas/Latinas

On a global scale Chicanas/Latinas' past experiences with reproductive technologies have not been pleasant ones. The use of third world countries of Latin America as places for experimentation and testing of new products for the distribution of chemicals limited or prohibited in the United States has become a common technique used by pharmaceutical companies and the practice is condoned by both the United States and Latin American governments. The most well known example of this practice is the testing of the first birth control pills in Puerto Rico. Sterilization abuse and reproductive maladies have been documented in Puerto Rico and among Puerto Rican women in the mainland United States (Clarke 1984 192). More recent examples of these types of abuses include the maquila (assembling) industries, built under the auspices of the Border Industrialization Program, located near the United States-Mexican border. Several authors have documented the situations in those industries where the majority of workers are women who are continually exposed to dangerous chemicals (Iglesias l986; Fernandez Kelly 1983).

The most blatant and commonly known example of control of Latina's reproduction is the use of sterilization as a means of birth control. Sterilization can be subtle or blatant, done with or without consent. Blatant sterilization involves the surgical removal of ovaries (oophorectemy), tubal ligation, hysterectomy, or some other form of permanent interference with the female reproductive system. It usually must be consented to either by the person involved or by a legal guardian. Subtle sterilization refers to means of preventing conception over which the woman has little or no control or of which she has no knowledge. Both types of sterilization can occur with informed consent, uninformed consent, or non-consent.

Sterilization as a means of population control among people of color throughout the world has been well-documented (Clarke l984). Clarke links modern efforts at worldwide population control with concepts of genetic control, ie. genetic engineering, and with the basic ideas of the eugenics movement. The eugenics movement exhibited both a positive and negative dimension. "Positive eugenics encouraged increased breeding among the 'fit,' while negative eugenics discouraged breeding among the 'defective'" (Corea 1985, 20). This attitude that the reproductive capacity of human populations can and must be selectively controlled has become widely accepted. Population control through sterilization, which is one concept underlying the eugenics movement, has now become an integral part of the value systems of a number of geneticists, biologists, medical practitioners, and public policy makers (Corea 1985, 12-30).

In the early l970's several examples of population control through sterilization ignited reproductive rights and civil rights activists to seek greater protection for women. These situations included the case of *Madrigal vs. Quilligan* (Velez-Ibañez 1980), a case which involved the unconsenting sterilization of Mexican women at the University of Southern California medical center, the sterilization of two young Black women in Alabama, and the patterned sterilization of Native American women by the United States Indian Health Service (Clarke 1984). Although the laws regarding surgical sterilization immediately following childbirth or abortion had changed prior to *Madrigal vs Quilligan*, those changes did not provide much protection for Chicanas/Latinas. The current one-month waiting period between consenting to a tubal ligation and the actual procedure effective in the U.S. is, however, at best a compromise, because it does not address the major issues.

The discussion of sterilization abuse has often shown a dichotomy between middle-class white women and working-class women of color, specifically Chicanas/Latinas. Let us consider, for example, the ideology of an appropriate family size. It is this ideology which underlies the so-called 'One hundred and twenty rule,' an "unofficial rule of thumb of the American College of Obstetricians and Gynecologists until about 1970, under which a woman's age multiplied by the number of children she already had must equal one hundred and twenty (120) or more in order for her to obtain sterilization for contraception" (Clarke 1984). Although seemingly designed to protect women from seeking sterilization while she was very young or had no children, this rule also protected physicians who 'encouraged' or induced women with four or more children and over thirty years of age to be sterilized. Chicanas/Latinas were overrepresented in this category. Conversely, these same physicians would not be as likely to allow a thirty year old woman with only one child, most likely to be a white female according to fertility statistics, to undergo such a procedure. Can we assume that although the 'one hundred and twenty rule' is no longer official policy it is no longer included in the values of many physicians?

Blatant sterilization is currently well regulated. Subtle sterilization, however, continues to be an issue for feminist groups concerned with reproductive rights, especially as it is applied to women of color. Subtle sterilization can take many different forms which are selectively applied to women of color. Clarke's list of forms of sterilization includes experiences all very familiar to Chicanas/Latinas either as "ideas" which have been put forth to them by their doctors, or situations with which they live on a daily basis, as follows: 1) lack of knowledge or access to abortion as an alternative to sterilization; 2) unnecessary hysterectomy; 3) economic constraints upon reproductive choice; 4) lack of knowledge of the permanence of sterilization; 5) surgical sterilization performed at the time of childbirth or abortion; 6) iatrogenic (medically-caused) sterility or infertility; 7) ideologies of 'appropriate' family size and structure; 8) lack of counseling to prevent regret of sterilization; 9) lack of knowledge or access to other means of contraception as alternative to sterilization (Clarke 1984).

An additional, and less recognized, form of subtle sterilization is unprotected exposure to teratogenic chemicals (chemicals known to cause malformation in a fetus) in the work place or in the home. This is a situation which affects everyone, but is most blatant in its effects on Chicanas/Latinas in the work place because of their overrepresentation in the three labor market categories which carry high risks of exposure: clerical (radiation exposure), service (chemicals for cleaning), and operatives and laborers (exposure to pesticides, herbicides, and chemicals used in the manufacturing processes). Concerns over the situation of farm workers unprotected exposure to chemicals are in this additional category. These known and suspected teratogenic chemicals contribute to infertility, still births, birth defects, and cancers such as those seen in McFarland, California and other Central Valley locations.

Finally, we add another word of caution here, and that is with respect to reproductive technology research on human beings. While human sperm for such research is easily obtainable, such is not the case for ova, or eggs. Until the early 1970s eggs ready for fertilization and/or research had to be obtained from ovaries surgically removed from the female. These ovaries often were "given" to researchers by hospitals. Since protection from sterilization procedures during other surgical or medical procedures did not come until the late 1970s, one may ask if non-essential surgeries were not a convenient way for researchers to obtain ovaries for research. And who's eggs were being utilized in all of this early research anyway? Evidence shows that oophorectomies (surgical removal of the ovaries) have been on the increase since the 1950s and perhaps before. Many physicians advocate hysterectomies and oophorectomies prior to menopause as a means of preventing cancers in otherwise healthy women. These surgically removed ovaries are those which were then available for use in early reproductive research (Arditti, Klein, and Minden, 1984, 47-51). Since the early 1970s, reproductive technology research has increased significantly because of the perfection of two techniques: superovulation (increasing the amount of ova production through the use of hormone therapy) and non-surgical recovery(flushing) of the eggs. More reproductive research than ever before can be conducted and with higher pregnancy and birth rates through in vitro fertilization, IVF (Corea 1985). More importantly, much of this research has been done through private or corporate funding by private individuals or in conjunction with university researchers in research programs sponsored by the corporations or individuals who will own the intellectual property or patentable products resulting from the research.

In view of past reproductive technological abuses, the current issues assume critical proportions. The lack of control Chicanas/ Latinas may experience over their reproductive lives must be linked to their material conditions. These material conditions include a socioeconomic status which places them in a high-risk category for continued reproductive victimization, increased health risks due to their occupational segregation, and exclusion from access to information, services, and decision-making in the area of reproductive technology policy making.

A brief summary of Chicanas/Latinas' employment and economic status in the United States underscores their high-risk status. In the area of employment and unemployment, Chicanas/ Latinas exhibit several characteristics: occupational segregation, high unemployment, and low wages. Chicanas/Latinas are concentrated in the three job categories with lowest pay and lowest job security—the clerical category with 42.1 percent for Mexican women and 44.7 percent for all Hispanics, the service category with 24.6 percent for Mexican and 20.7 percent for all Hispanics, and the operative category with 15.8 percent for Mexican and 13.9 percent for all Hispanics (Rix 1988). Chicanas/Latinas have an unemployment rate usually equivalent to that of Chicanos/Latinos, slightly lower than for African Americans and consistently higher than for whites, males or females. In 1975, Black men and women both had unemployment rates of 14.8 percent, while Hispanic women had a rate of 13.5 percent compared to 11.4 percent for Hispanic males. Ten years later in 1985 the rates were: Black women, 14.9 percent, Black men, 15.3 percent, Hispanic women 11.0 percent, and Hispanic men 10.2 percent (Rix 1988). Finally, Chicanas/Latinas have the lowest ratio of earnings: Chicanas/ Latinas earn on average 55.8 percent of white men's wages in compared with the percentages earned by white women, 68.2 percent, Black men, 72 percent, Black women, and men of Hispanic origin, 68.0 percent (Rix 1988).

The other important aspect of Chicana/Latina life that exacerbates their risk of reproductive victimization is the impact of poverty, a cumulative effect of employment segregation, unemployment, low wages, and the prevalence of single parenting, among other factors. Single female headed households in the Chicano/Latino population are more prevalent than among the white population and is a steadily increasing phenomenon. From 1975 to 1983, the number of single female-headed households among Chicanos/Latinos increased from 18.7 percent of total Chicano/Latino households to 23 percent. By 1988, 23.4 percent of Hispanic households were headed by females with no male present, compared to a rate of 13 percent for anglo (white) households (Rix 1988). In 1978, 53 percent of female-headed households among Chicanos/Latinos lived below the poverty line. By 1984, some sources argued that 71.0 percent of female-headed households among Chicanos/Latinos lived below the poverty line. March 1988 figures cite 51.8 percent of all Latino female-headed households living below the poverty level, with figures ranging from 47.1 percent to 65.3 percent for the different Latino sub-groups (Duany and Pittman 1990). Chicanas/Latinas, more so than any other group, either live in poverty or on the edge of it. Nationwide, the percentage of Chicano/Latino children living in poverty have either increased or remained at a very high rate, depending on the statistics utilized. The Children's Defense Fund publication on Latino youth indicates continuing high rates of 35.2 percent (Duany and Pittman 1990).

This statistical profile of Chicanas/Latinas and their households, coupled with their high-risk status for developing health problems, renders them vulnerable to a high degree of reproductive victimization. As members of the total Hispanic population, they have less health-care coverage than all other ethnic/racial groups in the United States. "Poverty, the absence of medical insurance, and the scarcity of Hispanics in health professions effectively bar many of them from good medical care" (Health/Medicine 1991). Moreover, researchers find that Hispanics' health appears to worsen as they adopt cultural patterns common to the United States, including smoking, drinking and eating patterns (Health/Medicine 1991). As acculturation occurs, it seems that poverty, segregation, and familial stress increase as health and educational status deteriorate.

Abortion is without question the focal point of reproductive issues in the 1990s. Chicanas/Latinas have been painfully confronted with this issue. Given the current threat to a woman's
right to publicly financed abortions, the health implications of an
end to legal abortions for Chicanas/Latinas, as well as all women
with limited means, would be devastating. As one team of researchers has noted:

> In the early 1970's, when legal abortion was available only on a lim-
> ited regional basis, over 40 percent of the women obtaining abortions
> had to travel outside their home state to do so. The 1973 U.S. Su-
> preme Court decision had a disproportionate impact on abortion rates
> of Black women, particularly teenagers, since improved geographic
> access to legal abortions, . . . allowed them to terminate unwanted
> pregnancies they would have either aborted through illegal channels
> or continued to term (Ezzard, Cates, et. al, 1982).

A later study of the impact of a ban on legal abortions on adolescent childbearing in New York suggested that banning abortion
would adversely impact childbearing of both Black and white
teenagers, that is, it would increase the number of unwanted
pregnancies resulting in significantly higher social welfare costs
(Joyce and Mocan 1990).

Although a comparable abortion study of Chicanas/Latinas
since *Roe vs. Wade* is not available, one can infer from studies on
low income women in general. For many women of color the significance of *Roe vs. Wade* was that it allowed states to provide abortion as a reproductive choice for women regardless of economic
status. This provided minority women with the critical opportunity to substitute high-risk, illegal procedures and unwanted pregnancies for safe, medically supervised abortions, thereby reducing
their risk of unnecessary deaths and future health complications.
Although in absolute numbers, more white females have abortions, the abortion ratio within the respective population cohorts
for Black females and for Chicana/Latina women is considerably
higher. Recent figures from the Center for Disease Control indicate that the ratio of Chicanas/Latinas receiving abortions is 13
percent within the national cohort, while they comprise only 8
percent of the total United States population. Thus, Chicanas/
Latinas are over represented among women receiving abortions.
Further, they are most highly represented in the age group fifteen

years of age or younger (McKay 1990). Safe, affordable, legal abortion may thus be a critical reproductive health issue for these young women.

Implications of New Reproductive Technologies

Reproductive technologies have come a very long way since the early 1960s and have taken many different directions. Embryology, fetal research, prenatal diagnosis and other similar bio-medical techniques underscore the need for a more complex and complete understanding of reproductive technology. At this point, it is useful to introduce a more complete definition of reproductive technologies, one which incorporates these complexities. Reproductive technologies of the 1990s are "visible manifestations of developments in bio-technology" (Hanmer, 1987, 697). This definition subsumes reproductive technologies under genetic or reproductive engineering defined as:

> ...anything to do with the manipulation of the gametes or the fetus, for whatever purpose, from conception other than by sexual union of two persons to treatment of disease in utero, to the ultimate manufacture of a human being to exact specifications. Thus the earliest procedure is artificial insemination,...next artificial fertilization or in vitro fertilization...next artificial implantation into a uterus...in the future ectogenesis or total extracorporal gestation of a fetus to term... and finally, what is popularly meant by genetic engineering, the production—or better, the biological manufacture—of a human being to desired specifications (Hanmer 1987, 698).

At present current technology enables us to perform three of the procedures mentioned above: donor and/or spousal artificial insemination, in vitro fertilization, and artificial implantation. Each of these procedures includes several variations, presents additional dangers, and causes greater dilemmas. Spousal artificial insemination possesses procedural complications which include danger of infection to the woman, psychological complications, and some pain. Donor insemination raises additional concerns related to the outcome of pregnancy including congenital malformations, genetic disease, the risk of intermarriage among genetically related individuals, genetic manipulation, and legal complications. The latest specter raised in artificial insemination is the potential transmission of Acquired Immune Deficiency Syndrome, (AIDS). Frozen embryos and their necessary implantation have already raised difficult issues such as whether they are private property, potential human beings, fetuses, gametes, or actual human beings. Other important concerns include the determination of who has legal and financial responsibility in case of defective fetuses, custodial battles, and possible unforeseen conflicts. Complex and painful ethical questions are raised by these latest technologies.

Older technologies such as birth control, sterilization, prenatal screening, and abortion raised moral issues and questions of access, legal rights, and control. New technologies such as in vitro fertilization, surrogate motherhood, artificial insemination, frozen embryos and uterine implantation, surgery in utero, and increased viability of premature fetuses raise new moral, ethical, psychological, legal and practical questions. Surrogate motherhood, achieved predominantly through artificial insemination or embryo transfer, has created a stir, culminating in the case of *Johnson vs Calvert*. This situation was highly publicized because it involved many controversial issues, racial differences, class differences, and a single parent on welfare, among other complex legal issues. Surrogate motherhood involving spousal artificial insemination of a woman other than the spousal mate is quickly becoming outdated as techniques for dealing with infertility (such as IVF) become simpler, cheaper, and safer.

A more complex, and interesting scenario has arisen with Arlette Schweitzer, the South Dakota grandmother who is pregnant with her daughter's twins. This was achieved through IVF, without any of the legal tangles surrounding the 1987 situation when Mary Beth Whitehead was the biological and surrogate mother. The concern here for Chicanas/Latinas is that they are vulnerable to the economic need to 'rent' their uterus just as, for centuries, poor and working class women have 'rented' their vaginas. Finally, we are barely beginning to understand the long-term social, legal and medical effects on the children born from these technologies.

Most importantly, as a society and particularly as women, we have not resolved many of these earlier issues and are not much further along in resolving the new ones. What is quite clear in all of these debates is that the issue of control of women is foremost.

Feminists have come to focus on this concern and view the ideological, legal, and practical struggle as one where men continue to maintain control over women's ability to procreate (Luker 1984; Arditti et al. 1984). "Each time a new technological development is hailed, the same question arises: is this liberation or oppression in a new guise?" (Arditti et al. 1984, 2).

Institutional racism/ethnocentrism and high poverty rates, coupled with the fact that Chicanas/Latinas have the highest fertility rates among all female groups, make Chicanas/Latinas particularly vulnerable to the negative aspects of new reproductive technologies. Reproductive technologies have traditionally been used to control the fertility of Chicanas/Latinas rather than to overcome infertility, and they will continue to be so used for several reasons. First, as Hanmer has explained, the latest reproductive technologies are being ideologically constructed as extensions of a patriarchal vision which is completely heterosexist—perfect children for perfect couples (Hanmer 1987). Secondly, reproductive technologies are commercialized and thus expensive—reproduction for profit—and thus beyond the means of most Latino/Latina families. Thirdly, as several feminist scholars have noted, some of the most noted researchers in reproductive technologies clearly espouse some of the concepts of the eugenics movement more respectable in the early part of this century. Finally, contemporary reproductive technologies negate or ignore cultural values and practices in reproduction itself. Thus Chicanas/Latinas, to date, have not generally benefitted from the development of reproductive technologies.

These latest developments in reproductive technologies threaten Chicanas/Latinas not because of some surrealistic, futuristic specter of the control of women described by feminist novelists such as Margaret Atwood, but because of the very real experiences which they have already had. Experiences with genocide, genocidal undercurrents, and teratogenesis lead us to conclude that Chicanas/Latinas will be easy targets for increasing patriarchal control over their bodies, even to the extent that they will be forced to sell their ovaries, their uteruses, in addition to their bodies to sustain themselves and their families (Spallone and Steinberg 1987). For Chicanas/Latinas, the critical questions are based on the constraints of class, race, and gender. How can Chicanas/Latinas control their fertility when they have little power in the medical, research, or policy making arenas? How can Chicanas/Latinas mobilize against the white minority worldwide which seeks to control people of color? How can Chicanas/Latinas address their infertility when the forms of intervention must be purchased at a cost usually out of their reach? How can Chicanas/Latinas begin to address these issues vital to their future? Where can they turn to inform, educate, and empower themselves?

This is an area of policy, research and activism to which the Chicano/Latino community must pay close attention. As Chicana feminists, whether we are activists, academics, or workers, we cannot consider ourselves unaffected by the new reproductive technologies simply because most of us do not benefit from them. Quite the contrary. Because of the potential for greater abuse of Chicanas/Latinas, more careful consideration must be given to this area of knowledge. As feminists we must develop a paradigm for understanding reproductive technologies which includes the impact of such research on women of color. As Chicanas/Latinas we must place the issues relating to the impact of reproductive technologies on Chicanas/Latinas among our uppermost concerns and on the first levels of our public policy concerns.

Selected
Bibliography

Chicana Studies:
An Updated List of Materials, 1980–1991

Lillian Castillo-Speed

The author would like to acknowledge the help of Lisa Hernandez and Carolyn Soto in compiling this update.

Introduction

The literature on Chicanas since 1980 documents a significant shift in perspective with the emergence of Chicana scholars in all disciplines of Chicano Studies. Chicanas are no longer merely the objects of study: they are also the critical observers and researchers. Furthermore, the study of Chicanas no longer represents only one facet of the Chicano experience. It pervades all aspects of that experience and with the emergence of more and more Chicana scholars has emerged as a discipline in its own right: Chicana Studies.

Since 1980, several reference works have provided useful information on various aspects of Chicana research. Beginning with the more general, Barbara J. and J. Cordell Robinson's *The Mexican American: A Critical Guide to Research Aids* should be mentioned first. It is a comprehensive bibliography of bibliographies on Chicanos, including a chapter on women. *The International Inventory of Current Mexico-Related Research* contains many references to on-going research projects on Chicanas. For a general index to articles published on Chicanos consult the *Chicano Periodical Index* (listed under Castillo-Speed and the Committee for the Development of Subject Access to Chicano Literature) and *The Chicano Index* (includes books and book articles as well as journal articles). Here will be found author and title indexes to poetry, essays and short stories, biographical sketches and book reviews, as well as subject access to all aspects of the Chicano experience. The *Chicano Anthology*

Index compiled by García-Ayvens opens up to bibliographical access articles, poems, short stories and book chapters appearing in anthologies. García-Ayvens also compiles and edits *Chicanos in These Times*, a cumulative subject guide to articles appearing in the *Los Angeles Times*. It includes many references to Chicanas under that heading and other related headings. Three very recent books dealing with women of color contain bibliographic references to works on Chicanas. Published in 1989, K. Lynn Stoner's *Latinas of the Americas* is a collection of bibliographical essays dealing with many different aspects of the Latin American woman, including Chicanas. There is no chapter on Chicanas per se, but the subject index contains 243 references under the term "Mexican Americans." *Women of Color in the United States*, edited by Bernice Redfern, was also published in 1989. It contains four sections: Afro-American Women, Asian American Women, Hispanic American Women, and Native American Women. The section on Hispanic American women includes ninety-nine annotated citations of publications on Puerto Rican and Cuban American women as well as on Chicanas, most from the last ten years. The third bibliography is *Women of Color and Southern Women*, edited by Andrea Timberlake, et al. Published in 1988, it is divided into six main areas: "Culture," "Education," "Employment," "Family," "Health," and "Political Activism/Social Movements." Each section includes subsections on six groups of women: African American, Asian American, Latina, Native American, Southern, and Women of Color. There are about 280 entries referring to Latinas.

Three bibliographic articles focusing specifically on Chicanas should be noted. Catherine Loeb's 1980 survey which appeared in *Frontiers* is a very good guide. Richard Chabrán's bibliographical essay "Chicana Reference Sources," which appeared in *Chicana Voices* (1986) is another excellent source. The most pertinent and most recent guide is Cynthia Orozco's "Getting Started in Chicana Studies" which appeared in *Women's Studies Quarterly* (1990). In the area of statistical information the most complete work is *The Hispanic Population of the United States* (1987) by Frank D. Bean and Marta Tienda. This 456 page book includes chapters on "Marriage, Family, and Household," and "Fertility Patterns Within the Spanish Origin Population." The extensive index includes many references under the heading "Women or Female."

The Bureau of the Census publishes a series of statistical updates called *Current Population Reports*. One update is "Hispanic Population in the United States." The most current update in this series should be consulted for current population figures.

In the area of mental health there is only one major reference source and that is *Hispanic Mental Health Research: A Reference Guide* (1982), compiled by Newton, Olmedo, and Padilla. The primary arrangement is by author but the subject index includes such terms as "Birth Control," "Family Planning," "Female," "Gender Identity," "Machismo," "Marital Stability," and "Marriage." It includes entries on books and reports as well as journal articles.

Three bibliographies on the maquiladora and border industries are Jorge V. Carrillo's *La industria maquiladora en México: bibliografía, directorio e investigaciones recientes/Border Assembly Industry and Recent Research* (1981), Rolando M. Villalobos' *Research Guide to the Literature on Northern Mexico's Maquiladora Assembly Industry* (1988), and Leslie Sklair's *Maquiladoras: Annotated Bibliography and Research Guide to Mexico's In-Bond Industry, 1980–1988*.

In the area of history and biography three works should be mentioned. Matt Meier's *Mexican American Biographies: A Historical Dictionary, 1836–1987* (1988) lists about 270 entries, forty of which are Chicanas ranging from Dolores Huerta to Lorna Dee Cervantes. Alberto Camarillo's *Latinos in the United States: A Historical Bibliography* (1986) contains many entries on Chicanas. A good place to begin when searching for archival sources on Chicanas is Barbara Driscoll's "Chicana Historiography: A Research Note Concerning Mexican Archival Sources," which appeared in *Chicana Voices* (1986).

Information on Chicana/Latina organizations can be found in Sylvia Gonzales' *Hispanic American Voluntary Organizations* (1985). A list of such organizations appears at the back of the book.

There are several resources on Chicano/Chicana literature which should be consulted. Ernestina Eger's *A Bibliography of Criticism of Contemporary Chicano Literature* (1982) contains a section on the image of Chicanas in literature as well as criticism on various Chicana authors. *Chicano Literature: A Reference Guide* (1985) by Julio A. Martinez and Francisco A. Lomelí includes an essay on Chicanas in Chicano literature as well as a few entries on specific Chicana writers. *Literatura Chicana: Creative and Critical Writings Through 1984* (1985) by Trujillo and Rodriguez contains many references to creative and critical works on Chicanas and also includes video interviews in the audio and sound recording sections. Bibliographies which focus on Chicana writings have appeared in Chicano literary journals. Elizabeth Ordonez's "Chicana Literature and Related Sources: A Selected and Annotated Bibliography" appeared in *Bilingual Review* in 1980. Iliana Sonntag's "Hacia una Bibliografía de Poesía Femenina Chicana" in *La Palabra* also appeared in 1980. As noted below, Norma Alarcón's bibliography is the most recent listing in this area. Chicanas are extensively represented in Goldman and Ybarra-Frausto's *Arte Chicano: A Comprehensive Annotated Bibliography of Chicano Art, 1965–1981* (1985). Each art exhibit which included a Chicana artist was so noted as well as books and articles which mentioned Chicanas.

The following list is an update to "Chicana Studies: A Selected List of Materials Since 1980," which was published in *Frontiers* (Vol. 11, no. 1 (1990)). The original list was compiled through an exhaustive search for items published since 1980 and the procedure for updating followed the same pattern. The search for articles began with the Chicano Database which contains over 38,000 journal article citations. The Chicano Database produces the *Chicano Periodical Index* and the *Chicano Index*, and is headquartered at the Chicano Studies Library at the University of California at Berkeley. It is now available in compact disc format as the *Chicano Database on CD-ROM*. Entering the subject heading "Chicanas" yielded almost 1000 citations. Other related terms such as "Family," "Sex Roles," "Sex Stereotypes," "Machismo," "Intermarriage," "Fertility," "Marriage," and "Feminism" produced more citations. Book articles were derived from a separate file on the Chicano Database which contains citations from the *Chicano Anthology Index*, compiled by Francisco García-Ayvens. Book citations were gathered by searching the resources of the Chicano Studies Library at UC Berkeley, the Chicano Research Center Library at UCLA and the Colección Tloque Nahuaque of UC Santa Barbara.

Materials included in the final list were chosen on the basis of usefulness for research. Biographical articles on Chicana engineers, businesspersons or government officials were excluded. On the other hand, critical articles on Chicana authors and their writings are represented here. Individual poems and short stories were excluded for the most part. These and the biographical articles are readily found in the *Chicano Database on CD-ROM*. Creative works such as novels and collections of poetry by a single author were also omitted. Norma Alarcón's "Chicana Writers and Critics in a Social Context: Towards a Contemporary Bibliography" is an excellent guide to creative works up to 1989.

Abrahamse, Allan F. *Beyond Stereotypes: Who Becomes a Single Teenage Mother?* Santa Monica, Calif.: RAND Corp., 1988.

Abrahamse, Allan F., Peter A. Morrison, and Linda J. Waite. "Teenagers Willing to Consider Single Parenthood: Who Is at Greatest Risk?" *Family Planning Perspectives* 20, no. 1 (January-February 1988): 13-18.

Achor, Shirley, and Aida G. Morales. "Chicanas Holding Doctoral Degrees: Social Reproduction and Cultural Ecological Approaches." *Anthropology and Education Quarterly* 21, no. 3 (September 1990): 269-287.

Acuña, Rodolfo. "Response to Cynthia Orozco." *La Red/The Net*, no. 79 (April 1984): 13-15.

_____. "The Struggles of Class and Gender: Current Research in Chicano Studies [Review Essay]." *Journal of American Ethnic History* 8, no. 2 (Spring 1989): 134-138.

"Adelante, mujer hispana." *Latino* 53, no. 2 (March-April, 1982): 26.

Agosin, Marjorie. "Elucubraciones y antielucubraciones: crítica feminista desde perspectivas poéticas." *Third Woman* 1, no. 2 (1982): 65-69.

Aguilar-Henson, Marcella. *The Multi-Faceted Poetic World of Angela de Hoyos*. Austin: Relámpago Books Press, 1985.

Ahern, Susan, Dexter Edward Bryan, and Reynaldo Baca. "Migration and la mujer fuerte." *Migration Today* 13, no. 1 (1985): 14-20.

Alarcón, Norma. "Chicana Feminism: In the Tracks of 'the' Native Woman." *Cultural Studies* 4, no. 3 (October 1990): 248-256.

_____. "Chicana's Feminist Literature: A Re-vision through Malintzin or Malintzin: Putting Flesh Back on the Object." In *This Bridge Called My Back: Writings by Radical Women of Color*, edited by Cherríe Moraga and Gloria Anzaldúa, 182-190. Watertown, Mass.: Persephone Press, 1981.

_____. "Chicana Writers and Critics in a Social Context: Towards a Contemporary Bibliography." *Third Woman* 4 (1989): 169-178.

_____. "Hay que inventarnos/We Must Invent Ourselves." *Third Woman* 1, no. 1 (1981): 4-6.

_____. "Latina writers in the United States." In *Spanish American Women Writers: A Bio-Bibliographical Source Book*, edited by Diane E. Marting, [557]-567. New York: Greenwood Press, 1990.

_____. "Making 'Familia' From Scratch: Split Subjectivities in the Work of Helena María Viramontes and Cherríe Moraga." *The Americas Review* 15, no. 3-4 (Fall-Winter, 1987): 147-159.

_____. "The Sardonic Powers of the Erotic in the Work of Ana Castillo." In *Breaking Boundaries: Latina Writing and Critical Readings*, edited by Asunción Horno-Delgado, et al., 94-107. Amherst: Univ. of Massachusetts Press, 1989.

_____. "The Theoretical Subject(s) of *This Bridge Called My Back* and Anglo-American Feminism." In *Criticism in the Borderlands: Studies in Chicano Literature, Culture, and Ideology*, edited by Hector Calderón and José David Saldívar, [28]-39. Durham, North Carolina: Duke Univ. Press, 1991. Also in *Making Face, Making Soul: Haciendo Caras: Creative and Critical Perspectives by Women of Color*, edited by Gloria Anzaldúa, 356-369. San Francisco: Aunt Lute Foundation Books, 1990.

_____. "Traddutora, traditora: A Paradigmatic Figure of Chicana Feminism." *Cultural Critique* 13, (Fall 1989): 57-87.

_____. "What Kind of Lover Have You Made Me, Mother?: Towards a Theory of Chicanas' Feminism and Cultural Identity through Poetry." In *Women of Color: Perspectives on Feminism and Identity*, edited by Audrey T. McCluskey, 85-110. Bloomington: Women's Studies Program, Indiana Univ., 1985.

Alarcón, Norma, Ana Castillo, and Cherríe Moraga. "The Sexuality of Latinas [Special Issue]." *Third Woman* 4 (1989).

Alarcón, Norma, and Cherríe Moraga. "Interview with Cherríe Moraga." *Third Woman* 3, no. 1-2 (1986): 127-134.

Alarcón, Norma, and Pat Mora. "Interview with Pat Mora." *Third Woman* 3, no. 1-2 (1986): 121-126.

Alcalay, Rina. "Hispanic Women in the United States: Family & Work Relations." *Migration Today* 12, no. 3 (1984): 13-20.

Alonso, Ana María, and María Teresa Koreck. "Silences: 'Hispanics,' AIDS, and Sexual Practices." *Differences: A Journal of Feminist Cultural Studies* 1, no. 1 (Winter 1989): 101-124.

Alvarez-Amaya, María. "Determinants of Breast and Cervical Cancer Behavior among Mexican American Women." *Border Health/Salud Fronteriza* 5, no. 3 (1989): 22-27.

Amaro, Hortensia. "Abortion Use and Attitudes Among Chicanas: The Need for Research." *Research Bulletin (Spanish Speaking Mental Health Research Center, UCLA)* 4, no. 3 (March 1980): 1-5.

_____. "Considerations for Prevention of HIV Infection among Hispanic Women." *Psychology of Women Quarterly*, 12, no. 4 (1988): 429-444.

_____. *Hispanic Women in Psychology: A Resource Directory*. Washington, D.C.: Committee on Women in Psychology, American Psychological Association, 1984.

_____. "Women in the Mexican-American Community: Religion, Culture, and Reproductive Attitudes and Experiences." *Journal of Community Psychology* 16, no. 1 (January 1988): 6-20.

Amaro, Hortensia, and Nancy Felipe Russo. "Hispanic Women and Mental Health: An Overview of Contemporary Issues in Research and Practice." *Psychology of Women Quarterly* 11, no. 4 (December 1987): 393-407.

Amaro, Hortensia, Nancy Felipe Russo, and Julie Johnson. "Family and Work Predictors of Psychological Well-Being among Hispanic Women Professionals." *Psychology of Women Quarterly* 11, no. 4 (1987): 505-521.

Amaro, Hortensia, Nancy Felipe Russo, and José A. Pares-Avila. "Contemporary Research on Hispanic Women: A Selected Bibliography of the Social Science Literature." *Psychology of Women Quarterly* 11, no. 4 (December 1987): 523-532.

Amodeo, Luiza B., Rosalyn Edelson, and Jeanette Martin. "The Triple Bias: Rural, Minority and Female." *Rural Educator* 3, no. 3 (Spring 1982): 1-6.

Anderson, Robert K. "Márez y Luna and the Masculine-Feminine Dialectic." *Crítica Hispánica* 6, no. 2 (1984): 97-105.

Andrade, Sally J. "Bibliography on Latino Families." In *Latino Families in the United States*, edited by Sally J. Andrade, 72-79. [S.l.]: Planned Parenthood Federation of America, Inc., 1983.

_____. "Chicana Adolescents and Contraception Issues." *La Red/The Net*, no. 35 (October 1980): 2, 14.

_____. *Latino Families in the United States: A Resource Book for Family Life Education.* [S.l.]: Planned Parenthood Federation of America, Inc., 1983.

_____. "Social Science Stereotypes of the Mexican American Woman: Policy Implications for Research." *Hispanic Journal of Behavioral Sciences* 4, no. 2 (June 1982): 223-244.

Aneshensel, Carol S., et al. "Onset of Fertility-Related Events During Adolescence: A Prospective Comparison of Mexican American and Non-Hispanic White Females." *American Journal of Public Health* 80, no. 8 (August 1990): 959-963.

_____. "Participation of Mexican American Female Adolescents in a Longitudinal Panel Survey." *Public Opinion Quarterly* 53, no. 4 (Winter 1989): 548-562.

Aneshensel, Carol S., Eve P. Fielder, and Rosina M. Becerra. "Fertility and Fertility-Related Behavior among Mexican-American and Non-Hispanic White Female Adolescents." *Journal of Health and Social Behavior* 30, no. 1 (March 1989): 56-76.

Angel, Ronald, and Marta Tienda. "Determinants of Extended Household Structure: Cultural Pattern or Economical Need?" *American Journal of Sociology* 87, no. 6 (May 1982): 1360-1383.

Angel, Ronald, and Jacqueline Lowe Worobey. "Single Motherhood and Children's Health." *Journal of Health and Social Behavior* 29, no. 1 (March 1988): 38-52.

Anzaldúa, Gloria. "Border Crossings." *Trivia: A Journal of Ideas*, no. 14 (Spring 1989): 46-51.

———. *Borderlands/La Frontera: The New Mestiza*. San Francisco: Spinsters/Aunt Lute, 1987.

———. "La prieta." In *This Bridge Called My Back: Writings by Radical Women of Color*, edited by Cherrie Moraga and Gloria Anzaldúa, 198-209. Watertown, Mass.: Persephone Press, 1981.

———, ed. *Making Face, Making Soul: Haciendo Caras: Creative and Critical Perspectives by Women of Color*. San Francisco: Aunt Lute Foundation Books, 1990.

Apodaca, Maria Linda. "A Double Edge Sword: Hispanas and Liberal Feminism." *Crítica* 1, no. 3 (Fall 1986): 96-114.

Aragón de Valdez, Theresa. "Organizing As a Political Tool for the Chicana." *Frontiers: A Journal of Women Studies* 5, no. 2 (Summer 1980): 7-13.

Arce, Carlos H., and Armando J. Abney-Guardado. "Demographic and Cultural Correlates of Chicano Intermarriage." *California Sociologist* 5, no. 2 (Summer 1982): 41-58.

Arenal, Sandra. *Sangre joven: las maquiladoras por dentro*. Mexico, D.F.: Editorial Nuestro Tiempo, 1986.

Arévalo, Rodolfo, and Marianne Minor, eds. *Chicanas and Alcoholism: A Socio-Cultural Perspective of Women*. San Jose, Calif.: School of Social Work, San Jose State Univ., 1981.

Argüelles, Lourdes, and Anne M. Rivero. "HIV Infection/AIDS and Latinas in Los Angeles County: Considerations for Prevention, Treatment, and Research Practice." *California Sociologist* 11, no. 1-2 (1988): 69-89.

Arizmendi, Yareli. "La mujer y el teatro chicano." In *Mujer y literatura mexicana y chicana: Culturas en contacto*, edited by Aralia López-González, et al., [85]-91. Mexico: Colegio de la Frontera Norte, 1988.

Atkinson, Donald R., Andrew Winzelberg, and Abby Holland. "Ethnicity, Locus of Control for Family Planning, and Pregnancy Counselor Credibility." *Journal of Counseling Psychology* 32, no. 3 (July 1985): 417-421.

Aulette, Judy, and Trudy Mills. "Something Old, Something New: Auxiliary Work in the 1983-1986 Copper Strike." *Feminist Studies* 14, no. 2 (Summer 1988): 251-268.

Ayers-Nackamkin, Beverly, et al. "Sex and Ethnic Differences in the Use of Power." *Journal of Applied Psychology* 67, no. 4 (August 1982): 464-471.

Baca, Reynaldo, and Dexter Edward Bryan. "Mexican Women, Migration and Sex Roles." *Migration Today* 13, no. 3 (1985): 14-18.

Baca Barragán, Polly. "La Chicana in Politics." In *La Chicana: Building for the Future*, 21-31. Oakland, Calif.: National Hispanic University, 1981.

Baca Barragan, Polly, Richard Hamner, and Lena Guerrero. "Untitled Interview with State Senators (Colorado) Polly Baca-Barrangan and Lena Guerrero." *National Hispanic Journal* 1, no. 2 (Winter 1982): 8-11.

Baca Zinn, Maxine. "Chicanas: Power and Control in the Domestic Sphere." In *Bridging Two Cultures: Multidisciplinary Readings in Bilingual, Bicultural Education*, edited by Martha Cotera and Larry Hufford, 270-281. Austin, Tex.: National Educational Laboratory Publishers, 1980.

_____. "Chicano Men and Masculinity." *Journal of Ethnic Studies* 10, no. 2 (Summer 1982): 29-44.

_____. "Employment and Education of Mexican-American Women: The Interplay of Modernity and Ethnicity in Eight Families." *Harvard Educational Review* 50, no. 1 (February, 1980): 47-62.

_____. "Gender and Ethnic Identity among Chicanos." *Frontiers: A Journal of Women Studies* 5, no. 2 (Summer, 1980): 18-24.

_____. "Mexican American Women in the Social Sciences." *Signs: Journal of Women in Culture and Society* 8, no. 2 (Winter 1982): 259-272.

_____. "Mexican Heritage Women: A Bibliographic Essay." *Sage Race Relations Abstracts* 9 (August 1984): 1-12.

_____. "Ongoing Questions in the Study of Chicano Families." In *The State of Chicano Research on Family, Labor, and Migration*, edited by Armando Valdez, Albert Camarillo, and Tomás Almaguer, 139-146. Stanford, Calif.: Stanford Center for Chicano Research, 1983.

_____. "Qualitative Methods in Family Research: A Look inside Chicano Families." *California Sociologist* 5, no. 2 (Summer 1982): 58-79.

_____. "Urban Kinship and Midwest Chicano Families: Evidence in Support of Revision." *De Colores* 6, no. 1-2 (1982): 85-98.

Badikian, Beatriz. "'Writing out of Necessity': An Interview with Sandra Cisneros." *The Feminist Writers Guild National Newsletter* 10, no. 1 (February 1987): 1, 6-8.

Baezconde-Garbanati, Lourdes and Nelly Salgado de Snyder. "Mexican Immigrant Women: A Selected Bibliography." *Hispanic Journal of Behavioral Sciences* 9, no. 3 (September 1987): 331-358.

Balkwell, Carolyn. "An Attitudinal Correlate of the Timing of a Major Life Event: The Case of Morale in Widowhood." *Family Relations* 34, no. 4 (October 1985): 577-581.

Barton, Amy E. "Women Farmworkers: Their Workplace and Capitalist Patriarchy." *Revista Mujeres* 3, no. 2 (June, 1986): 11-13.

Barton, Amy E., and California Commission on the Status of Women. *Campesinas: Women Farmworkers in the California Agricultural Labor Force: Re-*

port of a Study Project. Sacramento, Calif.: The Commission, [1978].

Bastida, Elena. "Sex-Typed Norms among Older Hispanics." *Gerontologist* 27, no. 1 (February 1987): 59-65.

Bauer, Richard L., and Richard A. Deyo. "Low Risk of Vertebral Fracture in Mexican American Women." *Archives of Internal Medicine* 147, no. 8 (August 1987): 1437-1439.

Bauer, Richard L., et al. "Risk of Postmenopausal Hip Fracture in Mexican-American Women." *American Journal of Public Health* 76, no. 8 (August 1986): 1020-1021.

Bauman, Raquel. "The Status of Chicanas in Medicine." *Research Bulletin (Spanish Speaking Mental Health Research Center, UCLA)* 4, no. 3 (March 1980): 6-7, 12-13.

Bean, Frank D. *Mexican American Fertility Patterns*. Austin: Univ. of Texas Press, 1985.

Bean, Frank D., and Gray Swicegood. "Generation, Female Education and Mexican American Fertility." *Social Science Quarterly* 63 (March 1982): 131-144.

Bean, Frank D., and Marta Tienda. *The Hispanic Population of the United States*. New York: Russell Sage Foundation, 1987.

Bean, Frank D., Elizabeth H. Stephen, and Wolfgang Opitz. "The Mexican Origin Population in the United States: A Demographic Overview." In *The Mexican American Experience: An Interdisciplinary Anthology*, edited by Rodolfo O. de la Garza, et al., 57-75. Austin: Univ. of Texas Press, 1985.

Bean, Frank D., Gray C. Swicegood, and Allan G. King. "Role Incompatibility and the Relationship between Fertility and Labor Supply among Hispanic Women." In *Hispanics in the U.S. Economy*, edited by George J. Borjas and Marta Tienda, 221-242. Orlando, Fla.: Academic Press, 1985.

Bean, Frank D., et al. "Generational Differences in Fertility among Mexican Americans: Implications for Assessing the Effects of Immigration." *Social Science Quarterly* 65, no. 2 (June, 1984): 573-582.

Becerra, Gloria V. "Chicana Employment—Options for the Future." In *La Chicana: Building for the Future*, 8-20. Oakland, Calif.: National Hispanic Univ., 1981.

Becerra, Rosina M., and Diane de Anda. "Pregnancy and Motherhood among Mexican American Adolescents." *Health and Social Work* 9, no. 2 (Spring 1984): 106-23.

Bello, Ruth T. "Being Hispanic in Houston: A Matter of Identity." *The Americas Review* 16, no. 1 (Spring 1988): 31-43.

Benardo, Margot L., and Darius Anthony. "Hispanic Women and Their Men." *Latina* 1, no. 3 (1983): 24-29.

Benton, Patricia Morán. "Mother's Day Reflections: Keepers of the

Faith." *Nuestro* 7, no. 4 (May 1983): 49.

Bergdolt-Munzer, Sara L. "Homemakers and Retirement Income Benefits: The Other Home Security Issue." *Chicano Law Review* 8 (1985): 61-80.

Berger, Peggy S. "Differences in Importance of and Satisfaction from Job Characteristics by Sex and Occupational Type among Mexican-American Employees." *Journal of Vocational Behavior* 28, no. 3 (June 1986): 203-213.

Bergmann, Barbara. "Trends in Occupational Segregation by Sex and Race, 1960-1981." In *Sex Segregation in the Workplace: Trends, Explanations and Remedies*, edited by Barbara F. Reskin, 11-26. Washington, D.C.: National Academy Press, 1984.

Billings, Linda M., and Alurista. "In Verbal Murals: A Study of Chicana Herstory and Poetry." *Confluencia* 2, no. 1 (Fall, 1986): 60-68.

Binder, Wolfgang. "Mothers and Grandmothers: Acts of Mythification and Remembrance in Chicano Poetry." In *Missions in Conflict: Essays on U.S.-Mexican Relations and Chicano Culture*, edited by Renate von Bardeleben, Dietrich Briesemeister, and Juan Bruce-Novoa, 133-143. Tubingen, W. Germany: Günter Narr Verlag, 1986.

———, ed. *Partial Autobiographies: Interviews with Twenty Chicano Poets*. Erlangen: Verlag Palm & Enke, 1985. Includes nine Chicanas.

Blackwelder, Julia Kirk. *Women of the Depression: Caste and Culture in San Antonio, 1929-1939*. College Station: Texas A & M Univ. Press, 1984.

Blanco, Iris. "La mujer en los albores de la conquista de México." *Aztlán* 11, no. 2 (Fall 1980): 249-270.

Blanco, Iris, and Rosalia Solórzano. "O te aclimatas o te aclimueres." *fem* 8, no. 34 (June-July 1984): 20-22.

Borland, Dolores C. "A Cohort Analysis Approach to the Empty Nest Syndrome among Three Ethnic Groups of Women: A Theoretical Position." *Journal of Marriage and the Family* 44, no. 1 (February 1982): 117-129.

Bornstein de Somoza, Miriam. "La poética chicana: visión panorámica." *La Palabra* 2, no. 2 (Fall 1980): 43-66.

Bouknight, Jon. "Language as a Cure: An Interview with Milcha Sánchez-Scott." *Latin American Theatre Review* 23, no. 2 (Spring 1990): 63-74.

Bourque, Linda B., Jess F. Kraus, and Beverly J. Cosand. "Attributes of Suicide in Females." *Suicide and Life-Threatening Behavior* 13, no. 2 (Summer 1983): 123-138.

Boza, María del Carmen, et al., eds. *Nosotras: Latina Literature Today*. Binghamton, NY: Bilingual Review Press, 1986.

Bridges, Julian C. "Family Life." In *Borderlands Sourcebook: A Guide to the Literature on Northern Mexico and the American Southwest*, edited by Ellwyn

R. Stoddard, Richard L. Nostrand, and Jonathan P. West, 259-262. Norman: Univ. of Oklahoma Press, 1983.

Brinson-Curiel, Barbara. "Lucha Corpi." In *Chicano Writers, First Series, Dictionary of Literary Biography* 82: 91-97. Detroit: Bruccoli Clark Layman, 1989.

Briody, Elizabeth K. "Patterns of Household Immigration into South Texas." *International Migration Review* 21, no. 1 (Spring 1987): 27-47.

Brown, Betty Ann. "Chicanas Speak Out." *Artweek* 15, no. 2 (January 14, 1984): 1 +.

Broyles-González, Yolanda. "Carmen Tafolla." In *Chicano Writers, First Series, Dictionary of Literary Biography* 82: 257-260. Detroit: Bruccoli Clark Layman, 1989.

_____. "Women in El Teatro Campesino: '¿Apoco estaba molacha la Virgen de Guadalupe?'" In *Chicana Voices: Intersections of Class, Race, and Gender*, edited by Teresa Córdova, et al., [162]-187. Austin: Center for Mexican American Studies, UT Austin, 1986.

Broyles-González, Yolanda, and Diane Rodríguez. "The Living Legacy of Chicana Performers: Preserving History through Oral Testimony." *Frontiers: A Journal of Women Studies* 11, no. 1 (1990): [46]-52.

Bruce-Novoa, Juan. "Bernice Zamora y Lorna Dee Cervantes: una estética feminista." *Revista Iberoamericana* 51 (July-December 1985: 132-133, 565-573.

_____. "Deconstructing the Dominant Patriarchal Text: Cecile Piñeda's Narratives." In *Breaking Boundaries: Latina Writing and Critical Readings*, edited by Asunción Horno-Delgado, et al., 72-81. Amherst: Univ. of Massachusetts Press, 1989.

Buriel, Raymond, et al. "Mexican-American Disciplinary Practices and Attitudes Toward Child Maltreatment: A Comparison of Foreign-and Native-Born Mothers." *Hispanic Journal of Behavioral Sciences* 13, no. 1 (February 1991): 78-94.

Buriel, Raymond, and Evangelina Saenz. "Psychocultural Characteristics of College-Bound and Non-College-Bound Chicanas." *Journal of Social Psychology* 110, second half (April,1980): 245-251.

Burnham, Linda. "Barbara Carrasco and Public Activist Art." *High Performance* 9, no. 3 (1986): 48.

_____. "Patssi Valdez." *High Performance* 9, no. 3 (1986): 54.

Buss, Fran Leeper. *La Partera: Story of a Midwife*. Ann Arbor: The Univ. of Michigan Press, 1980.

Bustamante, Jorge A. "Maquiladoras: A New Face of International Capitalism on Mexico's Northern Frontier." In *Women, Men and the International Division of Labor*, edited by June Nash and María Fernandez-Kelly, 224-256. Albany: State Univ. of New York Press, 1983.

Cabeza de Vaca, Darlene. "Knowing the Value God Places on Me..."

Revista Mujeres 2, no. 1 (January 1985): 26-29.

Calderón, Roberto, and Emilio Zamora. "Manuela Solís Sanger and Emma Tenayuca: A Tribute." In *Chicana Voices: Intersections of Class, Race, and Gender,* edited by Teresa Córdova, et al., 30-41. Austin: Center for Mexican American Studies, UT Austin, 1986.

Camarillo, Alberto. *Latinos in the United States: A Historical Bibliography.* Santa Barbara, Calif.: ABC-Clio, 1986.

Campoamor, Diana. "Gender Gap in Politics: No Laughing Matter." *Vista* 4, no. 8 (October 24, 1988): 14.

Campos Carr, Irene. "A Survey of Selected Literature on La Chicana." *NWSA (National Women's Studies Association) Journal* 1, no. 2 (Winter 1988-89): 253-273.

_____. "Proyecto La Mujer: Latina Women Shaping Consciousness." *Women's Studies International Forum* 12, no. 1 (1989): 45-49.

Canales, Genevieve, and Robert E. Roberts. "Gender and Mental Health in the Mexican Origin Population of South Texas." In *Mental Health Issues of the Mexican Origin Population in Texas: Proceedings of the Fifth Robert Lee Sutherland Seminar in Mental Health,* edited by Reymundo Rodríguez and Marion Tolbert Coleman, [89]-99. Austin: Hogg Foundation for Mental Health, Univ. of Texas, 1987.

Candelaria, Cordelia. "Another Reading of Three Poems by Zamora." *Melus* 7, no. 4 (Winter 1980): 78-81.

_____. "Film Portrayals of La Mujer Hispana." *Agenda* 11, no. 3 (May-June 1981): 32-36.

_____. "La Malinche, Feminist Prototype." *Frontiers: A Journal of Women Studies* 5, no. 2 (Summer 1980): 1-6.

_____. "Six Reference Works on Mexican-American Women: A Review Essay." *Frontiers: A Journal of Women Studies* 5, no. 2 (Summer 1980): 75-80.

_____. "Social Equity in Film Criticism." *Bilingual Review* 10, no. 2-3 (May-December 1983): 64-70.

Canino, Glorisa. "The Hispanic Woman: Sociocultural Influences on Diagnoses and Treatment." In *Mental Health and Hispanic Americans: Clinical Perspectives,* edited by Rosina M. Becerra, Marvin Karno, and Javier I. Escobar, 117-138. New York: Grune & Stratton, 1982.

Cantú, Norma. "Women Then and Now: An Analysis of the Adelita Image Versus the Chicana As Political Writer and Philosopher." In *Chicana Voices: Intersections of Class, Race, and Gender,* edited by Teresa Córdova, et al., 8-10. Austin: Center for Mexican American Studies, UT Austin, 1986.

Cárdenas, Gilbert. *The Migration and Settlement of Undocumented Women.* Austin: Center for Mexican American Studies Publications, 1986.

Cárdenas, Gilbert, Beth Anne Shelton, and Devon Peña. "Undocu-

212   *Lillian Castillo-Speed*

mented Immigrant Women in the Houston Labor Force." *California Sociologist* 5, no. 2 (Summer 1982): 98-118.

Cárdenas de Dwyer, Carlota. "Mexican American Women: Images and Realities." In *Bridging Two Cultures: Multidisciplinary Readings in Bilingual, Bicultural Education*, edited by Marta Cotera and Larry Hufford, 294-296. Austin: National Educational Laboratory Publishers, 1980.

Carranza, Ruth, Antonia Acevedo-Schoups, and Cynthia López. "Hispanas and AIDS." *Intercambios Femeniles* 3, no. 1 (Spring, 1988): 28-29.

Carrillo, Ana, et al. "History of Las Mujeres." *Revista Mujeres* 1, no. 1 (January 1984)): 4-5.

Carrillo, Jorge V. *La industria maquiladora en México: bibliografía, directorio e investigaciones recientes = Border Assembly Industry and Recent Research*. La Jolla: Program in United States-Mexican Studies, Univ. of California, San Diego, 1981.

Carrillo, Jorge V., and Alberto Hernández H. *Mujeres fronterizas en la industria maquiladora*. Mexico, D.F.: Secretaría de Educación Pública; Tijuana, B.C.N.: Centro de Estudios Fronterizos del Norte de México, 1985.

Carrillo, Loretta, and Thomas A. Lyson. "The Fotonovela As a Cultural Bridge of Hispanic Women in the United States." *Journal of Popular Culture* 17, no. 3 (Winter 1983): 59-64.

Carrillo, Teresa. "The Women's Movement and the Left in Mexico: The Presidential Candidacy of Doña Rosario Ibarra." In *Chicana Voices: Intersections of Class, Race, and Gender*, edited by Teresa Córdova, et al., 96-113. Austin: Center for Mexican American Studies, UT Austin, 1986.

Casas, J. Manuel, and Sylvia Ortíz. "Exploring the Applicability of the Dyadic Adjustment Scale for Assessing Level of Marital Adjustment with Mexican Americans." *Journal of Marriage and the Family* 47, no. 4 (November 1985): 1023-1027.

Casas, J. Manuel, and Joseph G. Ponterotto. "Profiling an Invisible Minority in Higher Education: The Chicana." *Personnel and Guidance Journal* 62, no. 6 (February 1984): 349-353.

Casaus, Luis, and Sally J. Andrade. "A Description of Latinos in the United States: Demographic and Sociocultural Factors of the Past and the Future." In *Latino Families in the United States*, edited by Sally J. Andrade, 9-23. [S.l.]: Planned Parenthood Federation of America, Inc., 1983.

Castañeda, Antonia. "Gender, Race, and Culture: Spanish-Mexican Women in the Historiography of Frontier California." *Frontiers: A Journal of Women Studies* 11, no. 1 (1990): [8]-20.

_____. "Spanish and European Women on World-wide Frontiers: The Women of Alta California and New Zealand." In *Western Women: Their*

Lands, Their Lives, edited by Lillian Schlissel, Vicki Ruiz, Janice Monk, 283-300. Albuquerque: Univ. of New Mexico Press, 1988.

Castillo, Ana. "La Macha: Toward a Beautiful Whole Self." In *Chicana Lesbians: The Girls Our Mothers Warned Us About,* edited by Carla Trujillo, 24-48. Berkeley: Third Woman Press, 1991.

Castillo, Sylvia. "A Guide to Hispanic Women's Resources: A Perspective on Networking among Hispanic Women." *California Women* (December 1983): 2-6.

Castillo-Speed, Lillian. "Chicana Studies: A Selected List of Materials Since 1980." *Frontiers: A Journal of Women Studies* 11, no. 1 (1990): [66]-84.

_____. "Chicana/Latina Literature and Criticism: Reviews of Recent Books." *WLW Journal* 11, no. 3 (September 1987): 1-4.

Castillo-Speed, Lillian, Richard Chabrán, and Francisco García-Ayvens, eds. *The Chicano Index: A Comprehensive Subject, Author, and Title Index to Chicano Materials.* Berkeley: Chicano Studies Library Publications Unit, 1989-.

_____, eds. *The Chicano Periodical Index.* Berkeley: Chicano Studies Library Publications Unit, 1985-1989.

Castro, Felipe G., Pauline Furth, and Herbert Karlow. "The Health Beliefs of Mexican, Mexican American and Anglo American Women." *Hispanic Journal of Behavioral Sciences* 6, no. 4 (December 1984): 365-383.

Castro, Felipe G., Gloria J. Romero, and Richard C. Cervantes. "Long-term Stress among Latino Women After a Plant Closure." *Sociology and Social Research* 71, no. 2 (January 1987): 85-88.

Castro, Rafaela. "Mexican Women's Sexual Jokes." Aztlán 13, no. 1-2 (Spring-Fall 1982): 275-293. Reprinted in *Perspectives in Mexican American Studies* 1 (1988): 129-143.

Cazares, Ralph B., Edward Murguía, and W. Parker Frisbie. "Mexican American Intermarriage in a Nonmetropolitan Context." In *The Mexican American Experience: An Interdisciplinary Anthology,* edited by Rodolfo O. de la Garza, et al., 393-401. Austin: Univ. of Texas Press, 1981. Also in *Social Science Quarterly* 65, no. 2 (June 1984): 626-634.

Center for U.S.-Mexican Studies; El Colegio de la Frontera Norte; and El Colegio de México. *International Guide to Research on Mexico/Guía internacional de investigaciones sobre México.* La Jolla: Center for U.S.-Mexican Studies, Univ. of California, San Diego, 1982-1987.

Cerra, Frances. "Live-in Child Care." *Nuestro* 9, no. 8 (October 1985): 17-19.

Chabrán, Richard. "Chicana Reference Sources." In *Chicana Voices: Intersections of Class, Race, and Gender,* edited by Teresa Córdova, et al., [146]-156. Austin: Center for Mexican American Studies, UT Austin, 1986.

Chacón, María A. *Chicanas in California Post Secondary Education: A Comparative Study of Barriers to the Program Progress.* Stanford, Calif.: Stanford Center for Chicano Research, 1985.

_____. "An Overdue Study of the Chicana Undergraduate College Experience." *La Luz* 8, no. 8 (October-November, 1980): 27.

Chacón, María A., Elizabeth G. Cohen, and Sharon Strover. "Chicanas and Chicanos: Barriers to Progress in Higher Education." In *Latino College Students*, edited by Michael A. Olivas, 296-324. New York: Teachers College Press, 1986.

Chacón, Peter. "Chicanas and Political Representation." In *La Chicana: Building for the Future*, 32-36. Oakland, Calif.: National Hispanic Univ., 1981.

Chan, Linda, et al. *Maternal and Child Health on the U.S.-Mexico Border.* Austin: Lyndon B. Johnson School of Public Affairs, Univ. of Texas, 1987.

Chávez, Denise. "Heat and Rain (Testimonio)." In *Breaking Boundaries: Latina Writing and Critical Readings*, edited by Asunción Horno-Delgado, et al., 27-32. Amherst: Univ. of Massachusetts Press, 1989.

Chávez, J.M., and R. Buriel. "Reinforcing Children's Efforts: A Comparison of Immigrant, Native-born Mexican American and European-American Mothers." *Hispanic Journal of Behavioral Sciences* 8, no. 2 (1986): 127-142.

Chavira, Alicia. "'Tienes que ser valiente:' Mexicana Migrants in a Midwestern Farm Labor Camp." In *Mexicanas at Work in the United States*, edited by Margarita B. Melville, 64-74. Houston: Mexican American Studies Program, Univ. of Houston, 1988.

Cisneros, Sandra. "Cactus Flowers: In Search of Tejana Feminist Poetry." *Third Woman* 3, no. 1-2 (1986):73-80.

_____. "Do You Know Me?: I Wrote *The House on Mango Street.*" *The Americas Review* 15, no. 1 (Spring 1987): 77-79.

_____. "Ghosts and Voices: Writing from Obsession." *The Americas Review* 15, no. 1 (Spring 1987): 69-73.

_____. "Living As a Writer: Choice and Circumstance." *The Feminist Writers Guild National Newsletter* 10, no. 1 (February 1987): 8-9. Also in *Revista Mujeres* 3, no. 2 (June 1986): 68-72.

_____. "Notes to a Young(er) Writer." *The Americas Review* 15, no. 1 (Spring 1987): 74-76.

Cochran, Jo, and Bettina Escudero, et al., eds. *Bearing Witness/Sobreviviendo: An Anthology of Native American/Latina Art and Literature [special issue]. Calyx: A Journal of Art and Literature by Women* 8, no. 2 (Spring 1984).

Codega, Susan A., B. Kay Pasley, and Jill Kreutzer. "Coping Behaviors of Adolescent Mothers: An Exploratory Study and Comparison of

Mexican-Americans and Anglos." *Journal of Adolescent Research* 5, no. 1 (January 1990): 34-53.

Committee for the Development of Subject Access to Chicano Literature. *The Chicano Periodical Index*. Boston: G.K. Hall, 1981-83.

Contreras, Gloria. "The Role of Hispanic Women in the Making of Texas." *Social Studies Texan* 5, no. 3 (Winter 1990): 33-35.

Cooney, Rosemary Santana, and Vilma Ortiz. "Nativity, National Origin, and Hispanic Female Participation in the Labor Force." *Social Science Quarterly* 64 (September 1983): 510-523.

Corbett, Kitty, Juana Mora, and Genevieve Ames. "Drinking Patterns and Drinking-Related Problems of Mexican-American Husbands and Wives." *Journal of Studies on Alcohol* 52, no. 3 (May 1991): 215-223.

Córdova, Teresa, et al., eds. *Chicana Voices: Intersections of Class, Race, and Gender*. Austin: Center for Mexican American Studies Publications, 1986.

Corrales, Ramona Jean. "Undocumented Hispanas in America." In *The State of Hispanic America II*, 100-107. Oakland, Calif.: National Hispanic Center for Advanced Studies and Policy Analysis and the National Hispanic Univ., 1982. Also in *La Chicana: Building for the Future*, 59-73. Oakland, Calif.: National Hispanic Univ., 1981.

Cortés, Carlos E. "Chicanas in Film: History of an Image." *Bilingual Review* 10, no. 2-3 (May-December 1983): 94-108.

Cotera, Martha P. "ERA: The Latina Challenge." *Nuestro* 5, no. 8 (November 1981): 47-48.

_____. "Sexism in Bilingual Bicultural Education." In *Bridging Two Cultures: Multidisciplinary Readings in Bilingual, Bicultural Education*, edited by Martha Cotera and Larry Hufford, 181-190. Austin: National Educational Laboratory Publishers, 1980.

Craver, Rebecca McDowell. "The Impact of Intimacy: Mexican-Anglo Intermarriage in New Mexico 1821-1846." *Southwestern Studies*, no. 66 (1982): 1-79.

_____. *The Impact of Intimacy: Mexican-Anglo Intermarriage in New Mexico, 1821-1846*. El Paso: Texas Western Press, Univ. of Texas at El Paso, 1982.

Crawford, John F. "Notes Toward a New Multicultural Criticism: Three Works by Women of Color." In *A Gift of Tongues: Critical Challenges in Contemporary American Poetry*, edited by Marie Harris and Kathleen Agüero, 155-195. Athens: Univ. of Georgia Press, 1987. Includes discussion of Lorna Dee Cervantes.

Cresswell, John L. "Sex-related Differences in the Problem-solving Abilities of Rural Black, Anglo, and Chicano Adolescents." *Texas Tech Journal of Education* 10, no. 1 (Winter 1983): 29-33.

Creswell, John L., and Roxanne H. Exezidis. "Research Brief: Sex and Ethnic Differences in Mathematics Achievement of Black and Mexican-American Adolescents." *Texas Tech Journal of Education* 9, no. 3 (Fall 1982): 219-222.

Cuellar, Israel, et al. "Clinical Psychiatric Case Presentation: Culturally Responsive Diagnostic Formulation and Treatment in an Hispanic Female." *Hispanic Journal of Behavioral Sciences* 5, no. 1 (March 1983): 93-103.

Cummins, Laura H., Susan C. M. Scrimshaw, and Patricia L. Engle. "Views of Cesarean Birth among Primiparous Women of Mexican Origin in Los Angeles." *Birth* 15, no. 3 (September 1988): 164-170.

Cummings, Michele, and Scott Cummings. "Family Planning among the Urban Poor: Sexual Politics and Social Policy." *Family Relations* 32, no. 1 (January 1983): 47-58.

Curry Rodríguez, Julia E. "Labor Migration and Familial Responsibilities: Experiences of Mexican Women." In *Mexicanas at Work in the United States*, edited by Margarita B. Melville, 47-63. Houston: Mexican American Studies Program, Univ. of Houston, 1988.

Curtis, Theodore T., and Maxine Baca Zinn. "Marital Role Orientation among Chicanos: An Analysis of Structural and Cultural Factors." *La Red/The Net*, no. 59 (October 1982): 2-4.

D'Andrea, Vaneeta-Marie. "Ethnic Women: A Critique of the Literature, 1971-1981." *Ethnic and Racial Studies* 9 (April, 1986): 235-246.

Daly, Mary B., Gary M. Clark, and William L. McGuire. "Breast Cancer Prognosis in a Mixed Caucasian-Hispanic Population." *JNCI: Journal of the National Cancer Institute* 74, no. 4 (April 1985): 753-757.

Darabi, Katherine F. *Childbearing among Hispanics in the United States*. New York: Greenwood Press, 1987.

Darabi, Katherine F., and Vilma Ortiz. "Childbearing among Young Latino Women in the United States." *American Journal of Public Health* 77, no. 1 (January 1987): 25-28.

Darabi, Katherine F., et al. "The Effect of Maternal Age on the Well-Being of Children." *Journal of Marriage and the Family* 46, no. 4 (November 1984): 933-934.

Darabi, Katherine F., Joy Dryfoos and Dana Schwartz. "Hispanic Adolescent Fertility." *Hispanic Journal of Behavioral Sciences* 8, no. 2 (June 1986): 157-171.

Davis, Cary, Carl Haub, and JoAnne Willette. "U.S. Hispanics: Changing the Face of America." *Population Bulletin* 38, no. 3 (June 1983): 1-43.

Davis, Sally M., and Mary B. Harris. "Sexual Knowledge, Sexual Interests, and Sources of Sexual Information of Rural and Urban Adolescents from Three Cultures." *Adolescence* 17, no. 66 (Summer 1982): 471-492.

de Anda, Diane. "A Study of the Interaction of Hispanic Junior High

School Students and Their Teachers." *Hispanic Journal of Behavioral Sciences* 4, no. 1 (March 1982): 57-74.

de Anda, Diane, and Rosina M. Becerra. "Support Networks for Adolescent Mothers." *Social Casework: Journal of Contemporary Social Work* 65, no. 3 (March 1984): 172-181.

de Anda, Diane, Rosina M. Becerra, and Eve Fielder. "In Their Own Words: The Life Experiences of Mexican-American and White Pregnant Adolescents and Adolescent Mothers." *Child and Adolescent Social Work* 7, no. 4 (August 1990): 301-318.

de la Fuente, Patricia. "Invisible Women in the Narrative of Tomás Rivera." *Revista Chicano-Riqueña* 13, no. 3-4 (Fall-Winter 1985): 81-89.

de la Fuente, Patricia, and María I. Duke dos Santos. "The Elliptic Female Presence as Unifying Force in the Novels of Rolando Hinojosa." *Revista Chicano-Riqueña* 12, no. 3-4 (Fall-Winter 1984):64-75.

de la Torre, Adela, and Lynda Rush. "The Determinants of Breastfeeding for Mexican Migrant Women." *International Migration Review* 21, no. 3 (Fall 1987): 728-742.

de León Siantz, Mary Lou. "Maternal Acceptance/Rejection of Mexican Migrant Mothers." *Psychology of Women Quarterly* 14, no. 2 (June 1990): 245-254.

de Lotbiniere-Harwood, Susanne, and Gloria Anzaldúa. "Conversations at the Book Fair: Interview with Gloria Anzaldúa." *Trivia: A Journal of Ideas*, no. 14 (Spring 1989): 37-45.

Del Castillo, Adelaida R. *Between Borders: Essays on Mexicana/Chicana History.* Encino, Calif.: Floricanto Press, 1990.

_____. "Sobre la experiencia educativa chicana." *fem* 10, no. 48 (October-November 1986): 7-10.

Del Castillo, Adelaida R., and María Torres. "The Interdependency of Educational Institutions and Cultural Norms: The Hispana Experience." In *The Broken Web: The Educational Experience of Hispanic American Women*, edited by Teresa McKenna and Flora Ida Ortiz, 39-60. Claremont, Calif.: Tomás Rivera Center; Berkeley: Floricanto Press, 1988.

Del Castillo, Adelaida R., et al. "An Assessment of the Status of the Education of Hispanic American Women." In *The Broken Web: The Educational Experience of Hispanic American Women*, edited by Teresa McKenna and Flora Ida Ortiz, 3-24. Claremont, Calif.: Tomás Rivera Center; Berkeley: Floricanto Press, 1988.

Del Rio, Carmen M. "Chicana Poets: Re-Visions from the Margin." *Revista Canadiense de Estudios Hispánicos* 14, no. 3 (Spring 1990): 431-445.

Del Zotto, Augusta. "Latinas with AIDS: Life Expectancy for Hispanic Women Is a Startling 45 Days After Diagnosis." *This World* (Sunday supplement to the *San Francisco Chronicle/Examiner*), (April 9, 1989).

Delgado, Abelardo "Lalo". "An Open Letter to Carolina . . . or Relations between Men and Women." *Revista Chicano-Riqueña* 10, no. 1-2 (Winter-Spring 1982): 279-284.

Delgado Campbell, Dolores. "Shattering the Stereotype: Chicanas as Labor Union Organizers." *Berkeley Women of Color*, no. 11 (Summer 1983): 20-23.

Delgado Votaw, Carmen. "Influencias culturales y feminismo en la mujer chicana." *fem* 10, no. 48 (October-November 1986): 27-30.

Desai, Parul, and Bernice Zamora. "Interview with Bernice Zamora, a Chicana Poet." *Imagine* 2, no. 1 (Summer 1985): 26-39.

Deutsch, Sarah. *No Separate Refuge: Culture, Class, and Gender on an Anglo-Hispanic Frontier in the American Southwest, 1880-1940*. New York: Oxford Univ. Press, 1987.

_____. "Women and Intercultural Relations: The Case of Hispanic New Mexico and Colorado." *Signs: Journal of Women in Culture and Society* 12, no. 4 (1987): 719-739.

Dewey, Janice. "Doña Josefa: Bloodpulse of Transition and Change." In *Breaking Boundaries: Latina Writing and Critical Readings*, edited by Asunción Horno-Delgado, et al., 39-47. Amherst: Univ. of Massachusetts Press, 1989.

Dixon, Marlene. "Theoretical Perspectives on Chicanas, Mexicanas and the Transnational Working Class." *Contemporary Marxism*, no. 11 (Fall 1985): 46-76.

Dixon, Marlene, Elizabeth Martínez, and Ed McCaughan. "Chicanas and Mexicanas within a Transnational Working Class: Theoretical Perspectives." *Review (Fernand Braudel Center)* 7, no. 1 (1983): 109-150.

Domenella, Ana Rosa. "Al margen de un coloquio fronterizo mujer y literatura mexicana y chicana." *fem* 14, no. 89 (May 1990): 32-34.

Dowling, Patrick T., and Michael Fisher. "Maternal Factors and Low Birthweight Infants: A Comparison of Blacks with Mexican-Americans." *Journal of Family Practice* 25, no. 2 (August, 1987): 153-158.

Dressel, Paula. "Symposium. Civil Rights, Affirmative Action, and the Aged of the Future: Will Life Chances Be Different for Blacks, Hispanics, and Women? An Overview of the Issues." *Gerontologist* 26, no. 2 (April 1986): 128-131.

Driscoll, Barbara A. "Chicana Historiography: A Research Note Regarding Mexican Archival Sources." In *Chicana Voices: Intersections of Class, Race, and Gender*, edited by Teresa Córdova, et al., [136]-145. Austin: Center for Mexican American Studies, UT Austin, 1986.

Dungy, Claibourne I. "Breast Feeding Preference of Hispanic and Anglo Women, 1978-1985." *Clinical Pediatrics* 28, no. 2 (February 1989): 92-94.

Durán Apodaca, María. "North from Mexico." In *With These Hands: Women Working on the Land*, edited by Joan M. Jensen, 120-122. New

York: McGraw-Hill, 1981.

Durón, Clementina. "Mexican Women and Labor Conflict in Los Angeles: The ILGWU Dressmakers' Strike of 1933." *Aztlán* 15, no. 1 (Spring 1984): 145-161.

Echaveste, Beatrice, and Dolores Huerta. "In the Shadow of the Eagle: Huerta/A la sombra del águila: Huerta." *Americas 2001* 1, no. 3 (November-December 1987): 26-30.

"Edición feminista (Special Issue)." *Imagine* 2, no. 1 (Summer 1985): ii-159.

Eger, Ernestina. *A Bibliography of Criticism of Contemporary Chicano Literature.* Berkeley: Chicano Studies Library Publications Unit, 1982.

Eisen, Marvin, and Gail L. Zellman. "Factors Predicting Pregnancy Resolution Decision Satisfaction of Unmarried Adolescents." *Journal of Genetic Psychology* 145, no. 2 (December 1984): 231-239.

Engle, Margarita Mondrus. "Mother's Day Reflections: A "Traditional" Latina." *Nuestro* 7, no. 4 (May 1983): 46.

Engle, Patricia L., et al. "Prenatal and Postnatal Anxiety in Mexican Women Giving Birth in Los Angeles." *Health Psychology* 9, no. 3 (1990): 285-299.

Escalante, Virginia, Nancy Rivera and Victor Valle. "Inside the World of Latinas." In *Southern California's Latino Community: A Series of Articles Reprinted From the Los Angeles Times*, 82-91. Los Angeles: Los Angeles Times, 1983.

Escobedo, Theresa Herrera, ed. "Thematic Issue: Chicana Issues." *Hispanic Journal of Behavioral Sciences* 4, no. 2 (June 1982): 145-286.

Espin, Oliva M. "Cultural and Historical Influences on Sexuality in Hispanic/Latin Women: Implications for Psychotherapy." In *Pleasure and Danger: Exploring Female Sexuality*, edited by Carole S. Vance, 149-164. Boston: Routledge & Kegan Paul, 1984.

_____. "Perceptions of Sexual Discrimination among College Women in Latin America and the United States." *Hispanic Journal of Behavioral Sciences* 2, no. 1 (March 1980): 1-19.

_____. "Psychological Impact of Migration on Latinas: Implications for Psychotherapeutic Practice." *Psychology of Women Quarterly* 11, no. 4 (December 1987): 489-503.

_____. "Spiritual Power and the Mundane World: Hispanic Female Healers in Urban U.S. Communities." *Women's Studies Quarterly* 16, no. 3 (Fall 1988): 33-47.

Estrada, Esther R. "The Importance of the 1980 Census." In *La Chicana: Building for the Future*, 2-7. Oakland, Calif.: National Hispanic Univ., 1981.

Estrada, Iliad. "Hispanic Feminists Meet—It's a Trip." *La Luz* 8, no. 7 (August-September 1980): 35.

Eysturoy, Annie O. "Isabella Rios (Diana López)." In *Chicano Writers, First Series, Dictionary of Literary Biography* 82: 201-205. Detroit: Bruccoli Clark Layman, 1989.

Eysturoy, Annie O., and Denise Chávez. "Denise Chávez: Interview." In *This Is About Vision: Interviews with Southwestern Writers*, edited by William Balassi, et al., [156]-169. Albuquerque: Univ. of New Mexico Press, 1990.

Facio, Elisa "Linda". "Gender and Aging: A Case of Mexicana/Chicana Elderly." *Trabajos Monográficos* 1, no. 1 (1985): 5-21.

_____. "The Interaction of Age and Gender in Chicana Older Lives: A Case Study of Chicana Elderly in a Senior Citizen Center." *Renato Rosaldo Lecture Series Monograph* 4, 1988, 21-38.

"Facts and Figures on Hispanic Americans, Women, and Education." In *The Broken Web: The Educational Experience of Hispanic American Women*, edited by Teresa McKenna and Flora Ida Ortiz, 195-217. Claremont, Calif.: Tomás Rivera Center; Berkeley: Floricanto Press, 1987.

Fajardo, Ramón. "Liberación femenil: canción corrido." *Missions in Conflict: Essays on U.S.-Mexican Relations and Chicano Culture*. Eds. Renate von Bardeleben, Dietrich Briesemeister, and Juan Bruce-Novoa. Tubingen, W. Germany: Günter Narr Verlag, 1986, p. 108-109.

Falasco, Dee, and David Heer. "Economic and Fertility Differences between Legal and Undocumented Migrant Mexican Families: Possible Effects of Immigration Policy Changes." *Social Science Quarterly* 65, no. 2 (June 1984): 495-504.

Falicov, Celia Jaes. "Mexican Families." In *Ethnicity and Family Therapy*, edited by Monica McGoldrick, John K. Pearce, and Joseph Giordano, 134-163. New York: The Guilford Press, 1982.

"La familia [special issue]." *De Colores* 6, no. 1-2 (1982): 1-149.

Farrell, Janice, and Kyriakos S. Markides. "Marriage and Health: A Three-Generation Study of Mexican Americans." *Journal of Marriage and the Family* 47, no. 4 (November 1985): 1029-1036.

Felice, Marianne E., et al. "Clinical Observations of Mexican-American, Caucasian, and Black Pregnant Teenagers." *Journal of Adolescent Health Care* 7, no. 5 (September 1986): 305-310.

_____. "Psychosocial Aspects of Mexican-American, White, and Black Teenage Pregnancy." *Journal of Adolescent Health Care* 8, no. 4 (July 1987): 330-335.

Fennelly, Katherine. *El embarazo precoz: Childbearing among Hispanic Teenagers in the United States*. New York: School of Public Health, Columbia Univ., 1988.

Fennelly, Katherine, Vasantha Kandiah, and Vilma Ortiz. "The Cross-Cultural Study of Fertility among Hispanic Adolescents in the Americas." *Studies in Family Planning* 20, no. 2 (March-April 1989): 96-101.

Fenster, Laura, and Molly J. Coye. "Birthweight of Infants Born to Hispanic Women Employed in Agriculture." *Archives of Environmental Health* 45, no. 1 (January-February 1990): 46-52.

Fernández, Celestino, and Louis M. Holscher. "Chicano-Anglo Intermarriage in Arizona, 1960-1980: An Exploratory Study of Eight Counties." *Hispanic Journal of Behavioral Sciences* 5, no. 3 (September 1983): 291-304.

Fernández, Roberta. "Lorna Dee Cervantes." In *Chicano Writers, First Series, Dictionary of Literary Biography* 82: 74-78. Detroit: Bruccoli Clark Layman, 1989.

Fernández-Kelly, María. *For We Are Sold, I and My People*. Albany: State Univ. of New York Press, 1983.

——. "'Maquila' Women." *NACLA Report on the Americas* 14, no. 5 (September-October 1980): 14-19.

——. "Mexican Border Industrialization, Female Labor Force, Participation, and Migration." *Women, Men, and the International Division of Labor*. Eds. June Nash and Maria Fernández-Kelly. Albany: State Univ. of New York Press, 1983, 205-223.

Fernández-Kelly, María, and Anna M. García. "Invisible amidst the Glitter: Hispanic Women in the Southern California Electronics Industry." In *The Worth of Women's Work: A Qualitative Synthesis*, edited by Anne Statham, Eleanor M. Miller, and Hans O. Mauksch, 265-292. Albany, N.Y.: State University of New York Press, 1989.

——. "The Making of an Underground Economy: Hispanic women, Home Work, and the Advanced Capitalist State." *Urban Anthropology* 14, No. 1-3 (Spring-Fall 1985): 59-90.

Fischer, Gloria J. "Hispanic and Majority Student Attitudes toward Forcible Date Rape as a Function of Differences in Attitudes toward Women." *Sex Roles* 17, no. 1-2 (July, 1987): 93-101.

Fischer, Nancy A., and John P. Marcum. "Ethnic Integration, Socioeconomic Status, and Fertility among Mexican Americans." *Social Science Quarterly* 65, no. 2 (June 1984): 583-593.

Flaskerud, Jacquelyn H., and Adeline M. Nyamathi. "Black and Latina Women's AIDS-Related Knowledge, Attitudes, and Practices." *Research in Nursing and Health* 12, no. 6 (December 1989): 339-346.

Fleming, Marilyn B. "Problems Experienced by Anglo, Hispanic and Navajo Indian Women College Students." *Journal of American Indian Education* 22, no. 1 (October 1982): 7-17.

Forste, Renata R., and Tim B. Heaton. "Initiation of Sexual Activity among Female Adolescents." *Youth and Society* 19, no. 3 (March 1988): 250-268.

"Fostering the Advancement of Latinas." *Nuestro* 6, no. 10 (December 1982): 48-49.

Fox, Linda C. "Obedience and Rebellion: Re-vision of Chicana Myths of Motherhood." *Women's Studies Quarterly* 11, no. 4 (Winter 1983): 20-22.

Franklin, Gerald S., and Karen S. Kaufman. "Group Psychotherapy for Elderly Female Hispanic Outpatients." *Hospital and Community Psychiatry* 33, no. 5 (May 1982): 385-387.

Franks, Adele L., Nancy J. Binkin, and Dixie E. Snider. "Isoniazid Hepatitis among Pregnant and Postpartum Hispanic Patients." *Public Health Reports* 104, no. 2 (March-April 1989): 151-155.

Fríaz, Guadalupe. "Chicanas in the Workforce = Chicanas en la fuerza de trabajo: 'Working 9 to 5.'" *Caminos* 2, no. 3 (May, 1981): 37-39, 61 +.

Frisbie, William Parker. "Recent Changes in Marital Instability among Mexican Americans: Convergence with Black and Anglo Trends?" *Social Forces* 58 (June 1980): 1205-1220.

_____. "Variation in Patterns of Marital Instability among Hispanics." *Journal of Marriage and the Family* 48, no. 1 (February 1986): 99-106.

Frisbie, William Parker, Wolfgang Opitz, and William R. Kelly. "Marital Instability Trends among Mexican Americans As Compared to Blacks and Anglos: New Evidence." *Social Science Quarterly* 66, no. 3 (September 1985): 587-601.

Fu, Victoria R., Dennis E. Hinkle, and Mary K. Korslund. "A Developmental Study of Ethnic Self-Concept among Pre-adolescent Girls." *Journal of Genetic Psychology* 14 (March 1983): 67-73.

Fuentes, Annette, and Barbara Ehrenreich. *Women in the Global Factory.* New York: Institute for New Communications; Boston: South End Press, 1983.

Galindo, Letticia. "Perceptions of Pachuquísmo and Use of Caló/Pachuco Spanish by Various Chicana Women." *La Red/The Net*, no. 48 (November 1981): 2, 10.

Gándara, Patricia. "Passing through the Eye of the Needle: High-Achieving Chicanas." *Hispanic Journal of Behavioral Sciences* 4, no. 2 (June 1982): 167-179.

García, Alma M. "El femenismo [sic] chicano: un panorama histórico." *fem* 10, no. 48 (October-November 1986): 23-24.

_____. "Studying Chicanas: Bringing Women into the Frame of Chicano Studies." In *Chicana Voices: Intersections of Class, Race, and Gender*, edited by Teresa Córdova, et al., 19-29. Austin: Center for Mexican American Studies, 1986.

_____. "The Development of Chicana Feminist Discourse, 1970-1980." *Gender & Society* 3, no. 2 (June 1989): 217-238. Also in *Unequal Sisters: A Multicultural Reader in U.S. Women's History*, edited by Ellen Carol DuBois and Vicki L. Ruiz, 418-431. New York: Routledge, 1990.

García, Mario T. "Family and Gender in Chicano and Border Studies Research." *Mexican Studies/Estudios Mexicanos* 6, no. 1 (Winter 1990): 109-119.

———. "La familia: the Mexican Immigrant Family, 1900-1930." In *Work, Family, Sex Roles, Language*, edited by Mario Barrera, Alberto Camarillo, and Francisco Hernández, 117-139. Berkeley: Tonatiuh-Quinto Sol, 1980.

———. "The Chicana in American History: The Mexican Women of El Paso, 1880-1920—A Case Study." *Pacific Historical Review* 49, no. 2 (May 1980): 315-337.

García-Ayvens, Francisco. *Chicanos in These Times: A Cumulative Subject Index to Articles about Chicanos in the Los Angeles Times*. Santa Fe Springs, Calif.: ATM Information Services, 1986-

———. *The Chicano Anthology Index*. Berkeley: Chicano Studies Library Publications Unit, 1990.

García Castro, Mary. "Migrant Women: Issues in Organization and Solidarity." *Migration World Magazine* 14, no. 1-2 (1986): 15-19.

Garn, Stanley M., and Marquisa LaVelle. "Reproductive Histories of Low Weight Girls and Women." *American Journal of Clinical Nutrition* 37, no. 5 (May 1983): 862-866.

Gettman, Dawn, and Devón Gerardo Peña. "Women, Mental Health, and the Workplace in a Transnational Setting." *Social Work* 31, no. 1 (January-February 1986): 5-11.

Gibbs, Jewelle Taylor. "Personality Patterns of Delinquent Females: Ethnic and Sociocultural Variations." *Journal of Clinical Psychology* 38, no. 1 (January 1982): 198-206.

Gibson, Guadalupe. "Hispanic Women: Stress and Mental Health Issues." *Women and Therapy* 2, no. 2-3 (Summer-Fall 1983), p. 113-133.

Gilbert, M. Jean. "Alcohol Consumption Patterns in Immigrant and Later Generation Mexican American Women." *Hispanic Journal of Behavioral Sciences* 9, no. 3 (September 1987): 299-313.

Glenn, Evelyn Nakano. "Racial Ethnic Women's Labor: Race, Gender, Class." *Review of Radical Political Economy* 17, no. 3 (Fall 1985): 86-108.

Golding, Jacqueline M. "Division of Household Labor, Strain, and Depressive Symptoms among Mexican Americans and Non-Hispanic Whites." *Psychology of Women Quarterly* 14, no. 1 (March 1990): 103-117.

Goldman, Shifra M. "Artistas chicanas texanas." *fem* 8, no. 34 (June-July 1984): 29-31.

———. "Artistas en acción: conferencia de las mujeres chicanas." *La Comunidad*, (Cultural Supplement to *La Opinión*, Los Angeles, Calif.) (August 10, 1980): 15.

———. "Trabajadoras mexicanas y chicanas en las artes visuales." In *A Través de la Frontera*, edited by Salvador Leal, 153-160. Mexico, D.F.:

Centro de Estudios Económicos y Sociales del Tercer Mundo, A.C.; Instituto de Investigaciones Estéticas, UNAM, 1983.

———. "Women Artists of Texas: MAS = More + Artists + Women = MAS." *Chismearte*, no. 7 (January 1981): 21-22.

Goldman, Shifra, and Tomás Ybarra-Frausto. *Arte Chicano: A Comprehensive Annotated Bibliography of Chicano Art, 1965-1981*. Berkeley: Chicano Studies Library Publications Unit, 1985.

Gómez, Alma, Cherríe Moraga, and Mariana Romo-Carmona, eds. *Cuentos: Stories by Latinas*. New York: Kitchen Table, Women of Color Press, 1983.

Gondolf, Edward W., Ellen Fisher, and J. Richard McFerron. "Racial Differences among Shelter Residents: A Comparison of Anglo, Black, and Hispanic Battered." *Journal of Family Violence* 3, no. 1 (March 1988): 39-51.

Gonzales, Sylvia Alicia. *Hispanic American Voluntary Organizations*. Westport, Conn.: Greenwood Press, 1985.

———. "The Latina Feminist: Where We've Been, Where We're Going." *Nuestro* 5, no. 6 (August-September, 1981): 45-47.

Gonzáles-Berry, Erlinda, and Tey Diana Rebolledo. "Growing up Chicano: Tomás Rivera and Sandra Cisneros." *Revista Chicano-Riqueña* 13, no. 3-4 (Fall-Winter 1985): 109-119.

González, Alex. "Sex Role of the Traditional Mexican Family: A Comparison of Chicano and Anglo Students' Attitudes." *Journal of Cross-Cultural Psychology* 13, no. 3 (September 1982): 330-339.

González, Deena J. "The Widowed Women of Santa Fe: Assessments on the Lives of an Unmarried Population, 1850-80." In *On Their Own: Widows and Widowhood in the American Southwest, 1848-1939*, edited by Arlene Scadron, 65-90. Urbana: Univ. of Illinois Press, 1988. Also in *Unequal Sisters: A Multicultural Reader in U.S. Women's History*, edited by Ellen Carol DuBois and Vicki L. Ruiz, 34-50. New York: Routledge, 1990.

González, Judith Teresa. "Dilemmas of the High-Achieving Chicana: The Double-Bind Factor in Male/Female Relationships." *Sex Roles: A Journal of Research* 18, no. 7-8 (April 1988): 367-380.

———. "Factors Relating to Frequency of Breast Self-Examination among Low-Income Mexican American Women: Implications for Nursing Practice." *Cancer Nursing* 13, no. 3 (June 1990): 134-142.

González, Judith Teresa, and Virginia M. González. "Initial Validation of a Scale Measuring Self-Efficacy of Breast Self-Examination among Low-Income Mexican American Women. *Hispanic Journal of Behavioral Sciences* 12, no. 3 (August 1990): 277-291.

González, Michelle. "Reflexiones de una estudiante chicana." *fem* 10, no. 48 (October-November 1986): 40-41.

González, Rosalinda M. "Chicana and Mexican Immigrant Families, 1920-1940: Women's Subordination and Family Exploitation." In *Decades of Discontent/The Women's Movement, 1920-1940*, edited by Louise Scharf and Joan M. Jensen, 59-84. Westport, Conn.: Greenwood Press, 1983.

_____. "The Chicana in Southwest Labor History, 1900-1975 (A Preliminary Bibliographic Analysis)." *Critical Perspectives of Third World America* 2, no. 1 (Fall 1984), p. 46-61.

González Borrero, María and, Angela M. Rodríguez. "Responding to Community Needs." In *Latino Families in the United States*, edited by Sally J. Andrade, 45-51. [S.l.]: Planned Parenthood Federation of America, Inc., 1983.

Grau, Ilda E. "Una utopia feminista." *fem* 8, no. 34 (June-July 1984): 4.

Gould, Jeffrey B., Becky Davey, and Randall S. Stafford. "Socioeconomic Differences in Rates of Cesarean Section." *The New England Journal of Medicine* 321, no. 4 (July 27, 1989): 223-239.

Green, Susan S. "Silicon Valley's Women Workers: A Theoretical Analysis of Sex-Segregation in the Electronics Industry Labor Market." In *Women, Men and the International Division of Labor*, edited by June Nash and María Fernández-Kelly, 273-331. Albany: State Univ. of New York Press, 1983.

Griswold del Castillo, Richard. "Chicano Family History Methodology and Theory: A Survey of Contemporary Research Direction." In *History, Culture, and Society: Chicano Studies in the 80s*, 95-106. National Association for Chicano Studies. Ypsilanti, Mich.: Bilingual Press/Editorial Bilingüe, 1983.

_____. *La Familia: Chicano Families in the Urban Southwest, 1848 to the Present*. Notre Dame, Ind.: Univ. of Notre Dame Press, 1984.

_____. "'Only for My Family...': Historical Dimensions of Chicano Family Solidarity—The Case of San Antonio in 1860." *Aztlán* 16, no. 1-2 (1985): 145-176.

Guendelman, Sylvia. "Double Lives: The Changing Role of Women in Seasonal Migration." *Women's Studies* 13, no. 3 (February, 1987): 249-271.

_____. "The Incorporation of Mexican Women in Seasonal Migration: A Study of Gender Differences." *Hispanic Journal of Behavioral Sciences* 9, no. 3 (September 1987), p. 245-264.

Gunther Enríquez, Martha. "Studying Infant Maternal Attachment: A Mexican-American Example." In *Anthropology of Human Birth*, edited by Margarita Artschwager Kay, 61-79. Philadelphia: F.A. Davis, 1981.

Gurak, Douglas T. "Assimilation and Fertility: A Comparison of Mexican American and Japanese American Women." *Hispanic Journal of*

Behavioral Sciences 2, no. 3 (September 1980): 219-239.

Gurak, Douglas T., and Joseph P. Fitzpatrick. "Intermarriage among Hispanic Ethnic Groups in New York City." *American Journal of Sociology* 87, no. 4 (January 1982): 921-934.

Gutiérrez, Jeannie, and Arnold Sameroff. "Determinants of Complexity in Mexican-American and Anglo-American Mothers' Conceptions of Child Development." *Child Development* 61, no. 2 (April 1990): 384-394.

Gutiérrez, Ramón A. "From Honor to Love: Transformation of the Meaning of Sexuality in Colonial New Mexico." In *Interpreting Kinship and Practice in Latin America*, edited by Raymond T. Smith, 237-263. Chapel Hill, North Carolina: Univ. of North Carolina Press, 1984.

_____. "Honor Ideology, Marriage Negotiation, and Class-Gender Domination in New Mexico, 1690-1846." *Latin American Perspectives* 12, no. 1 (Winter 1985): 81-104.

_____. *When Jesus Came the Corn Mothers Went Away: Power and Sexuality in New Mexico, 1500-1846*. Stanford: Stanford Univ. Press, 1991.

Gutiérrez Castillo, Dina. "La imagen de la mujer en la novela fronteriza." In *Mujer y literatura mexicana y chicana: Culturas en contacto*, edited by Aralia López-González, et al., [55]-63. Mexico: Colegio de la Frontera Norte, 1988.

Guttmacher, Sally. "Women Migrant Workers in the US." *Cultural Survival Quarterly* 8, no. 2 (Summer 1984): 60-61.

Hadley-Freydberg, Elizabeth. "Prostitutes, Concubines, Whores and Bitches: Black and Hispanic Women in Contemporary American Film." In *Women of Color: Perspectives on Feminism and Identity*, edited by Audrey T. McCluskey, 46-65. Bloomington: Women's Studies Program, Indiana Univ., 1985.

Hancock, Paula. "The Effect of Welfare Eligibility on the Labor Force Participation of Women of Mexican Origin in California." *Population Research and Policy Review* 5, no. 2 (1986): 163-185.

Harlow, Barbara. "Sites of Struggle: Immigration, Deportation, Prison, and Exile." In *Criticism in the Borderlands: Studies in Chicano Literature, Culture, and Ideology*, edited by Hector Calderón and José David Saldívar, [149]-163. Durham, North Carolina: Duke Univ. Press, 1991.

Harris, Mary G. *Cholas: Latino Girls and Gangs*. New York: AMS Press, 1988.

Hartzler, Kaye, and Juan N. Franco. "Ethnicity, Division of Household Tasks and Equity in Marital Roles: A Comparison of Anglo and Mexican American Couples." *Hispanic Journal of Behavioral Sciences* 7, no. 4 (December 1985): 333-344.

Hary-Fanta, Carol, and Priscilla Montana. "The Hispanic Female Adolescent: A Group Therapy Model." *International Journal of Group Psychotherapy* 32, no. 3 (1982): 351-366.

Hawley, Peggy, and Brenda Even. "Work and Sex-Role Attitudes in Relation to Education and Other Characteristics." *Vocational Guidance Quarterly* 31, no. 2 (December 1982): 101-108.

Hayghe, Howard. "Married Couples: Work and Income Patterns." *Monthly Labor Review* 106, no. 12 (December 1983): 26-29.

Hazuda, Helen P. "Employment Status and Women's Protection Against Coronary Heart Disease: Findings from the San Antonio Heart Study." *American Journal of Epidemiology* 123, no. 4 (April 1986): 623-640.

Heard, Martha E. "The Theatre of Denise Chávez: Interior Landscapes with *Sabor Nuevomexicano.*" *The Americas Review* 16, no. 2 (Summer 1988): 83-91.

Heathcote, Olivia D. "Sex Stereotyping in Mexican Reading Primers." *Reading Teacher* 36, no. 2 (November 1982): 158-165.

Hedderson, John J. "Fertility and Mortality." In *Borderlands Sourcebook: A Guide to the Literature on Northern Mexico and the American Southwest,* edited by Ellwyn R. Stoddard, Richard L. Nostrand, and Jonathan P. West, 232-236. Norman: Univ. of Oklahoma Press, 1983.

Hernández, Beatriz J. "Life As Art." *Vista* 3, no. 12 (August 7, 1988): 18, 34. About artist Yolanda López.

Hernández, Ines. "Sara Estela Ramírez: Sembradora." *Legacy: A Journal of Nineteenth-Century American Women Writers* 6, no. 1 (Spring 1989): 13-26.

Hernández, Leodoro. "The socialization of a Chicano family." *De Colores* 6, no. 1-2 (1982): 75-84.

Hernández, Lisa, and Tina Benítez, eds. *Palabras Chicanas: An Undergraduate Anthology.* Berkeley: Mujeres en Marcha, Univ. of California, Berkeley, 1988.

Herrera-Sobek, María. *Beyond Stereotypes: The Critical Analysis of Chicana Literature.* Binghamton, N.Y.: Bilingual Press/Editorial Bilingüe, 1985.

_____. "La Chicana: nuevas perspectivas." *La Comunidad* (Cultural Supplement to *La Opinión,* Los Angeles, Calif.), no. 10 (June 22, 1980): 14-15.

_____. "The Acculturation Process of the Chicana in the Corrido." *De Colores* 6, no. 1-2 (1982): 7-16.

_____. *The Mexican Corrido: A Feminist Analysis.* Bloomington: Indiana Univ. Press, 1990.

_____. "The Politics of Rape: Sexual Transgression in Chicano Fiction." *The Americas Review* 15, no. 3-4 (Fall-Winter 1987): 9-39.

_____. "The Treacherous Woman Archetype: A Structuring Agent in the

Corrido." *Aztlán* 13, no. 1-2 (Spring-Fall 1982): 135-148.

_____. "Women As Metaphor in the Patriarchal Structure of *Heart of Aztlán*." In *Rudolfo A. Anaya: Focus on Criticism*, edited by César A. González-T., [165]-182. La Jolla, Calif.: Lalo Press, 1990.

Herrera-Sobek, María, and Helena María Viramontes. "Bibliography [Chicana Creativity and Criticism Special Issue]." *The Americas Review* 15, no. 3-4 (Fall-Winter 1987): 182-188.

_____, eds. *Chicana Creativity and Criticism: Charting New Frontiers in American Literature.* Houston: Arte Publico Press, 1988. Also special issue of *The Americas Review* 15, no. 3-4 (Fall-Winter, 1987).

Hintz, Joy. *Valiant Migrant Women/Las mujeres valerosas.* Tiffin, Ohio: Sayger Printing, 1982.

"The Hispanic Woman: A Humanistic Perspective." *La Luz* 8, no. 8 (October-November 1980): 6-9.

"Hispanic Women Writers: An Interview with Rosaura Sánchez." *Lector* 2, no. 3 (November-December 1983): 5;7.

Hoffer, Thomas B. "Retention of Hispanic American High School Youth." In *The Broken Web: The Educational Experience of Hispanic American Women*, edited by Teresa McKenna and Flora Ida Ortiz, 107-135. Claremont, Calif.: Tomás Rivera Center; Berkeley: Floricanto Press, 1988.

Hogeland, Chris, and Karen Rosen. *Dreams Lost, Dreams Found: Undocumented Women in the Land of Opportunity.* San Francisco: Coalition for Immigrant and Refugee Rights and Services, 1991.

Holck, Susan E. "Lung Cancer Mortality and Smoking Habits: Mexican-American Women." *American Journal of Public Health* 72, no. 1 (January 1982): 38-42.

Holck, Susan E., et al. "Alcohol Consumption among Mexican American and Anglo Women: Results of a Survey along the U.S.-Mexico Border." *Journal of Studies on Alcoholism* 45, no. 2 (March 1984): 149-154.

_____. "Need for Family Planning Services among Anglo and Hispanic Women in the United States Counties Bordering Mexico." *Family Planning Perspectives* 14, no. 3 (May-June, 1982): 155-159.

Holscher, Louis M. "Hispanic Intermarriage: Changing Trends in New Mexico." *Agenda* 10, no. 6 (November-December 1980): 8-10.

Horno-Delgado, Asunción, et al., eds. *Breaking Boundaries: Latina Writing and Critical Readings.* Amherst: Univ. of Massachusetts Press, 1989.

Horowitz, Ruth. "Passion, Submission and Motherhood: The Negotiation of Identity by Unmarried Innercity Chicanas." *Sociological Quarterly* 22, no. 2 (Spring 1981): 241-252.

_____. "Femininity and Womanhood: Virginity, Unwed Motherhood, and Violence." In *Honor and the American Dream*, by Ruth Horowitz,

114-136. New Brunswick: Rutgers Univ. Press, 1983.

Hovell, Melbourne F., et al. "Occupational Health Risks for Mexican Women: The Case of the Maquiladora along the Mexican-United States Border." *International Journal of Health Services* 18, no. 4 (1988): 617-627.

Howell-Martínez, Vicky. "The Influence of Gender Roles on Political Socialization: An Experimental Study of Mexican-American Children." *Women & Politics* 2, no. 3 (Fall 1982), p. 33-46.

Huerta, Grace C. "Mother's Day Reflections: A Woman of Means." *Nuestro* 7, no. 4 (May 1983): 48-49.

Hunter, Kathleen I., Margaret W. Linn, and Shayna R. Stein. "Sterilization among American Indian and Chicano Mothers." *International Quarterly of Community Health and Education* 4, no. 4 (1983-1984): 343-352.

Hunt, Isabelle F., et al. "Zinc Supplementation During Pregnancy in Low-Income Teenagers of Mexican Descent: Effects on Selected Blood Constituents and on Progress and Outcome of Pregnancy." *American Journal of Clinical Nutrition* 42, no. 5 (November, 1985): 815-828.

_____. "Zinc Supplementation During Pregnancy: Zinc Concentration of Serum and Hair from Low-Income Women of Mexican Descent." *American Journal of Clinical Nutrition* 37, no. 4 (April 1983): 572-582.

Hurtado, Aida. "Midwife Practices in Hidalgo County, Texas." *Trabajos Monográficos* 3, no. 1 (1987): 1-30.

Hutchison, James. "Teenagers and Contraception in Cameron and Willacy Counties." *Borderlands Journal* 7, no. 1 (Fall, 1983): 75-90.

Iglesias, María, and María Luz Hernández. "Hermanas." In *Prophets Denied Honor: An Anthology on the Hispano Church of the United States*, edited by Antonio M. Stevens Arroyo, 141-142. Maryknoll, N.Y.: Orbis Books, 1980.

Iglesias, Norma. *La flor mas bella de la maquiladora: historias de vida de la mujer obrera en Tijuana, B.C.N.* Mexico, D.F.: Secretaría de Educación Pública, CEFNOMEX, 1985.

_____. "'Las mujeres somos mas responsables:' la utilización de mano de obra femenina en las maquiladoras fronterizas." *Trabajos Monográficos* 2, no. 1 (1986): 19-30.

Iglesias, Norma, and Jorge Carrillo. "¿Que me dejó el trabajo?: mi vida se pregunta." *Trabajos Monográficos* 2, no. 1 (1986), p. 10-18. English version appears on 1-10. Spanish version appears also in *fem* 10, no. 48 (October-November 1986): 43-45.

Irizarry, Estelle. "La abuelita in Literature." *Nuestro* 7, no. 7 (September 1983): 50.

Isasi-Díaz, Ada María. *Hispanic Women, Prophetic Voice in the Church: Toward* a Hispanic Women's Liberation Theology. San Francisco: Harper & Row, 1988.

Jaech, Richard E. "Latin American Undocumented Women in the United States." Currents in Theology and Mission 9, no. 4 (August 1982): 196-211.

Jaramillo, Mari Luci. "How to Succeed in Business and Remain Chicana." La Luz 8, no. 7 (August-September 1980): 33-35.

_____. "Institutional Responsibility in the Provision of Educational Experiences to the Hispanic American Female Student." In The Broken Web: The Educational Experience of Hispanic American Women, edited by Teresa McKenna and Flora Ida Ortiz, 25-35. Claremont, Calif.: Tomás Rivera Center; Berkeley: Floricanto Press, 1988.

_____. "Profile of Chicanas and International Relations." In La Chicana: Building for the Future, 37-58. Oakland, Calif.: National Hispanic Univ., 1981.

Jenoveva. "La Chicana: Principle of Life, Survival and Endurance." Calmécac 1 (Summer 1980): 7-10.

Jensen, Carol. "Cleofas M. Jaramillo on Marriage in Territorial Northern New Mexico." New Mexico Historical Review 58, no. 2 (April 1983): 153-171.

Jensen, Joan M. "Canning Comes to New Mexico: Women and the Agricultural Extension Service, 1914-1919." New Mexico Historical Review 57, no. 4 (October 1982): 361-386.

_____. "Crossing Ethnic Barriers in the Southwest: Women's Agricultural Extension Education, 1914-1940." Agricultural History 60, no. 2 (Spring 1986): 169-181.

_____. "'I've Worked, I'm Not Afraid of Work': Farm Women in New Mexico, 1920-1940." New Mexico Historical Review 61, no. 1 (January 1986): 27-52.

Job, Peggy. "La sexualidad en la narrativa femenina mexicana 1970-1987: una aproximación." Third Woman 4 (1989): 120-133.

John, A. Meredith, and Reynaldo Martorell. "Incidence and Duration of Breast-Feeding in Mexican-American Infants, 1970-1982." American Journal of Clinical Nutrition 50, no. 4 (October 1989): 868-874.

Johnson, Susan L. "Sharing Bed and Board: Cohabitation and Cultural Difference in Central Arizona Mining Towns." Frontiers: A Journal of Women Studies 7, no. 3 (1984): 36-42.

Jordan, Rosan A. "The Vaginal Serpent and Other Themes from Mexican-American Women's Lore." In Women's Folklore, Women's Culture, edited by Rosan A. Jordan and Susan J. Kalcik, 26-44. Philadelphia: Univ. of Pennsylvania Press, 1985.

Jorgensen, Stephen R., and Russell P. Adams. "Family Planning Needs and Behavior of Mexican American Women: A Study of Health Care

Professionals and Their Clientele." *Hispanic Journal of Behavioral Sciences* 9, no. 3 (September 1987): 265-286.

———. "Predicting Mexican-American Family Planning Intentions: An Application and Test of a Social Psychological Model." *Journal of Marriage and the Family* 50, no. 1 (February 1988): 107-119.

Kaigler-Walker, Karen, and Mary K. Ericksen. "General Values As Related to Clothing Values of Mexican-American Women." *Hispanic Journal of Behavioral Sciences* 11, no. 2 (May 1989): 156-167.

Kantorowski Davis, Sharon, and Virgina Chávez. "Hispanic Househusbands." *Hispanic Journal of Behavioral Sciences* 7, no. 4 (December 1985): 317-332.

Karnig, Albert K., Susan Welch, and Richard A. Eribes. "Employment of Women by Cities in the Southwest." *Social Science Journal* 21, no. 4 (October 1984): 41-48.

Kay, Margarita Artschwager, and Marianne Yoder. "Hot and Cold in Women's Ethnotherapeutics: The American-Mexican West." *Social Science & Medicine* 25, no. 4 (1987): 347-355.

Kearl, Michael C., and Edward Murguía. "Age Differences of Spouses in Mexican American Intermarriage: Exploring the Cost of Minority Assimilation." *Social Science Quarterly* 66, no. 2 (June 1985): 453-460.

Kernan, Lisa. "Keep Marching Sisters: The Second Generation Looks at *Salt of the Earth*." *Nuestro* 9, no. 4 (May 1985), p. 23-25.

Keremitsis, Dawn. "Del metate al molino: la mujer mexicana de 1910 a 1940." *Historia Mexicana* 33, no. 2 (1983): 285-302.

———. "Packaging the Product: Mexican Non-Durable Women Workers, 1910-1940." In *Women and Work in the Third World: The Impact of Industrialization and Global Economic Interdependence*, compiled by Nagat M. El-Sanabary, 235-244. Berkeley: Center for the Study, Education and Advancement of Women, Univ. of California, Berkeley, 1983.

Kimbel, Charles E., Nancy B. Marsh, and Andrew C. Kiska. "Sex, Age, and Cultural Differences in Self-Reported Assertiveness." *Psychological Reports* 55, no. 2 (October 1984): 419-422.

Kokinos, Mary, and Kathryn G. Dewey. "Infant Feeding Practices of Migrant Mexican-American Families in Northern California." *Ecology of Food and Nutrition* 18, no. 3 (June 1986): 209-220.

Klingenberg, Patricia. "Latin American Women Writers: Into the Mainstream (At Last)." *Tulsa Studies in Women's Literature* 6, no. 1 (Spring 1987): 97-107.

Kossoudji, Sherrie, and Susan Ranney. "The Labor Market Experience of Female Migrants: The Case of Temporary Mexican Migration to the U.S." *International Migration Review* 18, no. 4 (Winter 1984): 1120-1143.

Kranau, Edgar J., Vicki Green, and Gloria Valencia-Weber. "Acculturation and the Hispanic Woman: Attitudes toward Women, Sex-Role Attribution, Sex-Role Behavior, and Demographics." *Hispanic Journal of Behavioral Sciences* 4, no. 1 (March, 1982): 21-40.

Krause, Neal, and Kyriakos S. Markides. "Employment and Psychological Well-Being in Mexican American Women." *Journal of Health and Social Behavior* 26, no. 1 (March 985):15-26.

———. "Gender Roles, Illness Behavior in a Mexican American Population." *Social Science Quarterly* 68, no. 1 (March 1987): 102-121.

La Monica, Grace, Claire Gulino, and Irma Ortiz Soto. "A Comparative Study of Female Mexican and American Working Nurses in the Border Corridor." *Border Health/Salud Fronteriza* 5, no. 2 (April-June 1989): 2-6.

LaDuke, Betty. "Trivial Lives: Artists Yolanda López and Patricia Rodríguez." *Trivia: A Journal of Ideas* (Winter 1986): 74-85.

Lampe, Philip E. "Female Mexican Americans: Minority within a Minority." *Borderlands Journal* 6, no. 2 (Spring 1983): 99-109.

Laosa, Luis M. "Maternal Teaching Strategies and Cognitive Styles in Chicano Families." In *Latino Language and Communicative Behavior*, edited by Richard P. Durán, 295-310. Norwood, N.J.: ABLEX Publishing Corp., 1981.

———. "Maternal Teaching Strategies in Chicano and Anglo-American Families: The Influence of Culture and Education on Maternal Behavior." *Child Development* 51 (1980): 759-765.

Lara-Cantú, M. Asunción. "A Sex Role Inventory with Scales for 'Machismo' and 'Self-Sacrificing Woman'." *Journal of Cross-Cultural Psychology* 20, no. 4 (December 1989): 386-398.

Lara-Cantú, M. Asunción, and Roberto Navarro-Arias. "Positive and Negative Factors in the Measurement of Sex Roles: Findings from a Mexican Sample." *Hispanic Journal of Behavioral Sciences* 8, no. 2 (June 1986): 143-155.

Lavrin, Asunción. "El segundo sexo en México: experiencia, estudio e introspección, 1983-1987." *Mexican Studies/Estudios Mexicanos* 5, no. 2 (Summer 1989): 297-312.

Leal, Luis. "Arquetipos femeninos en la literatura mexicana." In *Aztlán y México: perfiles literarios e históricos*, by Luis Leal, 168-176. Binghamton, N.Y.: Bilingual Press/Editorial Bilingüe, 1985.

———. "Female Archetypes in Mexican Literature." In *Women in Hispanic Literature: Icons and Fallen Idols*, edited by Beth Miller. Berkeley: Univ. of California Press, 1983, 227-242.

———. "La soldadera en la narrativa de la Revolucion." In *Aztlán y México: perfiles literarios e históricos*, by Luis Leal, 185-193. Binghamton, N.Y.: Bilingual Press/Editorial Bilingue, 1985.

Lee, Bun Song. "A Comparison of Fertility Adaptation between Mexican Immigrants to the U.S. and Internal Migrants in Mexico." *Contemporary Policy Issues* 3, no. 3 (Spring 1985): 91-101.

Lee, Valerie. "Achievement and Educational Aspirations among Hispanic Female High School Students: Comparison between Public and Catholic Schools." In *The Broken Web: The Educational Experience of Hispanic American Women*, edited by Teresa McKenna and Flora Ida Ortiz, 137-192. Claremont, Calif.: Tomás Rivera Center; Berkeley: Floricanto Press, 1988.

León, Ana M., et al. "Self-Help Support Groups for Hispanic Mothers." *Child Welfare* 63, no. 3 (May-June 1984): 261-268.

Leonard, Jonathan S. "The Effect of Unions on the Employment of Blacks, Hispanics, and Women." *Industrial and Labor Relations Review* 39, no. 1 (October 1985): 115-132.

LeVine, Sarah Ethel, Clara Sunderland Correa, and F. Medardo Tapia Uribe. "The Marital Morality of Mexican Women—An Urban Study." *Journal of Anthropological Research* 42, no. 2 (Summer 1986): 183-202.

Levy-Oved, Albert, and Sonia Alcocer Marban. *Las maquiladoras en México*. Mexico, D.F.: Fondo de Cultura Económica, 1984.

Limón, José E. "La Llorona, the Third Legend of Greater Mexico: Cultural Symbols, Women, and the Political Unconscious." *Renato Rosaldo Lecture Series Monograph* 2 (Spring 1986): [59]-93.

Lindemann, Constance, and Wilbur Scott. "The Fertility Related Behavior of Mexican American Adolescents." *Journal of Early Adolescence* 2, no. 1 (Spring 1982): 31-38.

Lindstrom, Naomi. "Four Representative Hispanic Women Poets of Central Texas: A Portrait of Plurality." *Third Woman* 2, no. 1 (1984): 64-70.

Lizárraga, Sylvia S. "Chicana Women Writers and Their Audience." *Lector* 1, no. 1 (June 1982): 15-16;18.

———. "Hacia una teoria para la liberación de la mujer." In *In Times of Challenge: Chicanos and Chicanas in American Society*, edited by Juan R. Garcia, Julia Curry Rodriguez, and Clara Lomas, 25-31. National Association for Chicano Studies. Houston: Mexican American Studies Program, Univ. of Houston, 1988.

———. "Images of Women in Chicano Literature by Men." *Feminist Issues* 5, no. 2 (Fall 1985): 69-88.

———. "La mujer doblamente explotada: 'On the Road to Texas: Pete Fonseca.'" *Aztlán* 16, no. 1-2 (1985), p. 197-215.

———. "La mujer ingeniosa." *fem* 8, no. 34 (June-July 1984): 41.

———. "The Patriarchal Ideology in 'La noche que se apagaron las luces.'" *Revista Chicano-Riqueña* 13, no. 3-4 (Fall-Winter 1985): 90-95.

———. "The Resourceful Woman in *There Are No Madmen Here*." *Third*

Woman 2, no. 1 (1984): 71-74.

Lockert, Lucia Fox. *Chicanas: Their Voices, Their Lives.* Lansing: Michigan State Board of Education, 1988.

Loeb, Catherine. "La Chicana: A Bibliographic Survey." *Frontiers: A Journal of Women Studies* 5, no. 2 (Summer 1980): 59-74.

Lomas, Clara. "Libertad de no procrear: la voz de la mujer en 'A una madre de nuestros tiempos' de Margarita-Cota Cárdenas." In *Chicana Voices: Intersections of Class, Race, and Gender*, edited by Teresa Córdova, et al., [188]-194. Austin: Center for Mexican American Studies, UT Austin, 1986. [English translation], [195]-201. Spanish version also appears in Revista Mujeres 2, no. 1 (January 1985): 30-35.

———. "Mexican Precursors of Chicana Feminist Writing." In *Estudios Chicanos and the Politics of Community*, edited by Mary Romero and Cordelia Candelaria, [149]-160. Colorado Springs: National Association for Chicano Studies, 1989.

———. "Sylvia Lizárraga." In *Chicano Writers, First Series, Dictionary of Literary Biography* 82: 149-153. Detroit: Bruccoli Clark Layman, 1989.

Lomeli, Francisco A. "Chicana Novelists in the Process of Creating Fictive Voices." In *Beyond Stereotypes: The Critical Analysis of Chicana Literature*, edited by Maria Herrera-Sobek, 29-46. Binghamton, N.Y.: Bilingual Press/Editorial Bilingüe, 1985.

López-Garza, María C. "Toward a Reconceptualization of Women's Economic Activities: The Informal Sector in Urban Mexico." In *Chicana Voices: Intersections of Class, Race, and Gender*, edited by Teresa Córdova, et al., 66-76. Austin: Center for Mexican American Studies, UT Austin, 1986.

López-González, Aralia, et al., eds. *Mujer y literatura mexicana y chicana: Culturas en contacto.* Mexico: Colegio de la Frontera Norte, 1988.

Loustaunau, Martha Oehmke. "Hispanic Widows and Their Support Systems in the Mesilla Valley of Southern New Mexico, 1910-40." In *On Their Own: Widows and Widowhood in the American Southwest, 1848-1939*, edited by Arlene Scadron. Urbana: Univ. of Illinois Press, 1988, 91-116.

Lucero, Marcela C. "Resources for the Chicana Feminist Scholar." In *For Alma Mater: Theory and Practice in Feminist Scholarship*, edited by Paula A. Treichler, et al., 393-401. Urbana: Univ. of Illinois Press, 1985.

Luna-Lawhn, Juanita. "*El Regidor* and *La Prensa*: Impediments to Women's Self-Definition." *Third Woman* 4 (1989): 134-142.

———. "Victorian Attitudes Affecting the Mexican Woman Writing in La Prensa during the Early 1900s and the Chicana of the 1980s." In *Missions in Conflict: Essays on U.S.-Mexican Relations and Chicano Culture*, edited by Renate von Bardeleben, Dietrich Briesemeister, and Juan Bruce-Novoa, 65-71. Tubingen, W. Germany: Günter Narr Verlag, 1986.

MacCorquodale, Patricia. "Mexican-American Women and Mathematics: Participation, Aspirations, and Achievement." In *Linguistic and Cultural Influences on Learning Mathematics*, 137-160. Hillsdale, N. J.: Erlbaum, 1988.

Macias, Anna. *Against All Odds: The Feminist Movement in Mexico to 1940*. Westport, Conn.: Greenwood Press, 1982.

MacManus, Susan A., Charles S. Bullock, and Barbara P. Grothe. "A Longitudinal Examination of Political Participation Rates of Mexican-American Females." *Social Science Quarterly* 67, no. 3 (1986): 604-612.

Magnus, Peter D. "Breastfeeding among Hispanics." *American Journal of Public Health* 73, no. 5 (May 1983): 597.

Marin, Barbara VanOss et al. "Health Care Utilization by Low-Income Clients of a Community Clinic: An Archival Study." *Hispanic Journal of Behavioral Sciences* 3, no. 3 (September 1981): 257-273.

Marín, Christine. "La Asociación Hispano-Americana de Madres y Esposas: Tucson's Mexican American Women in World War II." *Renato Rosaldo Lecture Series Monograph* 1, (Summer 1985): [5]-18.

Marín, Gerardo, Eliseo J. Pérez-Stable, and Barbara VanOss Marin. "Cigarette Smoking among San Francisco Hispanics: The role of acculturation and gender." *American Journal of Public Health* 79, no. 2 (February 1989): 196-198.

Markides, Kyriakos S., and Janice Farrell. "Marital Status and Depression among Mexican Americans." *Social Psychiatry* 20, no. 2 (1985): 86-91.

Markides, Kyriakos S., and Sue K. Hoppe. "Marital Stratification in Three Generations of Mexican Americans." *Social Science Quarterly* 66, no. 1 (March 1985): 147-154.

Markides, Kyriakos S., and Sally W. Vernon. "Aging, Sex-Role Orientation and Adjustment: A Three-Generations Study of Mexican Americans." *Journal of Gerontology* 39, no. 5 (September, 1984): 586-591.

Markides, Kyriakos S., et al. "Sample Representativeness in a Three-Generation Study of Mexican Americans." *Journal of Marriage and the Family* 45, no. 4 (November 1983): 911-916.

Marlow, Christine. "Management of Family and Employment Responsibilities by Mexican American and Anglo American Women." *Social Work* 35, no. 3 (May 1990): 259-265.

Martínez, Douglas R. "Hispanic Origin Women in the U.S." *La Luz* 8, no. 8 (October-November 1980): 11-12.

Martínez, Elisa A. "Sharing Her Tiny Pieces of the Past." *Nuestro* 7, no. 7 (September 1983): 51-52.

Martínez, Estella A. "Child Behavior in Mexican American/Chicano

Families: Maternal Teaching and Child-Rearing Practices." *Family Relations* 37, no. 3 (July 1988): 275-280.

Martínez, Julio A., and Francisco A. Lomelí. *Chicano Literature: A Reference Guide*. Westport, Conn.: Greenwood Press, 1985.

Martínez, Marco Antonio. "Conversational Asymmetry between Mexican Mothers and Children." *Hispanic Journal of Behavioral Sciences* 3, no. 4 (December 1981): 329-346.

Martínez, Olivia. "The Three Rs of Chicana Leadership." In *La Chicana: Building for the Future*, 74-80. Oakland, Calif.: National Hispanic Univ., 1981.

Martínez, Ruben. "AIDS in the Latino Community." *Americas 2001* 1, no. 5 (March-April 1988): [14-18].

Martínez, Ruben, and Richard L. Dukes. "Race, Gender and Self-Esteem among Youth." *Hispanic Journal of Behavioral Sciences* 9, no. 4 (December 1987): 427-443.

Martínez, Virginia. "Chicanas and the Law." In *La Chicana: Building for the Future*, 134-146. Oakland, Calif.: National Hispanic Univ., 1981.

Mary, Nancy L. "Reactions of Black, Hispanic, and White Mothers to Having a Child with Handicaps." *Mental Retardation* 28, no. 1 (February 1990): 1-5.

Matute-Bianchi, María Eugenia. "A Chicana in Academe." *Women's Studies Quarterly* 10, no. 1 (Spring 1982): 14-17.

Mayers, Raymond Sánchez. "Use of Folk Medicine by Elderly Mexican-American Women." *Journal of Drug Issues* 19, no. 2 (1989): 283-295.

Mays, Vickie M., and Susan D. Cochran. "Issues in the perception of AIDS risk and risk reduction activities by Black and Hispanic/Latina women." *American Psychologist* 43, no. 11 (November 1988): 949-957.

McCracken, Ellen. "Latina Narrative and Politics of Signification: Articulation, Antagonism, and Populist Rupture." *Crítica* 2, no. 2 (Fall 1990): 202-207.

_____. "Sandra Cisneros' *The House on Mango Street*: Community-Oriented Introspection and the Demystification of Patriarchal Violence." In *Breaking Boundaries: Latina Writing and Critical Readings*, edited by Asunción Horno-Delgado, et al., 62-71. Amherst: Univ. of Massachusetts Press, 1989.

McKenna, Teresa, and Flora Ida Ortiz. "Select Bibliography on Hispanic Women and Education." In *The Broken Web: The Educational Experience of Hispanic American Women*, edited by Teresa McKenna and Flora Ida Ortiz, 221-254. Claremont, Calif.: Tomás Rivera Center; Berkeley: Floricanto Press, 1988.

_____. *The Broken Web: The Educational Experience of Hispanic American Women*. Claremont, Calif.: Tomás Rivera Center; Berkeley: Floricanto Press, 1988.

Meier, Matt. *Mexican American Biographies: A Historical Dictionary, 1836-1987.* Westport, Conn.: Greenwood Press, 1988.

Melville, Margarita B. "Female and Male in Chicano Theatre." In *Hispanic Theatre in the United States*, edited by Nicholás Kanellos, 71-79. Houston: Arte Publico Press, 1984.

_____. "Mexican Women Adapt to Migration." In *Mexican Immigrant Workers in the U.S.*, edited by Antonio Ríos-Bustamante, 119-124. Los Angeles: Chicano Studies Research Center Publications, Univ. of California, Los Angeles, 1981.

_____. "Mexican Women in the U.S. Wage Labor Force." In *Mexicanas at Work in the United States*, edited by Margarita B. Melville, 1-11. Houston: Mexican American Studies Program, Univ. of Houston, 1988.

_____. *Mexicanas at Work in the United States.* Houston: Mexican American Studies Program, Univ. of Houston, 1988.

Mendoza, Lupe. "Porque lo podemos hacer—¿a poco no?" *Revista Mujeres* 1, no. 2 (June 1984): 33-37.

Mesa-Bains, Amalia. "Quest for Identity: Profile of Two Chicana Muralists: Based on Interviews with Judith F. Baca and Patricia Rodríguez." In *Signs from the Heart: California Chicano Murals*, edited by Eva Sperling Cockcroft and Holly Barnet-Sánchez, [68-83]. Venice, Calif.: Social and Public Art Resource Center, 1990.

"La Mexicana/Chicana." *Renato Rosaldo Lecture Series Monograph* 1, (Summer 1985).

Michael, Robert T., and Nancy Brandon Tuma. "Entry into Marriage and Parenthood by Young Men and Women: The Influence of Family Background." *Demography* 22, no. 4 (November 1985): 515-544.

Miller, Darlis A. "Cross-Cultural Marriages in the Southwest: The New Mexico Experience, 1846-1900." *New Mexico Historical Review* 57, no. 4 (October 1982): 335-359.

Miller, Elaine N., and Nancy Saporta Sternbach. "Selected Bibliography." In *Breaking Boundaries: Latina Writing and Critical Readings*, edited by Asunción Horno-Delgado, et al., 251-263. Amherst: Univ. of Massachusetts Press, 1989.

Miller, George A. "Latinas on Border Patrol." *Vista* 4, no. 18 (January 1, 1989): 8-10.

Mindiola, Tatcho, Jr. "The Cost of Being a Mexican Female Worker in the 1970 Houston Labor Market." *Aztlán* 11, no. 2 (Fall, 1980): 231-247.

Miranda, Gloria E. "Hispano-Mexican Childrearing Practices in Pre-American Santa Barbara." *Southern California Quarterly* 65, no. 4 (Winter 1983): 307-320.

Mirandé, Alfredo. "Machismo." In *The Chicano Experience: An Alternative Perspective*, by Alfredo Mirandé, 165-181. Notre Dame, Ind.: Univ. of

Notre Dame Press, 1985.

———. "Machismo: rucas, chingazos y chingaderas." *De Colores* 6, no. 1-2 (1982): 17-31.

———. "The Chicano Family and Sex Roles: An Overview and Introduction." *De Colores* 6, no. 1-2 (1982): 1-6.

Mirandé, Alfredo, and Evangelina Enríquez. "Chicanas in the Struggle for Unions." In *Introduction to Chicano Studies*, edited by Livie Isauro Durán and H. Russell Bernard, 325-337. 2d ed. New York: Macmillan, 1982.

Molina, Carlos. "Family Health Promotion: A Conceptual Framework for "La Salud" and "El Bienestar" in Latino Communities." In *Latino Families in the United States*, edited by Sally J. Andrade, 35-42. [S.l.]: Planned Parenthood Federation of America, Inc., 1983.

Molina, Frieda. "The Social Impacts of the Maquiladora Industry on Mexican Border Towns." *Berkeley Planning Journal* 2, no. 1-2 (Spring-Fall 1985): 30-40.

Mondin, Sandra. "The Depiction of the Chicana in *Bless Me, Ultima* and *The Milagro Beanfield War*: A Study in Contrasts." In *Mexico and the United States: Intercultural Relations in the Humanities*, edited by Juanita Luna-Lawhn, et al., 137-150. San Antonio: San Antonio College, 1984.

Monk, Janice, and Vera Norwood. "Angles of Vision: Enhancing Our Perspectives on the Southwest." In *Old Southwest/New Southwest: Essays on a Region and Its Literature*, edited by Judy Nolte Lensink, 39-47. Tucson, Ariz.: The Tucson Public Library, 1989.

Moore, Helen A. "Hispanic Women: Schooling for Conformity in Public Education." *Hispanic Journal of Behavioral Sciences* 5, no. 1 (March 1983): 45-63.

Moore, Helen A., and Natalie K. Porter. "Leadership and Nonverbal Behaviors of Hispanic Females across School Equity Environments." *Psychology of Women Quarterly* 12, no. 2 (June 1988): 147-163.

Moore, Joan W. "Mexican-American Women Addicts: the Influence of Family Background." In *Drugs in Hispanic Communities*, edited by Ronald Glick and Joan Moore, 127-153. New Brunswick: Rutgers Univ. Press, 1990.

———. "The Paradox of Deviance in Addicted Mexican American Mothers." *Gender & Society* 3, no. 1 (March 1989): 53-70.

Mora, Magdalena. "The Tolteca Strike: Mexican Women and the Struggle for Union Representation." In *Mexican Immigrant Workers in the U.S.*, edited by Antonio Rios Bustamante, 111-117. Los Angeles: Chicano Studies Research Center Publications, Univ. of California, Los Angeles, 1981.

Mora, Magadalena, and Adelaida P. Del Castillo. *Mexican Women in the*

United States: Struggles Past and Present. Los Angeles: Chicano Studies Research Center Publications, Univ. of California, Los Angeles, 1980.

Mora, Pat, and Norma Alarcón. "A Poet Analyzes Her Craft." *Nuestro* 11, no. 2 (March 1987): 25-27.

Moraga, Cherríe. *Loving in the War Years: Lo que nunca pasó por sus labios*. Boston: South End Press, 1983.

———. "Third World Women in the United States—By and about Us: A Selected Bibliography." In *This Bridge Called My Back: Writings by Radical Women of Color*, edited by Cherríe Moraga and Gloria Anzaldúa, 251-261. Watertown, Mass.: Persephone Press, 1981.

Moraga, Cherríe, and Ana Castillo, eds. *Esta [sic] puente, mi espalda: voces de mujeres tercermundistas en los Estados Unidos*. San Francisco: Ism Press, 1988. Spanish translation and adaptation of *This Bridge Called My Back: Writings by Radical Women of Color*.

Morales, Patricia. "Femenismo [sic] chicano." *fem* 8, no. 39 (April-May 1985): 41-44.

Morales, Sylvia. "Chicano-Produced Celluloid Mujeres." *Bilingual Review* 10, no. 2-3 (May-December 1983): 89-93.

Moreno, José Adán, and Carmen Lomas Garza. "Carmen Lomas Garza: Traditional and Non-Traditional." *Caminos* 5, no. 10 (November 1984): 44-45, 53.

Mosher, William D., David P. Johnson, and Marjorie C. Horn. "Religion and Fertility in the United States: The Importance of Marriage Patterns and Hispanic Origin." *Demography* 23, no. 3 (August 1986): 367-379.

Moss, Nancy E. "Effects of Father-Daughter Contact on Use of Pregnancy Services by Mexican, Mexican-American, and Anglo Adolescents." *Journal of Adolescent Health Care* 8, no. 5 (September 1987): 419-424.

Mujeres en Marcha, University of California, Berkeley. *Chicanas in the 80s: Unsettled Issues*. Berkeley: Chicano Studies Library Publications Unit, 1983.

Muñoz, Daniel G. "Identifying Areas of Stress for Chicano Undergraduates." In *Latino College Students*, edited by Michael A. Olivas, 131-156. New York: Teachers College Press, 1986.

Murguía, Edward, and Ralph B. Cazares. "Intermarriage of Mexican Americans." *Marriage & Family Review* 5, no. 1 (Spring, 1982): 91-100.

Myres, Sandra Lynn. "Mexican Americans and Westering Anglos: A Feminine Perspective." *New Mexico Historical Review* 57, no. 4 (October 1982): 317-333.

Nava, Yolanda. "Chicanas in the Television Media." In *La Chicana: Building for the Future*, 120-133. Oakland, Calif.: National Hispanic Univ., 1981.

Navarro, Marta A., and Ana Castillo. "Interview with Ana Castillo." In *Chicana Lesbians: The Girls Our Mothers Warned Us About*, edited by Carla Trujillo, 113-132. Berkeley: Third Woman Press, 1991.

Nelson, Kathryn J. "Excerpts from Los Testamentos: Hispanic Women Folk Artists of the San Luis Valley, Colorado." *Frontiers: A Journal of Women Studies* 5, no. 3 (Fall 1980): 34-43.

Newton, Frank, Esteban L. Olmedo, and Amado M. Padilla. *Hispanic Mental Health Research: A Reference Guide*. Berkeley: Univ. of California Press, 1982.

Nieves-Squires, Sarah. *Hispanic Women: Making Their Presence on Campus Less Tenuous*. Washington, D.C.: Association of American Colleges, 1991.

Norris, Henri E. "AIDS, Women and Reproductive Rights." *Multicultural Inquiry and Research on AIDS (MIRA) Newsletter* 1, no. 3 (Summer 1987): [2-3].

Nyamathi, Adeline, and Rose Vásquez. "Impact of Poverty, Homelessness, and Drugs on Hispanic Women at Risk for HIV Infection." *Hispanic Journal of Behavioral Sciences* 11, no. 4 (November 1989): 299-314.

O'Connor, Mary I. "Women's Networks and the Social Needs of Mexican Immigrants." *Urban Anthropology* 19, no. 1-2 (Spring-Summer 1990): 81-98.

O'Donnell, Jo Anne. "Enhancing Educational Opportunities for Hispanic Women." *Journal of College Admissions*, no. 116 (Summer 1987): 20-25.

O'Guinn, Thomas C., Giovanna Imperia, and Elizabeth A. MacAdams. "Acculturation and Perceived Family Decision-making Input among Mexican American Wives." *Journal of Cross-Cultural Psychology* 18, no. 1 (March 1987): 78-92.

Olivares, Yvette. "The Sweatshop: The Garment Industry's Reborn Child." *Revista Mujeres* 3, no. 2 (June 1986): 55-62.

Oliveira, Annette. "Remarkable Latinas." In *Hispanics and Grantmakers: A Special Report of Foundation News*, 34. Washington, D.C.: Council on Foundations, 1981.

Olivera, Mercedes. "The New Hispanic Women." *Vista* 2, no. 11 (July 5, 1987): 6-8.

Olivero, Magaly. "Career Latinas: Facing the Challenges of a Family and a Career." *Nuestro* 5, no. 6 (August-September, 1981): 27-28.

Olvera-Ezzell, Norma, Thomas G. Power, and Jennifer H. Cousins. "Maternal Socialization of Children's Eating Habits: Strategies Used by Obese Mexican-American Mothers." *Child Development* 61, no. 2 (April 1990): 395-400.

Ordoñez, Elizabeth J. "Body, Spirit, and the Text: Alma Villanueva's Life Span." In *Criticism in the Borderlands: Studies in Chicano Literature, Cul-*

ture, and Ideology, edited by Hector Calderón and José David Saldivar, [61]-71. Durham, North Carolina: Duke Univ. Press, 1991.

_____. "Chicana Literature and Related Sources: A Selected and Annotated Bibliography." *Bilingual Review* 7, no. 2 (May-August 1980): 143-164.

_____. "Sexual Politics and the Theme of Sexuality in Chicana Poetry." In *Women in Hispanic Literature: Icons and Fallen Idols*, edited by Beth Miller, 316-339. Berkeley: Univ. of California Press, 1983.

_____. "The Concept of Cultural Identity in Chicana Poetry." *Third Woman* 2, no. 1 (1984): 75-82.

Orozco, Cynthia. "Chicana Labor History: A Critique of Male Consciousness in Historical Writing." *La Red/The Net*, no. 77 (January 1984): 2-5. Also *La Gente* [student newspaper from UCLA] (November-December 1983).

_____. "Getting Started in Chicana Studies." *Women's Studies Quarterly*, no. 1-2 (1990): 46-69.

_____. "Sexism in Chicano Studies and the Community." In *Chicana Voices: Intersections of Class, Race, and Gender*, edited by Teresa Córdova, et al., 11-18. Austin: Center for Mexican American Studies, UT Austin, 1986.

Ortega. E. Astrid. "Moving Hispanics into Nurses." *California Nurse* 83, no. 3 (April 1987): 8.

Ortega, Eliana, and Nancy Saporta Sternbach. "At the Threshold of the Unnamed: Latina Literary Discourse in the Eighties." In *Breaking Boundaries: Latina Writing and Critical Readings*, edited by Asunción Horno-Delgado, et al., [2]-23. Amherst: Univ. of Massachusetts Press, 1989.

Ortiz, Flora Ida. "Hispanic American Women in Higher Education: A Consideration of the Socialization Process." *Aztlán* 17, no. 2 (Fall 1986): 125-152.

_____. "The Distribution of Mexican American Women in School Organizations." *Hispanic Journal of Behavioral Sciences* 4, no. 2 (June 1982): 181-198.

Ortiz, Sylvia, and Jesus Manuel Casas. "Birth Control and Low-Income Mexican-American Women: The Impact of Three Values." *Hispanic Journal of Behavioral Sciences* 12, no. 1 (February 1990): 83-92.

Ortiz, Vilma, and Rosemary Santana Cooney. "Sex-Role Attitudes and Labor Force Participation among Young Hispanic Females and Non-Hispanic White Females." In *The Mexican American Experience: An Interdisciplinary Anthology*, edited by Rodolfo O. de la Garza, et al., 174-182. Austin: Univ. of Texas Press, 1985. Reprint of article in *Social Science Quarterly* 65, no. 2 (June 1984): 392-400.

Ortiz Ortega, Adriana. "Un camino por transitar." *fem* 8, no. 34 (June-

July 1984): 25-26.

Padilla, Amado M. "Mexican-American Adolescent Sexuality and Sexual Knowledge: An Exploratory Study." *Hispanic Journal of Behavioral Sciences* 13, no. 1 (February 1991): 95-104.

Padilla, Eligio R., and Kevin E. O'Grady. "Sexuality among Mexican Americans: A Case of Sexual Stereotyping." *Journal of Personality and Social Psychology* 52, no. 1 (1987): 5-10.

Padilla, Genaro. "Imprisoned Narrative? Or Lies, Secrets, and Silence in New Mexico Women's Autobiography." In *Criticism in the Borderlands: Studies in Chicano Literature, Culture, and Ideology*, edited by Hector Calderón and José David Saldívar, [43]-60. Durham, North Carolina: Duke Univ. Press, 1991.

_____. " 'Yo sola aprendí': Contra-Patriarchal Containment in Women's Nineteenth-Century California Personal Narratives." *The Americas Review* 16, no. 3-4 (Fall-Winter 1988), p. 91-109.

Padilla, Steve. "You've Come a Long Way, Baby. Or Have You?" *Nuestro* 7, no. 6 (August 1983): 38-41.

Palacios, Maria, and Juan N. Franco. "Counseling Mexican-American Women." *Journal of Multicultural Counseling and Development* 14 (July 1986): 124-131.

Pardo, Mary. "Mexican American Women Grassroots Community Activists: 'Mothers of East Los Angeles' " *Frontiers: A Journal of Women Studies* 11, no. 1 (1990): [1]-7.

Parra, Elena, and Ronald W. Henderson. "Mexican American Perceptions of Parent and Teacher Roles in Child Development." In *Bilingual Education for Hispanic Students in the United States*, edited by Joshua A. Fishman and Gary D. Keller, 289-299. New York: Teachers College Press, 1982.

Passman, Kristina. "Demeter, Kore and the Birth of the Self: The Quest for Identity in the Poetry of Alma Villanueva, Pat Mora y Cherríe Moraga." *Monographic Review* 6 (1990): 323-342.

Pavich, Emma Guerrero. "A Chicana Perspective on Mexican Culture and Sexuality." *Journal of Social Work and Human Sexuality* 4, no. 3 (Spring 1986): 47-65.

Peña, Devón Gerardo. "Between the Lines: A New Perspective on the Industrial Sociology of Women Workers in Transnational Labor Processes." In *Chicana Voices: Intersections of Class, Race, and Gender*, edited by Teresa Córdova, et al., 77-95. Austin: Center for Mexican American Studies, UT Austin, 1986.

_____. "Las Maquiladoras: Mexican Women in Class Struggle in the Border Industries." *Aztlán* 11, no. 2 (Fall, 1980): 159-229.

_____. "Tortuosidad: Shop Floor Struggles of Female Maquiladora Workers." In *Women on the U.S. Mexico Border: Repsonses to Change*, edited by

Vicki L. Ruiz and Susan Tiano, 129-154. Boston: Allen & Unwin, 1987.

Peña, Manuel. "Class, Gender, and Machismo: The 'Treacherous-Woman' Folklore of Mexican Male Workers." *Gender & Society* 5, no. 1 (March 1991): 30-46.

Pérez, Emma. "Sexuality and Discourse: Notes from a Chicana Survivor." In *Chicana Lesbians: The Girls Our Mothers Warned Us About*, edited by Carla Trujillo, 159-184. Berkeley: Third Woman Press, 1991.

Pérez, Robert. "Effects of Stress, Social Support and Coping Style on Adjustment to Pregnancy among Hispanic Women." *Hispanic Journal of Behavioral Sciences* 5, no. 2 (June 1983): 141-161.

Pérez-Erdelyi, Mireya, and Lucha Corpi. "Entrevista con Lucha Corpi: poeta chicana." *The Americas Review* 17, no. 1 (Spring 1989): 72-82.

Perrone, Bobette, H. Henrietta Stockel, and Victoria Krueger. *Medicine Women, Curanderas, and Women Doctors*. Norman: Univ. of Oklahoma Press, 1989.

Pesquera, Beatriz M., and Flo Durán. "Having a Job Gives You Some Sort of Power: Reflections of a Chicana Working Woman." *Feminist Issues* 4, no. 2 (Fall 1984): 79-96.

Peters, Ruth K., et al. "Risk Factors for Invasive Cervical Cancer among Latinas and Non-Latinas in Los Angeles County." *Journal of the National Cancer Institute* 77, no. 5 (November 1986): 1063-1077.

Phillips, Rachel. "Marina/Malinche." In *Women in Hispanic Literature: Icons and Fallen Idols*, edited by Beth Miller, 97-114. Berkeley: Univ. of California Press, 1983.

Pick, James B., et al. "Socioeconomic Influences on Fertility in the Mexican Borderlands Region." *Mexican Studies/Estudios Mexicanos* 6, no. 1 (Winter 1990): 11-42.

Pletsch, Pamela K. "Hispanics: At Risk for Adolescent Pregnancy?" *Public Health Nursing* 7, no. 2 (June 1990): 105-110.

Pohl, Frances K., and Judith F. Baca. "'The World War: A Vision of the Future without Fear,' an Interview with Judith F. Baca." *Frontiers: A Journal of Women Studies* 11, no. 1 (1990): [33]-43.

Ponce-Adame, Merrihelen. "Latinas and Breast Cancer." *Nuestro* 6, no. 8 (October 1982): 30-31.

———. "Women and Cancer." *Corazón de Aztlán* 1, no. 2 (March-April 1982): 32.

Popp, Gary E., and William F. Muhs. "Fears of Success and Women Employees." *Human Relations* 35, no. 7 (July 1982): 511-519.

Powell, Douglas R. "Designing Culturally Responsive Parent Programs: A Comparison of Low-Income Mexican and Mexican-American Mothers' Preferences." *Family Relations* 39, no. 3 (July 1990): 298-304.

Powers, Stephen, and Patricia Jones. "Factorial Invariance of the California Achievement Tests across Race and Sex." *Educational and Psychological*

Measurement 44, no. 4 (Winter 1984): 967-970.

Preciado Martin, Patricia. *Images and Conversations: Mexican Americans Recall a Southwestern Past.* Tucson: Univ. of Arizona Press, 1983. Includes seven Chicanas.

Pumariega, Andrés J. "Acculturation and Eating Attitudes in Adolescent Girls: A Comparative and Correlational Study." *Journal of the American Academy of Child Psychiatry* 25, no. 2 (March 1986): 276-279.

Queiro-Tajalli, Irene. "Hispanic Women's Perceptions and Use of Prenatal Health Care Services." *Affilia: Journal of Women and Social Work* 4, no. 2 (Summer 1989): 60-72.

Quezada, Rosa, and Katherine Jones-Loheyde. "Hispanic Women: Academic Advisees of High Potential." *Improving College & University Teaching* 32, no. 2-14 (1984): 95-98.

Quezada, Rosa, et al. "The Hispanic Woman Graduate Student: Barriers to Mentoring in Higher Education." *Texas Tech Journal of Education* 11, no. 3 (Fall 1984): 235-241.

Quintana, Alvina. "Ana Castillo's *The Mixquiahuala Letters*: The Novelist as Ethnographer." In *Criticism in the Borderlands: Studies in Chicano Literature, Culture, and Ideology*, edited by Hector Calderón and José David Saldívar, [72]-83. Durham, North Carolina: Duke Univ. Press, 1991.

———. "Challenge and Counter Challenge: Chicana Literary Motifs." *Against the Current* 2, no. 2 (March-April, 1987): 25, 28-32.

———. "Chicana Literary Motifs: Challenge and Counter-Challenge." *Images: Ethnic Studies Occasional Papers Series* (Fall 1986): 24-41.

———. "Expanding a Feminist View: Challenge and Counter-Challenge in the Relationship between Women." *Revista Mujeres* 2, no. 1 (January 1985): 11-18.

———. "Her story." *Revista Mujeres* 4, no. 1 (January 1987): 44-47.

———. "Language, Power, and Women: A Hermeneutic Interpretation." *Critical Perspectives of Third World America* 2, no. 1 (Fall 1984): 10-19.

———. "O Mama, With What's Inside of Me." *Revista Mujeres* 3, no. 1 (January 1986): 38-40.

———. "Politics, Representation and the Emergence of a Chicana Aesthetic." *Cultural Studies* 4, no. 3 (October 1990): 257-263.

———. "Women: Prisoners of the Word." In *Chicana Voices: Intersections of Class, Race, and Gender*, edited by Teresa Córdova, et al., [208]-219. Austin: Center for Mexican American Studies, UT Austin, 1986.

Quintanilla, Anita. "Images of Deceit." *Womanspirit* 10, no. 37, (Fall 1983): 25-26.

Radecki, Stephen E., and Gerald S. Bernstein. "Use of Clinic Versus Private Family Planning Care by Low-Income Women: Access, Cost and Patient Satisfaction." *American Journal of Public Health* 79, no. 6 (June 1989): 692-697.

Ramírez, Genevieve M., and Carmen Salazar Parr. "The Female Hero in Chicano Literature." In *Beyond Stereotypes: The Critical Analysis of Chicana Literature*, edited by María Herrera-Sobek, 48-60. Binghamton, N.Y.: Bilingual Press/Editorial Bilingüe, 1985.

Ramírez, Oscar, and Carlos H. Arce. "The Contemporary Chicano Family: An Empirically Based Review." In *Explorations in Chicano Psychology*, edited by Augustine Barón, Jr., 3-28. New York: Praeger, 1981.

Ramos, Juanita. *Compañeras: Latina Lesbians (an Anthology)*. New York: Latina Lesbian History Project, 1987.

Ramos, Reyes. "Discovering the Production of Mexican American Family Structure." *De Colores* 6, no. 1-2 (1982): 120-134.

Raney, Dana. "Hispanas Voice the Issues." *Intercambios Femeniles* 3, no. 2 (Summer 1988): 6-9.

Rapkin, Andrea J., and Pamela I. Erickson. "Differences in knowledge of and risk factors for AIDS between Hispanic and non-Hispanic women attending an urban family planning clinic." *AIDS* 4, no. 9 (1990): 889-899.

Rebolledo, Tey Diana. "Abuelitas: Mythology and Integration in Chicana Literature." *Revista Chicano-Riqueña* 11, no. 3-4 (Fall 1983): 148-158.

_____. "Game Theory in Chicana Poetry." *Revista Chicano-Riqueña* 11, no. 3-4 (Fall 1983): 159-168.

_____. "Hispanic Women Writers of the Southwest: Tradition and Innovation." In *Old Southwest/New Southwest: Essays on a Region and Its Literature*, edited by Judy Nolte Lensink, 49-61. Tucson, Ariz.: The Tucson Public Library, 1987.

_____. "Las escritoras: Romances and Realities." In *Pasó por aquí: Critical Essays on the New Mexican Literary Tradition*, edited by Erlinda Gonzales-Berry, 199-214. Albuquerque: Univ. of New Mexico, 1989.

_____. "Narrative Strategies of Resistance in Hispana Writing." *The Journal of Narrative Technique* 20, no. 2 (Spring 1990): 134-146.

_____. "Soothing Restless Serpents: The Dreaded Creation and Other Inspirations in Chicana Poetry." *Third Woman* 2, no. 1 (1984): 83-102.

_____. "The Bittersweet Nostalgia of Childhood in the Poetry of Margarita Cota-Cárdenas." *Frontiers: A Journal of Women Studies* 5, no. 2 (Summer 1980): 31-35.

_____. "The Maturing of Chicana Poetry: The Quiet Revolution of the 1980s." In *For Alma Mater: Theory and Practice in Feminist Scholarship*, edited by Paula A. Treichler, et al., 143-158. Urbana: Univ. of Illinois Press, 1985.

_____. "The Politics of Poetics: Or, What Am I, a Critic, Doing in This Text Anyhow?" *The Americas Review* 15, no. 3-4 (Fall-Winter 1987): 129-138. Also in *Making Face, Making Soul: Haciendo Caras: Creative and Critical Perspectives by Women of Color*, edited by Gloria Anzaldúa, 346-355. San Francisco: Aunt Lute Foundation Books, 1990.

_____. "Tradition and Mythology: Signatures of Landscape in Chicana Literature." In *The Desert Is No Lady: Southwestern Landscapes in Women's Writing and Art*, edited by Vera Norwood and Janice Monk, 96-124. New Haven: Yale Univ. Press, 1987.

———. "Walking the Thin Line: Humor in Chicana Literature." In *Beyond Stereotypes: The Critical Analysis of Chicana Literature*, edited by María Herrera-Sobek, 91-107. Binghamton, N.Y.: Bilingual Press/Editorial Bilingüe, 1985.

Rebolledo, Tey Diana, Erlinda Gonzales-Berry, and Teresa Márquez, eds. *Las Mujeres Hablan: An Anthology of Nuevo Mexicana Writers*. Albuquerque: El Norte Publications, 1988.

Rebolledo, Tey Diana, and Pat Mora. "Pat Mora: Interview." In *This Is About Vision: Interviews with Southwestern Writers*, edited by William Balassi, et al., [128]-139. Albuquerque: Univ. of New Mexico Press, 1990.

Redfern, Bernice. *Women of Color in the United States: A Guide to the Literature*. New York: Garland Publishing, 1989.

Reed-Sanders, Delores, Richard A. Dodder, and Lucia Webster. "The Bem Sex-Role Inventory across Three Cultures." *Journal of Social Psychology* 125, no. 4 (August 1985): 523-525.

Reimers, Cordelia W. "A Comparative Analysis of the Wages of Hispanics, Blacks, and Non-Hispanic Whites." In *Hispanics in the U.S. Economy*, edited by George J. Borjas and Marta Tienda, 27-75. Orlando, Fla.: Academic Press, 1985.

Remez, Lisa. "Rates of Adolescent Pregnancy and Childbearing Are High among Mexican-Born Mexican Americans." *Family Planning Perspectives* 23, no. 2 (March-April 1991): 88-89.

Richardson, Jean L., et al. "Frequency and Adequacy of Breast Cancer Screening among Elderly Hispanic Women." *Preventive Medicine* 16, no. 6 (November 1987): 761-774.

Rigg, Pat. "Petra: Learning to Read at 45." *Journal of Education* 167, no. 1 (1985): 129-139.

Rivera, Margarita T. "Cordelia Candelaria." In *Chicano Writers, First Series, Dictionary of Literary Biography* 82: 65-67. Detroit: Bruccoli Clark Layman, 1989.

Rivera, George, Aileen Lucero, and Robert M. Regoli. "Contemporary Curanderismo: A Study of Mental Health Agency and Home Clientele of a Practicing Curandera." *Issues in Radical Therapy* 13, no. 1-2 (Winter-Spring 1988): 52-57.

Rivera, Yvette. "Hispanic Women's Organizations and Periodicals Needed to Communicate New Options." *Media Report to Women* 12, no. 5 (September-October 1984): 15.

Rivero, Eliana S. "Escritura chicana: la mujer." *La Palabra* 2, no. 2 (Fall 1980): 2-9.

Roberts, Robert E., and Catherine Ramsay Roberts. "Marriage, Work and Depressive Symptoms among Mexican Americans." *Hispanic Journal of Behavioral Sciences* 4, no. 2 (June 1982): 199-221.

Robinson, Barbara J., and J. Cordell Robinson. *The Mexican-American: A Critical Guide to Research Aids*. Greenwich, Conn.: JAI Press, 1980.

Rocard, Marcienne. "The Remembering Voice in Chicana Literature." *The Americas Review* 14, no. 3-4 (Fall-Winter, 1986): 150-159.

Rockhill, Kathleen. "Gender, Language, and the Politics of Literacy." *British Journal of Sociology of Education* 8, no. 2 (1987): 153-167.

Rodríguez, Angela M., and Luis Casaus. "Latino Family Issues." In *Latino Families in the United States*, edited by Sally J. Andrade, 25-32. [S.l.]: Planned Parenthood Federation of America, Inc., 1983.

Rodríguez, Anita. "Las enjarradoras: Women of the Earth." *New Mexico* (February 1980): 46-47 +.

Rodríguez, Rogelio E., and Alan DeWolfe. "Psychological Distress among Mexican-American and Mexican Women as Related to Status on the New Immigration Law." *Journal of Consulting and Clinical Psychology* 58, no. 5 (October 1990): 548-553.

Rodríguez Aranda, Pilar E., and Sandra Cisneros. "On the Solitary Fate of Being Mexican, Female, Wicked and Thirty-Three: An Interview with Writer Sandra Cisneros." *The Americas Review* 18, no. 1 (Spring 1990): 64-80.

Rogers, Linda Perkowski, and Kyriakos S. Markides. "Well-Being in the Postparental Stage in Mexican-American Women." *Research on Aging* 11, no. 4 (December 1989): 508-516.

Romero, Bertha. "The Exploitation of Mexican Women in the Canning Industry and the Effects of Capital Accumulation on Striking Workers." *Revista Mujeres* 3, no. 2 (June 1986): 16-20.

Romero, Gloria J. "Attributions for the Occupational Success/Failure of Ethnic Minority and Nonminority Women." *Sex Roles* 14, no. 7-8 (April 1986): 445-452.

Romero, Gloria J., Felipe G. Castro, and Richard C. Cervantes. "Latinas without Work: Family, Occupational, and Economic Stress Following Unemployment." *Psychology of Women Quarterly* 12, no. 3 (September 1988): 281-297.

Romero, Mary. "Day Work in the Suburbs: The Work Experience of Chicana Private Household Workers." In *The Worth of Women's Work: A Qualitative Synthesis*, edited by Anne Statham, Eleanor M. Miller and Hans O. Mauksch. Albany: State Univ. of New York Press, 1988.

_____. "Domestic Service in the Transition from Rural to Urban Life: The Case of la Chicana." *Women's Studies Quarterly* 13, no. 3 (1987): 199-222.

_____. "Twice Protected? Assessing the Impact of Affirmative Action on

Mexican American Women." *Ethnicity and Women* 5 (1986): 135-156. Also in *Journal of Hispanic Policy* 3 (1989): 83-101.

Romero, Mary, and Eric Margolis. "Tending the Beets: Campesinas and the Great Western Sugar Company." *Revista Mujeres* 2, no. 2 (June 1985): 17-27.

Romero-Gwynn, Eunice, and Lucia Carías. "Breast-Feeding Intentions and Practice among Hispanic Mothers in Southern California." *Pediatrics* 84, no. 4 (October 1989): 626-632.

Rosaldo, Renato. "Fables of the Fallen Guy." In *Criticism in the Borderlands: Studies in Chicano Literature, Culture, and Ideology*, edited by Hector Calderón and José David Saldívar, [84]-93. Durham, North Carolina: Duke Univ. Press, 1991.

Rose, Margaret. "Traditional and Nontraditional Patterns of Female Activism in the United Farm Workers of America, 1962-1980." *Frontiers: A Journal of Women Studies* 11, no. 1 (1990): [26]-32.

Rosenhouse-Persson, Sandra, and Georges Sabagh. "Attitudes toward Abortion among Catholic Mexican-American Women: The Effects of Religiosity and Education." *Demography* 20, no. 1 (Fall 1983): 87-98.

Ross, Catherine E., John Mirowsky, and Patricia Ulbrich. "Distress and the Traditional Female Role: A Comparison of Mexicans and Anglos." *American Journal of Sociology* 89, no. 3 (November 1983): 670-682.

Rubio Goldsmith, Raquel. "Shipwrecked in the Desert: A Short History of the Adventures and Struggles for Survival of the Mexican Sisters of the House of the Providence in Douglas, Arizona During Their First Twenty-Two Years of Existence (1927-1949)." *Renato Rosaldo Lecture Series Monograph* 1 (Summer, 1985): [39]-67.

Ruelas, J. Oshi. "Moments of Change." *Revista Mujeres* 4, no. 1 (January 1987): 23-33.

Ruiz, Vicki L. "A Promise Fulfilled: Mexican Cannery Workers in Southern California." *The Pacific Historian* 30, no. 2 (1986): 51-61. Also in *Unequal Sisters: A Multicultural Reader in U.S. Women's History*, edited by Ellen Carol DuBois and Vicki L. Ruiz, 264-274. New York: Routledge, 1990.

———. "And Miles to Go . . .: Mexican Women and Work, 1930-1985." In *Western Women: Their Lands, Their Lives*, edited by Lillian Schlissel, Vicki L. Ruiz, and Janice Monk, 117-136. Albuquerque: Univ. of New Mexico Press, 1988.

———. "By the Day or Week: Mexicana Domestic Workers in El Paso." In *Women on the U.S.-Mexico Border: Responses to Change*, edited by Vicki L. Ruiz and Susan Tiano, 61-76. Boston: Allen & Unwin, 1987.

———. "California's Early Pioneers: Spanish/Mexican Women." *Social Studies Review* 29, no. 1 (Fall 1989): 24-30.

———. *Cannery Women/Cannery Lives: Mexican Women, Unionization, and the*

California Food Processing Industry, 1930-1950. Albuquerque: Univ. of New Mexico Press, 1987.

_____. "Obreras y madres: Labor Activism among Mexican Women and Its Impact on the Family." *Renato Rosaldo Lecture Series Monograph* 1 (Summer 1985): [19]-38.

Ruiz, Vicki L., and Susan Tiano, eds. *Women on the U.S.-Mexico Border: Responses to Change.* Boston: Allen & Unwin, 1987.

Sabagh, Georges. "Fertility Expectations and Behavior among Mexican Americans in Los Angeles, 1973-82." *Social Science Quarterly* 65, no. 2 (June 1984): 594-608.

Sabagh, Georges, and David López. "Religiosity and Fertility: The Case of Chicanas." *Social Forces* 59, no. 2 (1980): 431-439.

Sable, Martin H. *Las Maquiladoras: Assembly and Manufacturing Plants on the United States-Mexico Border.* New York: Haworth Press, 1989.

Sabogal, Fabio, et al. "Hispanic Familism and Acculturation: What Changes and What Doesn't?" *Hispanic Journal of Behavioral Sciences* 9, no. 4 (December 1987): 397-412.

Saenz, Rogelio, et al. "The Effects of Employment and Marital Relations on Depression among Mexican American Women." *Journal of Marriage and the Family* 51, no. 1 (February 1989): 239-251.

Salas, Elizabeth. *Soldaderas in the Mexican Military: Myth and History.* Austin: Univ. of Texas Press, 1990.

Salazar, Sandra A. "Chicanas As Healers." *La Chicana: Building for the Future*, 107-119. Oakland, Calif.: National Hispanic Univ., 1981.

Salazar Parr, Carmen. "La Chicana in Literature." In *Chicano Studies: A Multidisciplinary Approach*, edited by Eugene E. Garcia, Francisco Lomeli, and Isidro D. Ortiz, 120-134. New York: Teachers College Press, 1984.

Salazar Parr, Carmen, and Genevieve M. Ramírez. "The Chicana in Chicano Literature." In *Chicano Literature: A Reference Guide*, edited by Julio A. Martínez and Francisco A. Lomeli, 97-107. Westport, Conn.: Greenwood Press, 1985.

Saldívar, José David. "Towards a Chicano Poetics: The Making of the Chicano Subject." *Confluencia* 1, no. 2 (Spring 1986), p. 10-17.

Saldívar, Ramón. "Dialectics in the Chicano Novel: Gender and Difference." In *Mexico and the United States: Intercultural Relations in the Humanities*, edited by Juanita Luna-Lawhn, et al., 151-160. San Antonio: San Antonio College, 1984.

_____. "The Dialectics of Subjectivity: Gender and Difference in Isabella Ríos, Sandra Cisneros, and Cherríe Moraga." In *Chicano Narrative: The Dialectics of Difference*, edited by Ramón Saldívar, 171-199. Madison: Univ. of Wisconsin Press, 1990.

Saldívar-Hull, Sonia. "Feminism on the Border: From Gender Politics to

Geopolitics." In *Criticism in the Borderlands: Studies in Chicano Literature, Culture, and Ideology*, edited by Hector Calderón and José David Saldívar, [203]-220. Durham, North Carolina: Duke Univ. Press, 1991.

Salgado de Snyder, Nelly. "Factors Associated with Acculturative Stress and Depressive Symptomatology among Married Mexican Immigrant Women." *Psychology of Women Quarterly* 11, no. 4 (December 1987): 475-488.

_____. "The Role of Ethnic Loyalty among Mexican Immigrant Women." *Hispanic Journal of Behavioral Sciences* 9, no. 3 (September 1987): 287-298.

Salgado de Snyder, Nelly, Richard C. Cervantes, and Amado M. Padilla. "Gender and Ethnic Differences in Psychosocial Stress and Generalized Distress among Hispanics." *Sex Roles* 22, no. 7-8 (April 1990): 441-453.

Salgado de Snyder, Nelly, and Amado M. Padilla. "Cultural and Ethnic Maintenance of Interethnically Married Mexican-Americans." *Human Organization* 41, no. 4 (Winter 1982): 359-362.

Salgado de Snyder, Nelly, Cynthia M. López, and Amado M. Padilla. "Ethnic Identity and Cultural Awareness among the Offspring of Mexican Interethnic Marriages." *Journal of Early Adolescence* 2, no. 3 (Fall 1982): 277-282.

San Miguel, Rachel. "Being Hispanic in Houston: My Name Is Carmen Quezada." *The Americas Review* 16, no. 1 (Spring, 1988): 44-52.

Sánchez, George J. "'Go After the Women': Americanization and the Mexican Immigrant Woman, 1915-1929." In *Unequal Sisters: A Multicultural Reader in U.S. Women's History*, edited by Ellen Carol DuBois and Vicki L. Ruiz, 250-263. New York: Routledge, 1990.

Sánchez, Marta Ester. *Contemporary Chicana Poetry: A Critical Approach to an Emerging Literature*. Berkeley: Univ. of California Press, 1985.

_____. "Gender and Ethnicity in Contemporary Chicana Poetry." *Critical Perspectives of Third World America* 2, no. 1 (Fall 1984): 147-166.

_____. "The Birthing of the Poetic "I" in Alma Villanueva's *Mother May I?*: The Search for a Feminine Identity." In *Beyond Stereotypes: The Critical Analysis of Chicana Literature*, edited by María Herrera-Sobek, 108-152. Binghamton, N.Y.: Bilingual Press/Editorial Bilingüe, 1985.

Sánchez, Rosaura. "Chicana Prose Writers: The Case of Gina Valdés and Sylvia Lizárraga." In *Beyond Stereotypes: The Critical Analysis of Chicana Literature*, edited by María Herrera-Sobek, 61-70. Binghamton, N.Y.: Bilingual Press/Editorial Bilingüe, 1985.

_____. "El discurso femenino en la literatura chicana." In *Mujer y literatura mexicana y chicana: Culturas en contacto*, edited by Aralia López-González, et al., 37-43. Mexico: Colegio de la Frontera Norte, 1988.

Santiago, Myrna I. "La Chicana." *fem* 8, no. 34 (June-July 1984): 5-9.

Santillán, Richard. "Rosita the Riveter: Midwest Mexican American Women During World War II, 1941-1945." *Perspectives in Mexican American Studies* 2 (1989): 115-147.

Saracho, Olivia N. "Women and Education: Sex Role Modifications of Mexican American women." *Education* 109, no. 3 (Spring 1989): 295-301.

Saragoza, Alex M. "The Conceptualization of the History of the Chicano Family." In *The State of Chicano Research on Family, Labor, and Migration*, edited by Armando Valdez, Albert Camarillo, and Tomás Almaguer, 111-138. Stanford, Calif.: Stanford Center for Chicano Research, 1983.

Schecter, Hope Mendoza. *Activist in the Labor Movement, the Democratic Party, and the Mexican-American Community: An Interview.* Berkeley: Regional Oral History Office, Bancroft Library, Univ. of California, Berkeley, 1980.

Schlissel, Lillian, Vicki L. Ruiz, and Janice Monk, eds. *Western Women: Their Land, Their Lives.* Albuquerque: Univ. of New Mexico Press, 1988.

Schwartz-Lookinland, Sandra, Linda C. McKeever, and Mary Saputo. "Compliance with Antibiotic Regimens in Hispanic Mothers." *Patient Education and Counseling* 13, no. 2 (April 1989), p. 171-182.

Scrimshaw, Susan C. M., et al. "Factors Affecting Breastfeeding among Women of Mexican Origin or Descent in Los Angeles." *American Journal of Public Health* 77. no. 4 (April 1987): 467-470.

Segura, Denise. "Chicana and Mexican Immigrant Women at Work: Barriers to Employment and Mobility." In *Women of Color in American Society*, edited by Maxine Baca Zinn and B. T. Dill. Philadelphia: Temple Univ. Press, in press.

_____. "Chicana and Mexican Immigrant Women at Work: The Impact of Class, Race and Gender on Occupational Mobility." *Gender & Society* 3, no. 1 (March 1989): 37-52.

_____. "Conflict in Social Relations at Work: A Chicana Perspective." In *Estudios Chicanos and the Politics of Community*, edited by Mary Romero and Cordelia Candelaria, 110-131. Colorado Springs: National Association for Chicano Studies, 1989.

_____. "Familism and Employment among Chicanas and Mexican Immigrant Women." In *Mexicanas at Work in the United States*, edited by Margarita B. Melville, 24-32. Houston: Mexican American Studies Program, Univ. of Houston, 1988.

_____. "Labor Market Stratification: The Chicana Experience." *Berkeley Journal of Sociology* 29 (1984): 57-91.

_____. "The Interplay of Familism and Patriarchy on the Employment of

Chicana and Mexican Immigrant Women." In *Renato Rosaldo Lecture Series Monograph* 5, (1989): 35-53.

Seligson, Mitchell, and Edward J. Williams. *Maquiladoras and Migration Workers in the Mexico-United States Border Industrialization Program.* Austin: Mexico-United States Border Research Program, Univ. of Texas at Austin, 1981.

Shapiro, Johanna, and Eleanor B. Saltzer. "Attitudes toward Breast-feeding among Mexican-American Women." *Journal of Tropical Pediatrics* 31, no. 1 (February 1985): 13-16.

Shapiro, Johanna, and Ken Tittle. "Maternal Adaptation to Child Disability in a Hispanic Population." *Family Relations* 39, no. 2 (April 1990): 179-185.

Shapiro, Peter. "Watsonville Shows 'It Can Be Done.'" *Guardian* 39, no. 24 (March 25, 1987): 1, 9.

Sheridan, Thomas E. "From Luisa Espinel to Lalo Guerrero: Tucson's Mexican Musicians Before World War II." *Journal of Arizona History* 25, no. 3 (Fall 1984): 285-300.

Sierra, Christine Marie. "The University Setting Reinforces Inequality." In *Chicana Voices: Intersections of Class, Race, and Gender,* edited by Teresa Córdova et al., 5-7. Austin: Center for Mexican American Studies, UT Austin, 1986.

Simon, Rita J., and Margo DeLey. "The Work Experience of Undocumented Mexican Women Migrants in Los Angeles." *International Migration Review* 18, no. 4 (Winter 1984): 1212-1229.

Simoniello, Katina. "On Investigating the Attitudes toward Achievement and Success in Eight Professional U.S. Mexican Women." *Aztlán* 12, no. 1 (Spring 1981): 121-137.

Sklair, Leslie. *Maquiladoras: Annotated Bibliography and Research Guide to Mexico's In-Bond Industry, 1980-1988.* La Jolla: Center for U.S.-Mexican Studies, Univ. of California, San Diego, 1989.

Slesinger, Doris P., and Yoshitka Okada. "Fertility Patterns of Hispanic Migrant Farm Women: Testing the Effect of Assimilation." *Rural Sociology* 49, no. 3 (Fall 1984): 430-440.

Smith, Bradford M. "The Measurement of Narcissism in Asian, Caucasian, and Hispanic American Women." *Psychological Reports* 67, no. 3 (December 1990): 779-785.

Smith, Jack C. "Trends in the Incidence of Breastfeeding for Hispanics of Mexican Origin and Anglos on the US-Mexican Border." *American Journal of Public Health* 72, no. 1 (January, 1982): 59-61.

Smith, Peggy B. "Sociologic Aspects of Adolescent Fertility and Child-bearing among Hispanics." *Journal of Developmental and Behavioral Pediatrics* 7, no. 6 (December 1986): 346-349.

Smith, Peggy B., Laurilynn McGill, and Raymond B. Wait. "Hispanic

Adolescent Conception and Contraception Profiles." *Journal of Adolescent Health Care* 8, no. 4 (July 1987): 352-355.

Solorzano Torres, Rosalía. "Female Mexican Immigrants in San Diego County." In *Women on the U.S.-Mexico Border: Responses to Change*, edited by Vicki L. Ruiz and Susan Tiano, 41-59. Boston: Allen & Unwin, 1987.

_____. "Women, Labor, and the U.S.-Mexico Border: Mexican Maids in El Paso, Texas." In *Mexicanas at Work in the United States*, edited by Margarita B. Melville, 75-83. Houston: Mexican American Studies Program, Univ. of Houston, 1988.

Sonntag, Iliana. "Hacia una bibliografía de poesía femenina chicana." *La Palabra* 2, no. 2 (Spring [Fall] 1980): 91-109.

Sorenson, Ann Marie. "Fertility, Expectations and Ethnic Identity among Mexican-American Adolescents: An Expression of Cultural Ideals." *Sociological Perspectives* 28, no. 3 (July 1985): 339-360.

_____. "The Fertility and Language Characteristics of Mexican-American and Non-Hispanic Husbands and Wives." *Sociological Quarterly* 29, no. 1 (March 1988): 111-130.

Sosa Riddell, Adaljiza, ed. *Policy Development: Chicana/Latina Summer Research Institute [handbook]*. Davis: Chicano Studies Program, Univ. of California, Davis, 1989.

Soto, Shirlene. *Emergence of the Modern Mexican Woman: Her Participation in Revolution and Struggle for Equality, 1910-1940*. Denver: Arden Press, 1990.

_____. "La Malinche: 16th Century Leader." *Intercambios Femeniles* 2, no. 6 (Spring 1987): 13.

_____. "Tres modelos culturales: la Virgen de Guadalupe, la Malinche y la Llorona." *fem* 10, no. 48 (October-November 1986): 13-16.

Spector, Rachel E. *The Utilization of Parteras as a Source of Maternal/Child Health Care along the U.S./Mexico Border*. Austin: Lyndon B. Johnson School of Public Affairs, Univ. of Texas, 1983.

Staudt, Kathleen. "Programming Women's Empowerment: A Case from Northern Mexico." In *Women on the U.S. Mexico Border: Responses to Change*, edited by Vicki L. Ruiz and Susan Tiano, 155-173. Boston: Allen & Unwin, 1987.

Steigelfest, Annette. "Ethnicity and Sex Role Socialization." *Bilingual Journal* 6, no. 3 (Spring 1982): 11-15, 24.

Sternbach, Nancy Saporta. "'A Deep Racial Memory of Love:' The Chicana Feminism of Cherríe Moraga." In *Breaking Boundaries: Latina Writing and Critical Readings*, edited by Asunción Horno-Delgado, et al., 48-61. Amherst: Univ. of Massachusetts Press, 1989.

Stephen, Elizabeth Hervey. *At the Crossroads: Fertility of Mexican-American Women*. New York: Garland Publishing, 1989.

Stewart, Kenneth L., and Arnoldo de León. "Fertility among Mexican Americans and Anglos in Texas, 1900." *Borderlands Journal* 9, no. 1 (Spring 1986): 61-67.

———. "Work Force Participation among Mexican Immigrant Women in Texas, 1900." *Borderlands Journal* 9, no. 1 (Spring 1986): 69-74.

Stoddard, Ellwyn R. *Maquila: Assembly Plants in Northern Mexico.* El Paso: Texas Western Press, 1987.

Stolp, Chandler, and David Warner. "Mental Health Service Utilization of California Hospitals by Age, Ethnicity, and Sex in 1983." In *Mental Health Issues of the Mexican Origin Population in Texas: Proceedings of the Fifth Robert Lee Sutherland Seminar in Mental Health*, edited by Reymundo Rodríguez and Marion Tolbert Coleman, [116]-134. Austin: Hogg Foundation for Mental Health, Univ. of Texas, 1987.

Stoner, K. Lynn. *Latinas of the Americas: A Source Book.* New York: Garland Publishing, 1989.

Stroup-Benham, Christine A., and Fernando M. Treviño. "Reproductive Characteristics of Mexican-American, Mainland Puerto Rican, and Cuban-American Women: Data from the Hispanic Health and Nutrition Examination Survey." *JAMA: Journal of the American Medical Association* 265, no. 2 (January 9, 1991): 222-226.

Stroup-Benham, Christine A., Fernando M. Treviño, and Dorothy B. Treviño. "Alcohol Consumption Patterns among Mexican American Mothers and among Children from Single-and Dual-Headed Households: Findings from HHANES 1982-84." *American Journal of Public Health* 80 (December 1990): 36-41.

Suárez, Cecilia Cota Robles, and Lupe Anguiano. *Every Woman's Right: The Right to Quality Education and Economic Independence.* Montebello, Calif.: National Chicana Foundation, [1981].

Sullivan, Teresa A. "The Occupational Prestige of Women Immigrants: A Comparison of Cubans and Mexicans." *International Migration Review* 18, no. 4 (Winter 1984): 1045-1062.

Summar, Polly. "A Marriage of Old & New: A Traditional Ceremony in El Rito." *New Mexico Magazine* 62 (April 1984): 60-66.

Sweeney, Mary Anne, and Claire Gulino. "The Health Belief Model As an Explanation for Breast-feeding Practices in a Hispanic Population." *ANS: Advances in Nursing Science* 9, no. 4 (July 1987): 35-50.

Swicegood, Gray, et al. "Language Usage and Fertility in the Mexican-Origin Population of the United States." *Demography* 25, no. 1 (February 1988): 17-33.

Tafolla, Carmen. "Chicano Literature: Beyond Beginnings." In *A Gift of Tongues: Critical Challenges in Contemporary American Poetry*, edited by Marie Harris and Kathleen Agüero, 206-225. Athens: Univ. of Georgia Press, 1987.

_____. *To Split a Human: Mitos, machos y la mujer chicana.* San Antonio, Tex.: Mexican American Cultural Center, 1985.

Tavera Rivera, Margarita. "Autoridad in absentia: La censura patriarcal en la narrativa chicana." In *Mujer y literatura mexicana y chicana: Culturas en contacto,* edited by Aralia López-González, et al., [65]-69. Mexico: Colegio de la Frontera Norte, 1988.

Taylor, Elena. "Conversations with a Chicana Physician." *Revista Mujeres* 1, no. 2 (June 1984): 44-46.

Taylor, Paul S. "Mexican Women in Los Angeles Industry in 1928." *Aztlán* 11, no. 1 (Spring 1980): 99-131.

"Three Latina Artists." *Americas 2001* 1, no. 5 (March-April 1988): 21.

Three times a woman: Chicana poetry. Tempe, Ariz.: Bilingual Press/Editorial Bilingüe, 1989. Poetry by Alicia Gaspar de Alba, María Herrera-Sobek and Demetria Martínez.

Tiano, Susan. "Labor Composition and Gender Stereotypes in the Maquila." *Journal of Borderland Studies* 5, no. 1 (Spring 1990): 20-24.

_____. "Maquiladoras in Mexicali: Integration or Exploitation?" In *Women on the U.S.-Mexico Border: Responses to Change,* edited by Vicki L. Ruiz and Susan Tiano, 77-101. Boston: Allen & Unwin, 1987.

_____. "Maquiladoras, Women's Work, and Unemployment in Northern Mexico." *Aztlán* 15, no. 2 (Fall 1984): 341-378.

_____. "Women's Work and Unemployment in Northern Mexico." In *Women on the U.S.-Mexico Border: Responses to Change,* edited by Vicki L. Ruiz and Susan Tiano, 17-39. Boston: Allen & Unwin, 1987.

Tienda, Marta. "Headship and Household Composition among Blacks, Hispanics and Other Whites." *Social Forces* 61 (Fall 1982): 508-531.

Tienda, Marta, and Jennifer Glass. "Household Structure and Labor-Force Participation of Black, Hispanic, and White Mothers." *Demography* 22, no. 3 (August 1985): 381-394.

Tienda, Marta, and Patricia Guhleman. "The Occupational Position of Employed Hispanic Women." In *Hispanics in the U.S. Economy,* edited by George J. Borjas and Marta Tienda, 243-273. Orlando, Fla.: Academic Press, 1985.

Timberlake, Andrea, et al., eds. *Women of Color and Southern Women: A Bibliography of Social Science Research, 1975-1988.* Memphis, Tenn: Center for Research on Women, Memphis State Univ., 1988. See also updates.

Torano, María Elena, and Lourdes Alvarez. "Hispanas: Success in America." In *The State of Hispanic America* II, 151-167. Oakland, Calif.: National Hispanic Center for Advanced Studies and Policy Analysis and the National Hispanic Univ., 1982.

Torres, Aida, and Susheela Singh. "Contraceptive Practice among Hispanic Adolescents." *Family Planning Perspectives* 18, no. 4 (July-August 1986): 193-194.

Torres Raines, Rosario. "The Mexican American Woman and Work: Intergenerational Perspectives of Comparative Ethnic Groups." In *Mexicanas at Work in the United States*, edited by Margarita B. Melville, 33-46. Houston: Mexican American Studies Program, Univ. of Houston, 1988.

Treacy, Mary Jane. "The Ties That Bind: Women and Community in Evangelina Vigil's *Thirty an' Seen a Lot.*" In *Breaking Boundaries: Latina Writing and Critical Readings*, edited by Asunción Horno-Delgado, et al., 82-93. Amherst: Univ. of Massachusetts Press, 1989.

Trevathan, Wenda R. "First Conversations: Verbal Contact of Mother-Newborn Interaction." *Journal of Cross-Cultural Psychology* 19, no. 1 (March 1988): 65-77.

Triandis, Harry C., et al. "Role Perceptions of Hispanic Young Adults." *Journal of Cross-Cultural Psychology* 15, no. 3 (September 1984): 297-320.

Trotter, Robert T. "Ethnic and Sexual Patterns of Alcohol Use: Anglo and Mexican American College Students." *Adolescence* 17, no. 66 (Summer 1982): 305-325.

Trujillo, Carla. "Chicana Lesbians: Fear and Loathing in the Chicano Community." In *Chicana Lesbians: The Girls Our Mothers Warned Us About*, edited by Carla Trujillo, 186-194. Berkeley: Third Woman Press, 1991.

_____, ed. *Chicana Lesbians: The Girls Our Mothers Warned Us About.* Berkeley: Third Woman Press, 1991.

Trujillo, Roberto G., and Andrés Rodríguez. *Literatura chicana: Creative and Critical Writings through 1984.* Oakland, Calif.: Floricanto Press, 1985.

Tucker, Barbara, and Carolyn Huerta. "A Study of Developmental Tasks As Perceived by Young Adult Mexican-American Females." *Lifelong Learning* 10, no. 4 (January 1987): 4-7.

U.S. Department of Labor, Women's Bureau. *Adelante mujer hispana: A Conference Model for Hispanic Women.* Washington, D.C.: The Bureau, 1980.

U.S. National Institute of Education. *Conference on the Educational and Occupational Needs of Hispanic Women, June 29-30, 1976; December 10-12, 1976.* Washington, D.C.: U.S. Department of Education, 1980.

Valadez, Esther. "[The Role of the Latina]." *Chicano Law Review* 6 (1983): 21-24.

Valdés, Guadalupe, and Manuel Cárdenas. "Positive Speech Accommodation in the Language of Mexican American Bilinguals: Are Women Really More Sensitive?" *Hispanic Journal of Behavioral Sciences* 3, no. 4 (December 1981): 347-359.

Valdés, Guadalupe, Herman García, and Diamantina Storment. "Sex-Related Speech Accommodations among Mexican-American Bilinguals: A Pilot Study of Language Choice in Customer-Server Interactions." In *Bilingualism and Language Contact: Spanish, English, and Native American Languages*, edited by Florence Barkin, Elizabeth A. Brandt, and Jacob Ornstein-Galicia, 187-200. New York: Teachers College, 1982.

Valdez, Avelardo. "Recent Increases in Intermarriage by Mexican American Males: Bexar County, Texas from 1971 to 1980." *Social Science Quarterly* 64 (March 1983): 136-144.

Valdez, Diana. "Mexican American Family Research: A Critical Review and Conceptual Framework." *De Colores* 6, no. 1-2 (1982): 48-63.

Valenzuela-Crocker, Elvira. "Women, Power and the Vote." *Nuestro* 8, no. 6 (August 1984): 43-44.

Varela, Vivian. "Hispanic Women's Resource Guide." *Commonground Magazine* 1, no. 3 (May 1983): 14-15.

Vargas-Willis, Gloria, and Richard C. Cervantes. "Consideration of Psychosocial Stress in the Treatment of the Latina Immigrant." *Hispanic Journal of Behavioral Sciences* 9, no. 3 (September 1987): 315-329.

Vásquez, Mario F. "Immigrant Workers in the Apparel Manufacturing Industry in Southern California." In *Mexican Immigrant Workers in the U.S.*, edited by Antonio Ríos Bustamante, 85-96. Los Angeles: Chicano Studies Research Center Publications, Univ. of California, Los Angeles, 1981.

Vásquez, Melba J. T. "Confronting Barriers to the Participation of Mexican American Women in Higher Education." *Hispanic Journal of Behavioral Sciences* 4, no. 2 (June 1982): 147-165.

_____. "Power and Status of the Chicana: A Social-Psychological Perspective." In *Chicano Psychology*. 2d ed., edited by Joe L. Martínez, Jr. and Richard H. Mendoza, 269-287. Orlando, Fla.: Academic Press, 1984.

Vásquez, Melba J. T., and Anna M. González. "Sex Roles among Chicanos: Stereotypes, Challenges and Changes." In *Explorations in Chicano Psychology*, edited by Augustine Barón, Jr, 50-70. New York: Praeger, 1981.

Vásquez-Nuttall, Ena, Ivonne Romero-García, and Brunilda De León. "Sex Roles and Perceptions of Femininity and Masculinity of Hispanic Women: A Review of the Literature." *Psychology of Women Quarterly* 11, no. 4 (December 1987): 409-425.

Vega, Alicia. "Three Latinas in Hollywood." *Americas 2001* 1, no. 7 (July-August 1988): 4-6.

Vega, William A., Bohdan Kolody, and Juan Ramón Valle. "Marital Strain, Coping, and Depression among Mexican-American Women." *Journal of Marriage and the Family* 50, no. 2 (May, 1988): 391-403.

_____. "Migration and Mental Health: An Empirical Test of Depression Risk Factors among Immigrant Mexican Women." *International*

Migration Review 21, no. 3 (Fall 1987): 512-530.

———. "The Relationship of Marital-Status, Confidante Support, and Depression among Mexican Immigrant Women." *Journal of Marriage and the Family* 48, no. 3 (1986): 597-605.

Vega, William A., George Warheit, and Kenneth Meinhardt. "Marital Disruption and the Prevalence of Depressive Symptomatology among Anglos and Mexican Americans." *Journal of Marriage and the Family* 46 no. 4 (November 1984): 817-824.

Vega, William A., et al. "Depressive Symptoms and Their Correlates among Immigrant Mexican Women in the United States." *Social Science and Medicine* 22, no. 6 (1986): 645-652.

Velásquez, Roberto J., Wendell J. Callahan, and Ricardo Carrillo. "MMPI Differences among Mexican-American Male and Female Psychiatric Inpatients." *Psychological Reports* 68, no. 1 (February 1991): 123-127.

Velázquez Treviño, Gloria. "Jovita González: una voz de resistencia cultural en la temprana narrativa chicana." In *Mujer y literatura mexicana y chicana: Culturas en contacto,* edited by Aralia López-González, et al., [77]-83. Mexico: Colegio de la Frontera Norte, 1988.

Ventura, Stephanie J., and Selma M. Taffel. "Childbearing Characteristics of U.S.-and Foreign-born Hispanic Mothers." *Public Health Reports* 100, no. 6 (November-December 1985), p. 647-652.

Veyna, Angelina F. "Una vista al pasado: la mujer en Nuevo Mexico, 1744-1767." *Trabajos Monográficos* 1, no. 1 (1985), p. 28-42.

———. "Women in Early New Mexico: A Preliminary View." In *Chicana Voices: Intersections of Class, Race, and Gender,* edited by Teresa Córdova, et al., 120-135. Austin: Center for Mexican American Studies, UT Austin, 1986.

Vigil, Evangelina, ed. "Woman of Her Word: Hispanic Women Write [special issue]." *Revista Chicano-Riqueña* 11, no. 3-4 (Fall, 1983).

Vigil, James Diego. "The Nexus of Class, Culture and Gender in the Education of Mexican American Females." In *The Broken Web: The Educational Experience of Hispanic American Women,* edited by Teresa McKenna and Flora Ida Ortiz, 79-103. Claremont, Calif.: Tomás Rivera Center; Berkeley: Floricanto Press, 1988.

Villalobos, Rolando M. *Research Guide to the Literature on Northern Mexico's Maquiladora Assembly Industry.* [Stanford, Calif.?]: Zapata Underground Press, 1988.

Viramontes, Helena María. "'Nopalitos:' The Making of Fiction." In *Breaking Boundaries: Latina Writing and Critical Readings,* edited by Asunción Horno-Delgado, et al., 33-38. Amherst: Univ. of Massachusetts, Press, 1989.

Vivo, Paquita. "Voces de Hispanas: Hispanic Women and Their Conerns." In *Hispanics and Grantmakers: A Special Report of Foundation News*, 35-39. Washington, D.C.: Council on Foundations, 1981.

Vogeley, Nancy. "Bernice Zamora." In *Chicano Writers, First Series, Dictionary of Literary Biography* 82: 289-294. Detroit: Bruccoli Clark Layman, 1989.

Votaw, Carmen Delgado. "Cultural Influences on Hispanic Feminism." *Agenda* 11, no. 4 (1981): 44-49.

Warren, Charles W., Jack C. Smith, and Roger W. Rochat. "Differentials in the Planning Status of the Most Recent Live Birth to Mexican Americans and Anglos." *Public Health Reports* 98, no. 2 (March-April 1983): 152-160.

Watkins, Elizabeth L., Mary D. Peoples, and Connie Gates. "Health and Social Needs of Women Farmworkers: Receiving Maternity Care at a Migrant Health Center." *Migration Today* 13, no. 2 (1985): 39-42.

Weller, Susan C., and Claibourne I. Dungy. "Personal Preferences and Ethnic Variations among Anglo and Hispanic Breast and Bottle Feeders." *Social Science & Medicine* 23, no. 6 (1986): 539-548.

Whiteford, Linda. "Migrants No Longer: Changing Family Structure of Mexican Americans in South Texas." *De Colores* 6, no. 1-2 (1982): 99-108.

Williams, Brett. "Why Migrant Women Feed Their Husbands Tamales: Foodways as a Basis for a Revisionist View of Tejano Family Life." In *Ethnic and Regional Foodways in the United States*, edited by Linda Keller Brown and Kay Mussell, 113-126. Knoxville: Univ. of Tennessee Press, 1984.

Williams, Joyce E. "Mexican American and Anglo Attitudes about Sex Roles and Rape." *Free Inquiry in Creative Sociology* 13, no. 1 (May 1985): 15-20.

Williams, Norma. "Changes in Funeral Patterns and Gender Roles among Mexican Americans." In *Women on the U.S.-Mexico Border: Responses to Change*, edited by Vicki L. Ruiz and Susan Tiano, 197-217. Boston: Allen & Unwin, 1987.

——. "Role Making among Married Mexican American Women: Issues of Class and Ethnicity." *Journal of Applied Behavioral Science* 24, no. 2 (1988): 203-217.

——. *The Mexican American Family: Tradition and Change*. Dix Hills, New York: General Hall, Inc., 1990.

Williams, Ronald L., et al. "Pregnancy Outcomes among Spanish-surname Women in California." *American Journal of Public Health* 76, no. 4 (April 1986): 387-391.

Winkler, Karen J. "Scholars Say Issues of Diversity Have 'Revolutionized' Field of Chicano Studies." *Chronicle of Higher Education* 37, no. 4 (September 26, 1990): A4-A9.

Winter, Michael, Nancy Felipe Russo, and Hortensia Amaro. "The Use of Inpatient Mental Health Services by Hispanic Women." *Psychology of Women Quarterly* 11, no. 4 (December 1987): 427-441.

Woodward, Carolyn. "Dare to Write: Virginia Woolf, Tillie Olsen, Gloria Anzaldúa." In *Changing Our Power: An Introduction to Women Studies*, edited by Jo Whitehorse Cochran, et al., 336-349. Dubuque, Iowa: Kendall/Hunt, 1988.

Yarbro-Bejarano, Yvonne. "Cherríe Moraga." In *Chicano Writers, First Series, Dictionary of Literary Biography* 82: 165-177. Detroit: Bruccoli Clark Layman, 1989.

_____. "Cherríe Moraga's *Giving up the Ghost*: The Representation of Female Desire." *Third Woman* 3, no. 1-2 (1986): 113-120.

_____. "Chicana Literature from a Chicana Feminist Perspective." *The Americas Review* 15, no. 3-4 (Fall-Winter 1987): 139-145.

_____. "Chicanas' Experience in Collective Theatre: Ideology and Form." *Women & Performance* 2, no. 2 (1985): 45-58.

_____. "De-Constructing the Lesbian Body: Cherríe Moraga's *Loving in the War Years*." In *Chicana Lesbians: The Girls Our Mothers Warned Us About*, edited by Carla Trujillo, 143-155. Berkeley: Third Woman Press, 1991.

_____. "Primer encuentro de lesbianas feministas latinoamericanas y caribeñas." *Third Woman* 4 (1989): 143-146.

_____. "Teatropoesia by Chicanas in the Bay Area: Tongues of Fire." *Revista Chicano-Riqueña* 11, no. 1 (Spring 1983): 78-94.

_____. "The Female Subject in Chicano Theater: Sexuality, Race, and Class." *Theatre Journal* 38, no. 4 (December 1986): 389-407.

_____. "The Image of the Chicana in Teatro." In *Gathering Ground: New Writing and Art by Northwest Women of Color*, edited by Jo Cochran, J.T. Stewart and Mayumi Tsutakawa, 90-96. Seattle, Wash.: Seal Press, 1984.

Ybarra, Lea. "Empirical and Theoretical Developments in the Study of Chicano Families." In *The State of Chicano Research on Family, Labor, and Migration*, edited by Armando Valdez, Albert Camarillo, and Tomás Almaguer, 91-110. Stanford, Calif.: Stanford Center for Chicano Research, 1983.

_____. "Marital Decision-making and the Role of Machismo in the Chicano Family." *De Colores* 6, no. 1-2 (1982): 32-47.

_____. "Separating Myth from Reality: Socio-Economic and Cultural Influences on Chicanas and the World of Work." In *Mexicanas at Work in the United States*, edited by Margarita B. Melville, 12-23. Houston: Mexican American Studies Program, Univ. of Houston, 1988.

_____. "When Wives Work: The Impact on the Chicano Family." *Journal of Marriage and the Family* 44 (February 1982): 169-178.

Young, Gay. "Gender Identification and Working-Class Solidarity among Maquila Workers in Ciudad Juárez: Stereotypes and Realities." In *Women on the U.S.-Mexico Border: Responses to Change*, edited by Vicki L. Ruiz and Susan Tiano, 105-127. Boston: Allen & Unwin, 1987.

_____. "Women, Development and Human Rights: Issues in Integrated Transnational Production." *Journal of Applied Behavioral Science* 20, no. 4 (November 1984): 383-401.

Zambrana, Ruth E. *Bibliography on Maternal and Child Health Across Class, Race and Ethnicity.* Memphis, Tenn.: Memphis State Univ. Center for Research on Women, 1990.

_____. *Hispanic Professional Women: Work, Family and Health.* Los Angeles: National Network of Hispanic Women, 1987.

_____. "Research Issues: Family, Health, and Employment Patterns of Hispanic Women." *Research Bulletin (Spanish Speaking Mental Health Research Center, UCLA)* 3, no. 3 (July 1980): 10-11.

_____. "Toward Understanding the Educational Trajectory and Socialization of Latina Women." In *The Broken Web: The Educational Experience of Hispanic American Women*, edited by Teresa McKenna and Flora Ida Ortiz, 61-77. Claremont, Calif.: Tomás Rivera Center; Berkeley: Floricanto Press, 1988.

_____. *Work, Family, and Health: Latina Women in Transition.* Bronx, N.Y.: Hispanic Research Center, Fordham Univ., 1982.

Zambrana, Ruth E., and Sandra Frith. "Mexican-American Professional Women: Role Satisfaction Differences in Single and Multiple Role Lifestyles." *Journal of Social Behavior and Personality* 3, no. 4 (1988): 347-361.

Zambrano, Myrna. *Mejor sola que mal acompañada: para la mujer golpeada.* Seattle, Wash.: Seal Press, 1985.

Zapata, Jesse T., and Pat T. Jaramillo. "The Mexican American Family: An Adlerian Perspective." *Hispanic Journal of Behavioral Sciences* 3, no. 3 (September 1981): 275-290.

_____. "Research on the Mexican American Family." *Journal of Industrial Psychology* 77, no. 1 (1981): 72-85.

Zavala, Iris M. "Ideologías y autobiografías: perspectivas femeninas." *Third Woman* 1, no. 2 (1982): 35-39.

Zavella, Patricia. "'Abnormal intimacy': The Varying Work Networks of Chicana Cannery Workers." *Feminist Studies* 11, no. 3 (Fall 1985): 541-557.

_____. "The Impact of 'Sun Belt Industrialization' on Chicanas." *Frontiers: A Journal of Women Studies* 8, no. 1 (1984): 21-27.

_____. "The Impact of the Women's Factory Work on Chicano Families." *Revista Mujeres* (January 1988): 41-53.

_____. "The Politics of Race and Gender: Organizing Chicana Cannery

Workers in Northern California." In *Women and Politics of Empowerment: Perspectives from the Workplace and the Community*, edited by Ann Bookman and Sandra Morgan, 202-224. Philadelphia: Temple Univ. Press, 1988.

_____. "The Problematic Relationship of Feminism and Chicana Studies." *Women Studies Quarterly* 17, no. 1-2 (1989): 25-36.

_____. *Women's Work and Chicano Families: Cannery Workers of the Santa Clara Valley*. Ithaca: Cornell Univ. Press, 1987.

Zayas, Luis H. "Toward an Understanding of Suicide Risks in Young Hispanic Females." *Journal of Adolescent Research* 2, no. 1 (Spring 1987): 1-11.

Zeff, Shirley B. "A Cross-Cultural Study of Mexican American, Black American and White American Women of a Large Urban University." *Hispanic Journal of Behavioral Sciences* 4, no. 2 (June 1982): 245-261.

Zepeda, Marlene. "Selected Maternal-Infant Care Practices of Spanish-speaking Women." *JOGN Nursing* 11, no. 6 (November, December 1982): 371-374.

Zúñiga, María E. "Assessment Issues with Chicanas: Practice Implications." *Psychotherapy* 25, no. 2 (Summer 1988): 288-293.

Works Cited

Acuña, Rodolfo. 1981. *Occupied America: A History of Chicanos*. 2nd ed. New York: Harper and Row.

Adorno, Rolena. 1990. "New Perspectives in Colonial Spanish-American Literary Studies." *Journal of the Southwest* 32 (Summer): 173-91.

Alarcón, Norma. 1983. "Chicana Feminist Literature: A Re-Vision Through Malintzin/or Malintzin: Putting Flesh Back on the Object." In *This Bridge Called My Back: Writings By Radical Women of Color*, eds. Cherríe Moraga and Gloria Anzaldúa. 2nd ed. New York: Kitchen Table Press.

———. 1989. "*Traddutora, Traditora*: A Paradigmatic Figure of Chicana Feminism." *Cultural Critique* 13 (Fall): 57-88.

———. 1990. "The Theoretical Subject(s) of *This Bridge Called My Back and Anglo-American Feminism*." In *Making Face, Making Soul: Haciendo Caras*, ed. Gloria Anzaldúa, 356-69. San Francisco: Aunt Lute Foundation.

Alarcón, Norma, Ana Castillo, and Cherríe Moraga, eds. 1989. "The Sexuality of Latinas," *Third Woman* 4.

Almaguer, Tomás. 1971. "Toward the Study of Chicano Colonialism." *Aztlán, Chicano Journal of the Social Sciences and Arts* 2: 7-22.

Almaguer, Tomás, and Albert Camarillo. 1983. "Urban Chicano Workers in Historical Perspective: A Review of the Literature." In *The State of Chicano Research on Family, Labor and Migration*, eds. Armando Valdez, Albert Camarillo, and Tomás Almaguer, 3-32. Stanford: Stanford Center for Chicano Research.

Alvarez, R. 1971. "The Unique Psycho-historical Experience of the Mexican American." *Social Sciences Quarterly* 52: 15-29.

Anaya, R. A., and F. Lomeli. 1989. *Aztlán: Essays on the Chicano Homeland*. Albuquerque: Universisty of New Mexico Press.

Andersen, M. L. 1988. *Thinking About Women, Sociological Perspectives on Sex and Gender*. 2nd ed. New York: Macmillan.

Anzaldúa, Gloria. 1987. *Borderlands/ La Frontera: The New Mestiza*. San Francisco: Spinster/Aunt Lute.

Apodaca, María Linda. 1986. "A Double-Edged Sword: Hispanas and Liberal Feminism." *Crítica: A Journal of Critical Essays* 1 (Fall): 96-114.

Archibald, Robert. 1978. *The Economic Aspects of the California Missions*. Washington, D.C.: Academy of Franciscan History.

Archives of California. 62 vols. Bancroft Library, University of California, Berkeley.

Ardener, Edwin. 1975. "Belief and the Problem of Women." In *Perceiving*

Women, ed. Shirley Ardner. London: Malaby Press.

Ardener, Shirley, ed. 1975. *Perceiving Women*. London: Malaby Press.

Arditti, Rita, Renate Duelli Klein, and Shelly Minden. 1984. *Test-Tube Women: What Future for Motherhood?* London: Pandora Press.

Argüelles, Lourdes. 1990. A Survey of Latina Immigrant Sexuality. Paper read at National Association for Chicano Studies Conference, 29 March-1 April, Albuquerque. New Mexico.

Baca Zinn, M., L. Weber Cannon, E. Higginbotham, and B. Thorton Dill. 1986. "The Costs of Exclusionary Practices in Women's Studies." *Signs: Journal of Women in Culture and Society* 11 (Winter): 290-303.

Bakhtin, Mikhail M. 1981. *The Dialogic Imagination*. Ed. Michael Holquist, trans. Carly Emerson, and Michael Holquist. Austin: University of Texas Press.

———. 1964. *Rabelais and His World*. *Trans*. Helene Iswolsky. Bloomington: Indiana University Press.

Bancroft, Hubert Howe. 1884, 1885. *History of California*. 7 vols. San Francisco: A.L. Bancroft and Co.

Bannon, John Francis. 1970. *The Spanish Borderlands Frontier, 1531-1821*. New York: Holt, Rinehart and Winston.

Barber-Madden, R., and J. B. Kotch. 1990. "Maternity Care Financing: Universal Access of Universal Care.: *Journal of Health Politics Policy and Law* 15 (4): 803.

Barrera, Mario. 1978. *Race and Class in the Southwest*. Notre Dame: University of Notre Dame Press.

Barrera, Mario, Carlos Muñoz, and C. Ornelas. 1972. "The Barrio as an Internal Colony." In *People and Politics in Urban Society, Urban Affairs Annual Review*, Vol. 6, ed. H. H. Hahn, 465-99. Beverly Hills: Sage Publications.

Barrett, Michèle. 1988. *Women's Oppression Today*. London: Verso.

Beauchamp, Dan E., and Ronald L. Rouse. 1990. "Universal New York Health Care: A Single-Payer Strategy Linking Cost Control and Universal Access." *The New England Journal of Medicine* 323 (10): 640-44.

Beauvoir, Simone de. [1949] 1979. *The Second Sex*. Trans. H. M. Parshley. Reprint. New York: Knopf.

Beilharz, Edwin A. 1971. *Felipe de Neve: First Governor of California*. San Francisco: California Historical Society.

Benson, Susan Porter. 1978. "'The Clerking Sisterhood,' Rationalization and the Work Culture of Saleswomen in American Department Stores, 1890-1960." *Radical America* 12: 41-55.

———. 1983. "'The Customers Ain't God': The Work Culture of Department Store Saleswomen, 1890-1940." In *Working Class America, Essays on Labor, Community and American Society*, eds. Michael H. Frisch, and Daniel J. Walkowitz, 185-211. Urbana: University of Illinois Press.

Bernal, G. 1980. "Parentification and De-parentification in Family Therapy." In *Questions and Answers in Family Therapy*, Vol. II, ed. A.S. Gurman, 125-142. New York: Brunner/Mazel.

Bernal, G., and A.I. Alvarez. 1983. "Culture and Class in the Study of Families." In *Cultural Perspectives in Family Therapy*, ed. C. Falicov, 33-50. Rockville, Md.: Aspen Publications.

Bernal, G., and Yvette Flores-Ortiz. 1982. "Latino Families in Therapy: Engagement and Evaluation." *Journal of Marital and Family Therapy* 8 (3): 357-365.

_____. 1984. "Latino Families: Socio-historical perspectives and Cultural Issues." *Nueva Epoca* 1 (1): 4-9.

Bernal, G, Yvette Flores-Ortiz, and C. Rodríguez-Dragín. 1986. "Terapia familiar intergeneracional con Chicanos y familias Mejicanas imigrantes a los Estados Unidos." *Revista de Psicología* (Cali, Colombia) 12 (2): 26-48.

Bernal, G., and C. Rodríguez-Dragín. 1985. *Terapia familiar intergeneracional: intervención breve en una familia con problemas de alcholismo y depresión.* Monografías EIRENE, 10. New York: Brunner/Mazel.

Blauner, R. 1972. *Racial Oppression in America.* New York: Harper and Row.

Bodenheimer, Thomas. 1990. "Should We Abolish the Private Health Insurance Industry?" *International Journal of Health Services* 20 (2): 199-220.

Bolton, Herbert E., trans. and ed. 1930. *Anza's California Expeditions.* 5 vols. Berkeley: University of California Press.

Bonnicksen, Andrea L. 1989. *In Vitro Fertilization: Building Policy from Laboratories to Legislatures.* New York: Columbia University Press.

Boszormeyi-Nagy, I., and G.M. Spark. 1984. *Invisible Loyalties.* New York: Brunner/Mazel.

Brading, David A. 1973. "Los españoles en México hacia 1792." *Historia mexicana* 23 (julio-septiembre 1973): 126-44.

Braverman, Paula, Geraldine Oliva, Ilarie G. Miller, Randy Reitter, and Susan Egerter. "Adverse Outcomes and Lack of Health Insurance Among Newborns in an Eight-County Area of California, 1982-1986." *The New England Journal of Medicine* 321 (8): 508-12.

Brinkerhoff, Sidney B., and Odie B. Faulk. 1965. *Lancers for the King: A Study of the Frontier Military System of Northern New Spain, with a Translation of the Royal Regulations of 1772.* Phoenix: Arizona Historical Foundation.

Brown, M. 1981. A Historical Economic Analysis of the Wage Structure of the California Fruit and Vegetable Canning Industry. Ph.D. diss., University of California, Berkeley.

Broyles-González, Yolanda. 1990. "What Price Mainstream? Luis

266

Valdéz's *Corridos* On Stage and Film." *Cultural Studies* 4 (3): 281-93.

Campbell, Leon. 1974. "The First Californios: Presidal Society in Spanish California, 1769-1822." In *The Spanish Borderlands*, ed. Oakah L. Jones Jr., 106-118. Los Angeles: Lorrin L. Morrison.

———. 1977. "The Spanish Presidio in Alta California During the Mission Period, 1769-1784." *Journal of the West* 16 (October): 63-77.

Candelaria, Cordelia. 1978. "Women in the Academy." *Rendezvous: Journal of Arts and Letters* 13: 9-18.

———. 1980. "La Malinche, Feminist Prototype." *Frontiers: A Journal of Women Studies* 5: 1-16.

———. 1989. "The Multicultural 'Wild Zone' of Ethnic-identified American Literatures." In *Multiethnic Literatures of the United States: Critical Introductions and Classroom Resources*, ed. Cordelia Candelaria, i-xiv. Boulder: University of Colorado Press.

Cantarow, Ellen, with Susan Gushee O'Malley, and Sharon Hartman Strom. 1980. "Jessie Lopez de la Cruz, The Battle for Farmworkers' Rights." *Moving the Mountain: Women Working for Social Change*, 94-151. Old Westbury, N.Y.: Feminist Press.

Carrillo, R.C. 1983. Male Batterers: A Multivariate and Social Learning Analysis. Ph.D. diss., California School of Professional Psychology, Fresno.

———. 1989. La familia latinoamericana y la violencia. Paper presented at XXII Interamerican Congress of Psychology, Buenos Aires, Argentina.

Castañeda, Antonia I. 1990. "Presidarias y Pobladoras: Spanish-Mexican Women in Frontier Monterey, Alta California, 1770-1821." Ph.D. diss., Stanford University.

Castillo, Ana. 1977. *Otro Canto*. Chicago: Privately printed.

———. 1979. *The Invitation*. Chicago: Privately printed.

———. 1984. *Women Are Not Roses*. Houston: Arte Público Press.

———. 1986. *The Mixquiahuala Letters*. Binghamton, N.Y.: Bilingual Review Press.

———. 1988. *My Father Was a Toltec*. Novato, Calif: West End Press.

———. 1991. "La Macha: Toward a Beautiful Whole Self." In *Chicana Lesbians: The Girls Our Mothers Warned Us About*, ed. Carla Trujillo. Berkeley: Third Woman Press.

Chabram, Angie, and Rosalinda Fregoso, eds. 1990. *Cultural Studies* 4 (October): 3.

Chapman, Charles E. 1916. *The Founding of Spanish California: The Northwestward Expansion of New Spain, 1687-1783*. New York: The Macmillan Co.

———. 1930. *A History of California: The Spanish Period*. New York: The Macmillan Co.

Chartkoff, Joseph L. and Kerry Kona Chartkoff. 1984. *The Archeology of California*. Stanford: Stanford University Press.

Chávez, Denise. 1986. *The Last of the Menu Girls*. Houston: Arte Público Press.

Chicano Coordinating Committee on Higher Education. 1969. *El Plan de Santa Barbara: A Chicano Plan for Higher Education*. Santa Barbara: La Causa Publications.

Cisneros, Sandra. 1983. *The House on Mango Street*. Houston: Arte Público Press.

_____. 1987. *My Wicked Wicked Ways*. Bloomington, Ind: Third Woman Press.

Cixous, Hélène. 1981. "Castration or Decapitation." *Signs: Journal of Women in Culture and Society* 7 (1): 41-55.

Clarke, Adele. 1984. "Socialist-Feminism and Reproductive Rights: Movement Work and Its Contradictions." *Socialist Review* 78 (14, 6): 110-121.

Collier, Jane, Michelle Z. Rosaldo, and Sylvia Yanagisako. 1982. "Is There Family? New Anthropological Views." In *Rethinking the Family, Some Feminist Questions*, eds. Barrie Thorne and Marilyn Yalom, 25-39. New York: Longman.

Cook, E. A. 1989. "Measuring Feminist Consciousness." *Women and Politics* 9: 71-88.

Cook, Sherburne F. 1976a. *The Population of the California Indians, 1769-1970*. Berkeley: University of California Press.

_____. 1976b. *The Conflict Between the California Indian and White Civilization*. Berkeley: University of California Press. Originally published as "The Indians versus the Spanish Mission." *Ibero-Americana* 2 (1943).

Córdova, T., N. Cantú, G. Cárdenas, J. Garcia, and C. M. Sierra, eds. 1986. *Chicana Voices: Intersections of Class, Race, and Gender*. National Association for Chicano Studies, conference proceedings. Austin: University of Texas Center for Mexican American Studies.

Corea, Gena. 1977. *The Hidden Malpractice*. New York: William Morrow and Company.

_____. 1985. *The Mother Machine: Reproductive Technologies From Artificial Insemination to Artificial Wombs*. New York: Harper & Row.

COSSMH0, National Coalition of Hispanic Health and Human Services Organization. 1990. *. . .And Access For All*. Washington, D.C.

Costello, Cynthia B. 1985. "'WEA're Worth It!' Work Culture and Conflict at the Wisconsin Education Association Insurance Trust." *Feminist Studies* 11 (3): 497-518.

Cotera, M. P. 1977. *The Chicana Feminist*. Austin: Information Systems Development.

_____. 1980. "Feminism: The Chicana and Anglo Versions, A Historical

Analysis." In *Twice a Minority: Mexican American Women*, ed. Margarita Melville, 217-234. St. Louis: C. V. Mosby.

Coyle, Laurie, Gail Hershatter, and Emily Honig. 1980. "Women at Farah: An Unfinished Story." In *Mexican American Women in the United States*, eds. Magdalena Mora and Adelaida Del Castillo, 117-144. Los Angeles: University of California Chicano Research Center Publications.

CSA. 1991. "Hispanic Health in the United States." *Journal of the American Medical Association* 265 (2): 248-52.

Culleton, James. 1950. *Indians and Pioneers of Old Monterey*. Fresno: Academy of California Church History.

Czarnowski, Lucille K. 1950. *Dances of Early California*. Palo Alto: Pacific Books.

Davis, Angela. Y. 1981. *Women, Race and Class*. New York: Random House.

de la Torre, Adela. 1990. "Latino Health in the 1980s: Critical Health Policy Issues." In *Income and Status Differences Between White and Minority Americans*, ed. Sucheng Chan. Lewiston, Maine: Edwin Mellon Press.

de la Torre, Adela, and Refugio Rochin. 1990. "Hispanic Poor and the Effects of Immigration Reform." *Chicago Law Review* 10: 1.

Del Castillo, Adelaida. 1974. "La Visión Chicana." *Encuentro Femenil* 12: 46-48.

———. 1977. "Malintzin Tenepal: A Preliminary Look Into a New Perspective." In *Essays on La Mujer*, eds. Rosaura Sánchez and Rosa Martínez Cruz, 124-150. Los Angeles: University of California Chicano Studies Research Center.

Department of Health and Human Services. 1989. *A Profile of Uninsured Americans*. Research Findings 1, National Medical Expenditure Survey. Washington, D.C.: U.S. Government Printing Office.

Díaz-Guerrero, R. 1955. "Neurosis and the Mexican Family Structure." *American Journal of Psychiatry* 112: 411-417.

Dill, B. 1983. "Race, Class, and Gender: Prospects for an All-Inclusive Sisterhood." *Feminist Studies* 9: 131-50.

Du Bois, W. E. B. 1965. *The Souls of Black Folk: Three Negro Classics*. New York: Knopf.

Duany, Luis, and Karen Pittman. 1990. *Latino Youths at a Crossroads*. Adolescent Pregnancy Prevention Clearing House Report. Washington, D.C.: Children's Defense Fund.

Duron, Clementina. 1984. "Mexican Women and Labor Conflict in Los Angeles: The ILGWU Dressmakers' Strike of 1933." *Aztlán, Chicano Journal of the Social Sciences and Arts*. 15: 145-161.

Duras, Marguerite. 1985. *The Lover*. Trans. Barbara Bray. New York: Harper and Row.

Employees Benefits Research Institute. 1990. Health Market Survey, 6 August. 5-6.

Eisenstein, Sarah. 1983. *Give Us Bread but Give Us Roses*. London: Routledge & Kegan Paul.

Escheveste reglamento. Instrucción que debe observar el comandante nombrado para los establecimientos de San Diego y Monterey, 23 de julio de 1773. Manuscript collection, Bancroft Library, University of California, Berkeley.

Ezzard, N.V., W. Cates, D.G. Kramer, and C. Tietze. 1982. "Race Specific Patterns of Abortion Use by American Teen-agers." *American Journal of Public Health* 72: 8.

Fages, Pedro. 1774. Año de 1774, Californias: Representación de Don Pedro Fages sobre el estupro violento que cometieron los tres soldados que espresa. Archivo General de la Nación, Californias. Microfilm. Bancroft Library, University of California, Berkeley.

_____. 1937. *A Historical, Political, and Natural Description of California by Pedro Fages, Soldier of Spain, Dutifully Made for the Viceroy in the Year 1775.* Trans. H. I. Priestly. Reprint. 1972. Ramona, Calif: Ballena Press.

Falicov, C. 1982. "Mexican Families." In *Ethnicity and Family Therapy*, ed. M. McGoldrick, J.K. Pearce, and J. Giodano, 134-163. New York: Guidford Press.

Family Violence Project. 1989. *Family Violence: The Facts*. San Francisco.

Faragher, John Mack. 1979. *Women and Men on the Overland Trail*. New Haven: Yale University Press.

Fernández-Kelly, María Patricia. 1983. *For We Are Sold, I and My People*. Albany: State University of New York Press.

Firestone, S., and A. Koedt, eds. 1970. *Notes from the Second Year: Women's Liberation Major Writings of the Radical Feminist*. New York: Radical Feminist.

Flores, F. 1971. "Conference of Mexican Women: Un Remolino." *Regeneración* 1: 1-4.

_____. 1973. "Equality." *Regeneración* 2: 4-5.

Flores-Ortiz, Yvette. 1982. The Impact of Acculturation on the Chicano Family: An Analysis of Selected Variables. Ph.D. diss., University of California, Berkeley.

_____. 1990. Workshop on Chicana Lesbians at MALCS (Mujeres Activas en Letras y Cambio Social) Summer Research Institute, 3-6 August, at University of California, Los Angeles.

Flores-Ortiz, Yvette, and G. Bernal. 1989. "Contextual Family Therapy of Addiction with Latinos." In *Minorities and Family Therapy*, ed. G.W. Saba, B.M. Karrer, and K.V. Hardy, 123-142. New York: Haworth Press.

Flores-Ortiz, Yvette, and R.C. Carrillo. 1989. La familia latinoamericana y la violencia: un modelo contextual de terapia intergeneracional. Workshop presentation at XXII Interamerican Congress of Psychology, Buenos Aires, Argentina.

Flores-Ortiz, Yvette, R.C. Carrillo, and M. Esteban. 1991. La Violencia en la Familia: un modelo contextual de terapia intergeneracional. Paper presented at XXIII Interamerican Congress of Psychology, San José, Costa Rica.

Foucault, Michel. 1978. *The History of Sexuality: Volume I, An Introduction.* Trans. Robert Hurley. New York: Pantheon.

Fouque, Antoinette. 1980. "Quoted in 'The MLF is you, is me.'" In *New French Feminisms*, eds. Elaine Marks and Isabelle De Courtivron, 117-118. Amherst: University of Massachusetts Press.

Freedman, Estelle. 1979. "Separatism as Strategy: Female Institution Building and American Feminism, 1870-1930." *Feminist Studies* 5 (Fall): 512-529.

Freeman, J. 1984. "The Women's Liberation Movement: Its Origins, Structure, Activities, and Ideas." In *Women, A Feminist Perspective*, ed. J. Freeman, 3rd ed., 543-556. Palo Alto: Mayfield Publishing.

Freire, Paolo. 1970. *Pedagogy of the Oppressed.* Trans. M. B. Ramos. New York: Herder and Herder.

Friedland, William J., and Robert J. Thomas. 1974. "Paradoxes of Agricultural Unionism in California." *Society* 11: 54-62.

Furino, Antonio, and Eric Muñoz. 1991. "Hispanic Health: Time for Data, Time for Action." *Journal of the American Health Association* 265 (2): 253-57.

Galarza, Ernesto. 1964. *Merchants of Labor.* Santa Barbara: McNally & Loftin.

_____. 1977. *Farm Workers and Agri-business in California, 1947-1960.* Notre Dame: University of Notre Dame Press.

Gantz McKay, Emily. 1991. *The Hispanic Population: 1990 A Chartbook "Snapshot."* Washington, D.C.: National Council of La Raza.

GAO. 1991a. *Health Insurance Coverage: A Profile of the Uninsured in Selected States.* Washington, D.C.: U.S. Government Printing Office.

_____. 1991b. *Private Health Insurance Problems Caused by a Segmented Market.* Human Resources Division. Washington, D.C.: U.S. Government Printing Office.

García, Alma M. 1989. "The Development of Chicana Feminist Discourse, 1970-1980." *Gender and Society* 3 (June): 217-38.

García, F. Chris, ed. 1974. *La Causa Politica, A Chicano Politics Reader.* Notre Dame: University of Notre Dame Press.

García, J. 1981. "*Yo Soy Mexicano...*: Self-Identity and Sociodemographic Corrolates." *Social Science Quarterly* 62, (1): 88-98.

García, Mario T. 1980. "The Chicana in American History: The Mexican Women of El Paso, 1880-1920—A Case Study." *Pacific Historical Review* 49: 315-337.

Gauthier, Xaviere. 1980. "Is There Such a Thing As Women's Writing?" In *New French Feminisms*, eds. Elaine Marks and Isabelle De Courtivron, 161-164. Amherst: University of Massachusetts Press.

Gilbert, Sandra M., and Susan Gubar. 1979. *The Madwoman in the Attic: The Woman Writer and the Nineteenth-Century Literary Imagination.* New Haven: Yale University Press.

Ginsberg, Eli. 1989. Keynote address to the "Health Policy and the Hispanic: A National Action Forum." 6-7 October. San Antonio, Texas.

_____. 1992. "Access to Health Care for Hispanics." In *Health Policy and the Hispanic*, ed. Antonio Furino. Boulder: Westview Press.

Glenn, Evelyn Nakano. 1985. "Racial Ethnic Women's Labor: The Intersection of Race, Gender and Class Oppression." *Review of Radical Political Economics* 17: 86-108.

Gonzáles, P. 1986. "Spanish Heritage and Ethnic Protest in New Mexico: The Anti-Fraternity Bill of 1933." *New Mexico Historical Review* 61, (4): 281-99.

González, Deena J. 1985. The Women of Santa Fé. Ph.D. diss., University of California, Berkeley.

_____. Forthcoming. *Resisting Colonization: The Spanish Mexican Women of Santa Fe, 1820-1880.*

González-Block, Miguel A., and David E. Hayes-Bautista. 1990. AIDS: The Silent Threat to Bi-National Security. Working paper, UC-Mexus Conference on Bi-National Security Issues. Los Angeles: University of California.

Gordon-Bradshaw, Ruth H. 1988. "A Social Essay on Special Issues Facing Poor Women of Color." 243-59. Haworth Press.

Gramick, Jeannine, and Pat Furey, eds. 1988. *The Vatican and Homosexuality.* New York: Crossroad Publishing Co.

Haley, J., and C. Madanes. 1988. "Abuse in the Family." Workshop presentation in San Francisco, July.

Hammer, Jalna. 1987. "Reproductive Trends and the Emergence of Moral Panic." *Social Science and Medicine* 25 (6): 607-704.

Hartmann, Heidi. 1981. "The Unhappy Marriage of Marxism and Feminism: Toward a More Progressive Union." In *Women and Revolution*, ed. Lydia Sargent, 2-41. Boston: South End Press.

Hennessy, Alistar. 1978. *The Frontier in Latin American History.* Albuquerque: University of New Mexico Press.

Hernández, Carmen. 1971. "Carmen Speaks Out." *Paper Chicano* 1 (June): 8-9.

Herrera-Sobek, María. 1982. "The Treacherous Woman Archetype: A

Structuring Agent in the Corrido." *Aztlán, Chicano Journal of the Social Sciences and Arts* 13: 135-147.

Hinojosa, Rolando. 1973. *Estampas del Valle y Otras Obras.* Berkeley: Quinto Sol.

———. 1977. *Generaciones y semblanzas.* Berkeley: Editorial Justa.

———. 1981. *Mi querido Rafa.* Houston: Arte Público Press.

Hittell, Theodore S. 1879-98. *History of California.* 4 vols. San Francisco: N. J. Stone.

hooks, bell. 1981. *Ain't I a Woman: Black Women and Feminism.* Boston: South End Press.

———. 1984. *Feminist Theory: From Margin to Center.* Boston: South End Press.

Horta, María Teresa, María Isabel Barreno, and María Velho da Costa. 1975. *The Three Marias.* Trans. Helen R. Lane. New York: Doubleday.

Hull, G., P. Bell Scott, and B. Smith. 1982. *All Men Are Black, All Women Are White, But Some of Us Are Brave.* Old Westbury, N.Y.: Feminist Press.

Hunter College Women's Studies Collective. 1983. *Women's Realities Women's Choices.* New York: Oxford University Press.

Hurtado, Aida. 1989. "Relating to Privilege: Seduction and Rejection in the Subordination of White Women and Women of Color." *Signs, Journal of Women in Culture and Society* 14 (Summer): 833-855.

Iglesias, Norma. 1986. *Las mujeres somos más responsables: Utilización de mano de obra femenina en las maquiladoras fronterizas.* Trabajos Monográficos 2 (1): 1-30. Davis: University of California Chicano Studies Program.

Irigary, Luce. 1983. "Interview." In *Women Writers Talking,* ed. Janet Todd, 231-246. New York: Holmes and Meier.

———. 1985a. *This Sex Which Is Not One.* Trans. Catherine Porter with Carolyn Burke. Ithaca: Cornell University Press.

———. 1985b. *Speculum of the Other Woman.* Trans. Gillian. G. Gill. Ithaca: Cornell University Press.

Jaggar, A. M. 1983. *Feminist Politics and Human Nature.* Totowa, N.J.: Rowman and Allanheld.

Jameson, Fredric. 1975. "The Ideology of the Text." *Salmagundi* 31-32 (Fall 1975/Winter 1976): 225.

Jardine, Alice. A. 1985. *Gynesis: Configurations of Woman and Modernity.* Ithaca: Cornell University Press.

Jones, Oakah L., Jr. 1979. *Los Paisanos: Spanish Settlers on the Northern Frontier of New Spain.* Norman: University of Okalhoma Press.

Joseph, Gloria. 1981. "The Incomplete Menage à Trois: Marxism, Feminism, and Racism." In *Women and Revolution, A Discussion of the Unhappy Marriage of Marxism and Feminism,* ed. Lydia Sargent, 109-143. Boston:

South End Press.

Joyce, T.J., and N.H. Mocan. 1990. "The Impact of Legalized Abortion on Adolescent Childbearing in New York City." *American Journal of Public Health* 80 (3): 273-278.

Kasl, Charlotte Davis. 1989. *Women, Sex and Addiction: A Search for Love and Power.* New York: Ticknor and Fields.

Kern, Rosemary, and Jack E. Bresch. 1990. "Systemic Health Care Reform: Is it Time?" *Health Progress* (January-February): 32-44.

Kessler-Harris, Alice. 1982. *Out To Work, A History of Wage-Earning Women in the United States.* New York: Oxford University Press.

Kinnard, Lawrence, ed. 1958. *The Frontiers of New Spain: Nicholás de Lafora's Description, 1766-1768.* Berkeley: The Quivera Society.

Klein, E. 1984. *Gender Politics.* Cambridge: Harvard University Press.

Klein, Renate, ed. 1989. *Infertility: Women Speak Out About Their Experiences with the New Reproductive Technologies.* London: Pandora Press.

Kolodny, Annette. 1985. "A Map for Rereading: Gender and the Interpretation of Literary Texts." In *The New Feminist Criticism*, ed. Elaine Showalter, 46-62. New York: Pantheon.

Konetzke, Richard. 1945. "La emigración de mujeres españolas a América durante la época colonial." *Revista internacional de sociología* 3 (enero-marzo): 123-50.

Kristeva, Julia. 1977. *About Chinese Women.* Trans. Anita Barrows. London: Boyars.

———. [1979] 1981. "Women's Time." Trans. Alice Jardine and Harry Blake. *Signs: Journal of Women in Culture and Society* 7 (May): 55-69.

———. 1984. *Revolution in Poetic Language.* Trans. Margaret Waller. New York: Columbia University Press.

Kushner, Sam. 1975. *Long Road to Delano.* New York: International Publications.

Lacan, Jacques. 1977. *Écrits.* Trans. Alan Sheridan. London: Tavistock.

———. [1958] 1986. "The Agency of the Letter in the Unconscious, or Reason since Freud." Trans. Alan Sheridan. In *Critical Theory Since 1965*, ed. Hazard Adams and Leroy Searle, 738-754. Tallahassee: Florida State University Press.

———. [1977] 1986. "The Mirror Stage as Formative of the Function of the I as Revealed in Psychoanalytic Experience." Trans. Alan Sheridan. In *Critical Theory Since 1965*, ed. Hazard Adams and Leroy Searle, 734-738. Tallahassee: Florida State University Press.

Lamphere, Louise. 1985. "Bringing the Family to Work: Women's Culture on the Shop Floor." *Feminist Studies* 11 (3): 519-540.

Lasuén, Fermín Francisco de. 1965. "Refutation of Charges, Mission of San Carlos of Monterey, 19 June 1801." In *Writings of Fermín Francisco de Lasuén*, trans. and ed. Finbar Kenneally, 2: 210. 2 vols. Washing-

274

ton, D. C.: Academy of American Franciscan History.

Latino Community Project. 1990. *Latino AIDS Information Resources*. Los Angeles: University of California Chicano Studies Research Center.

Levy, Jacques. 1975. *César Chavez: Autobiography of La Causa*. New York: Farrar, Straus & Giroux.

Lewis, D. K. 1983. "A Response to Inequality: Black Women, Racism and Sexism." In *The Signs Reader: Women, Gender and Scholarship*, eds. E. Abel and E. K. Abel, 169-91. Chicago: University of Chicago Press.

Libro de Matrimonios. Misión San Carlos Borromeo, Vol. 1, 1772-1855. Pastoral Office, Diocese of Monterey, California.

Limón, José. 1981. "The Folk Performance of Chicano and the Cultural Limits of Political Ideology." In *"And Other Neighborly Names": Social Process and Cultural Image in Texas Folklore*, eds. Richard Bauman and Roger D. Abrahams, 197-225. Austin: University of Texas Press.

———. 1990. "La Llorona, the Third Legend of Greater Mexico: Cultural Symbols, Women, and the Political Unconscious." In *Between Borders: Essays on Mexicana/Chicana History*, ed. Adelaida R. Del Castillo, 399-432. Encino, Calif: Floricanto Press.

Lizárraga, Sylvia S. 1977. "From a Woman to a Woman." In *Essays on La Mujer*, eds. Rosaura Sánchez and Rosa Martínez Cruz, 91-96. Los Angeles: University. of California Chicano Studies Research Center.

Longeaux y Vásquez, Enriqueta. 1970. "The Mexican-American Woman." In *Sisterhood is Powerful: An Anthology of Writings from the Women's Liberation Movement*, ed. Robin Morgan, 379-384. New York: Vintage.

———. 1971. "Soy Chicana Primero." *El Grito del Norte* 4 (April 26): 11-14.

López, S. A. 1977. "The Role of the Chicana Within the Student Movement." In *Essays on La Mujer*, ed. Rosaura Sánchez and Rosa Martínez Cruz, 16-29. Los Angeles: University of California Chicano Studies Research Center.

Lorenzana, Apolinaria. 1878. Memorias de Apolinarina Lorenzana, mayo de 1878, Santa Barbara. Manuscript collection, Bancroft Library, University of California, Berkeley.

Luepnitz, D.A. 1988. *The Family Interpreted: Feminist Theory in Clinical Practice*. New York: Basic Books.

Luker, Kristin. 1984. *Abortion and the Politics of Motherhood*. Berkeley: University of California Press.

Lynd, S. 1979. "Where is the Teamster Rebellion Going?" *Radical America* 13 (2): 7-74.

Macias, Anna. 1982. *Against All Odds*. Westport, Conn: Greenwood Press.

Macias, Y. R. 1974. "Nuestros Antepasados y el Movimiento." *Aztlán, Chicano Journal of the Social Sciences and the Arts* 5 (Spring/Fall): 143-53.

Maranda, Pierre. 1980. "The Dialectic of Metaphor: An Anthropological Essay on Hermenutics." In *The Reader in the Text: Essays on Audience and Interpretation*, eds. Susan R. Suleiman and Inge Corsman, 183-204. Princeton: Princeton University Press.

Machachlan, Colin M., and Jaime E. Rodríguez O. 1980. *The Forging of the Cosmic Race: A Reinterpretation of Colonial Mexico*. Berkeley: University of California Press.

Marks, Elaine, and Isabelle De Courtivron, eds. 1980. *New French Feminisms*. Amherst: University of Massachusetts Press.

Martin, D. 1976. *Battered Wives*. New York: Pocket Books.

Martin, Luis. 1983. *Daughters of the Conquistadores: Women of the Viceroyalty of Peru*. Albuquerque: University of New Mexico Press.

Martínez, E. 1972. "La Chicana." In *Third World Women*, 130-132. San Francisco: Third World Communications.

Matthiessen, Peter. 1969. *Sal Sí Puedes, César Chávez and the New American Revolution*. New York: Random House.

McGoldrick, M., and B. Carter, eds. 1989. *Women in Families*. New York: Gardner Press.

McKay, Trent. 1990. Remarks at "Abortion: Beyond the Debate" conference, 15 September, Sacramento, Calif.

Melosh, Barbara. 1982. *"The Physician's Hand": Work Culture and Conflict in American Nursing*. Philadelphia: Temple University Press.

Melville, Margarita, ed. 1980. *Twice a Minority: Mexican-American Women*. St. Louis: C.V. Mosby.

Milkman, Ruth. 1976. "Women's Work and the Economic Crisis: Some Lessons Learned from the Great Depression." *The Review of Radical Political Economics* 8: 73-97.

———, ed. 1985. *Women, Work and Protest: A Century of U.S. Women's Labor History*. Boston: Routledge & Kegan Paul.

Miller, M. 1976. "Mexican Americans, Chicanos, and Others: Ethnic Self-Identification and Selected Social Attributes of Rural Texas Youth." *Rural Sociology* 4, (2): 234-247.

Millman, Marcia, and Rosabeth Moss Kanter, eds. 1975. *Another Voice: Feminist Perspectives on Social Life and Social Science*. New York: Doubleday.

Minuchin, S. 1974. *Families and Family Therapy*. Cambridge: Harvard University Press.

Mirandé, Alfredo. 1985. *The Chicano Experience: An Alternative Perspective*. Notre Dame: University of Notre Dame Press.

Mirandé, Alfredo, and Evangelina Enríquez. 1979. *La Chicana*. Chicago: University of Chicago Press.

Mitchell, Gregg. 1989. "Barrier Crusaders." *Pomona College Today* (Summer): 17.

Mitchell, Juliet. 1973. *Women's Estate*. New York: Vintage.

_____. 1974. *Psychoanalysis and Feminism*. New York: Penguin.

Moi, Toril. 1985. *Sexual/Textual Politics*. New York: Routledge.

Montejano, David. 1987. *Anglos and Mexicans in the Making of Texas, 1836-1986*. Austin: University of Texas Press.

Moorhead, Max L. 1974. "The Soldado de Cuera: Stalwart of the Spanish Borderlands." In *The Spanish Borderlands*, ed. Oakah L. Jones Jr., 85-195. Los Angeles: Lorrin L. Morrison.

_____. 1975. *The Presidio Bastion of the Spanish Borderlands*. Norman: University of Oklahoma Press.

Mora, Magdalena. 1981. "The Role of Mexican Women in the Richmond Tolteca Strike." In *Mexican Immigrant Workers in the U.S.*, ed. Antonio Rios-Bustamante, 111-118. Los Angeles: University. of California Chicano Studies Research Center Publications.

Moraga, Cherríe. 1983. *Loving in the War Years: Lo que nunca pasó pos sus labios*. Boston: South End Press.

_____. 1986. *Giving Up the Ghost*. Los Angeles: West End Press.

Moraga, Cherríe, and Gloria Anzaldúa, eds. 1983. *This Bridge Called My Back: Writings by Radical Women of Color*. 2d. ed. New York: Kitchen Table Press.

Morales, Alejandro. 1975. *La verdad sin voz*. México: Joaquín Mortiz.

Morner, Magnus. 1967. *Race Mixture in the History of Latin America*. Boston: Little, Brown, and Co.

Myres, Sandra L. 1982. *Westering Women and the Frontier Experience, 1800-1915*. Albuquerque: University of New Mexico Press.

Nash, Madeleine. 1991. "All in the Family." *Time* 138 (19 August): 7-58.

Nelson, Eugene. 1966. *Huelga, the First Hundred Days of the Great Delano Grape Strike*. Delano, Calif: Farm Worker Press.

Neve, Felipe de. Reglamento para el gobierno de la provincia de Californias, 24 octubre 1781. Manuscript collection, Bancroft Library, University of California, Berkeley.

Nieto, C. 1974. "Chicanas and the Women's Rights Movements." *Civil Rights Digest* 4 (Spring): 38-42.

Nieto-Gómez, Anna. 1973. "La Feminista." *Encuentro Femenil* 1: 34-47.

_____. 1974. "Chicana Feminism." *Encuentro Femenil* 1: 3-5.

Northrop, Marie E. 1984-1987. *Spanish-Mexican Families of Early California, 1769-1850*. 2 vols. Burbank: Southern California Geneological Society.

Orozco, Cynthia. 1986. "Sexism in Chicano Studies and the Community." In *Chicana Voices: Intersections of Class, Race, and Gender*, ed. Teresa Córdova, et al., 11-18. Austin: University of Texas Center for Mexican American Studies.

Ostriker, Alicia. 1982. "The Thieves of Language: Women Poets and Revisionist Mythmaking." *Signs: Journal of Women and Culture in Society*

8 (1): 68-90.

Ots y Capdequi, José María. 1934. *Instituciones sociales de la América Española en el período colonial*. La Plata, Argentina: Biblioteca Humanidades.

Palóu, Francisco. 1926. *Historical Memoirs of New California*. Ed. Herbert Eugene Bolton. 4 vols. Berkeley: University of California Press.

Paz, Octavio. 1961. *The Labyrinth of Solitude*. Trans. Lysander Kemp. New York: Grove Press.

Pérez, Emma. 1988. Through Her Love and Sweetness: Women, Revolution and Reform in Yucatán, 1910-1918. Ph.D. diss., University of California, Los Angeles.

_____. 1990. "A La Mujer: A Critique of the Mexican Liberal Party's Ideology on Women." In *Between Borders: Essays on Mexicana/Chicana History*, ed. Adelaida Del Castillo, 459-482. Los Angeles: Floricanto Press.

_____. 1991. "Sexuality and Discourse: Notes from a Chicana Survivor." In *Chicana Lesbians: The Girls Our Mothers Warned Us About*, ed. Carla Trujillo, 159-184. Berkeley: Third Woman Press.

Pérez, Eulalia. 1877. Una Vieja y Sus Recuerdos, 1877, Mission San Gabriel. Manuscript collection, Bancroft Library, University of California, Berkeley.

Perry, Ruth. 1980. *Women, Letters, and the Novel*. New York: AMS Press.

Pinderhughes, E. 1982. "Afro-American Families and the Victim System." In *Ethnicity and Family Therapy*, ed. M. McGoldrick, J.K. Pearce, and J. Giodano, 108-122. New York: Guilford Press.

Pineda, Magaly. 1986. "Feminism and Popular Education: A Critical But Necessay Relationship." *Isis International* 6: 111-13.

Ponce, Arcelia. 1989. "La Preferida." *Third Woman* 4: 85-89.

Portillo-Trambley, Estela. 1975. *Rain of Scorpions and Other Writings*. Berkeley: Tonatiuh-Quinto Sol International.

Rabine, Leslie Wahl. 1988. "A Feminist Politics of Non-Identity." *Feminist Studies* 14 (Spring): 11-31.

Radway, Janice. 1984. *Reading the Romance: Women, Patriarchy, and Popular Literature*. Chapel Hill: University of North Carolina Press.

Rapp, Reyna. 1978. "Family and Class in Contemporary America: Notes Toward an Understanding of Ideology." *Science and Society* 42: 278-300.

"Redstockings Manifesto." 1970. In *Notes from the Second Year: Women's Liberation Major Writings of the Radical Feminist*, eds. S. Firestone and A. Koedt, 112-113. New York: Radical Feminist.

Rich, Adrienne. 1980. "Cumpulsory Heterosexuality and Lesbian Existence." In *Women: Sex and Sexuality*, eds. Catherine R. Stimpson and Ethel Spector Person, 62-91. Chicago: University of Chicago Press.

Richman, Irving Berdine. 1911. *California Under Spain and Mexico, 1535-*

278

1847. Boston: Houghton Mifflin Co.

Rix, Sara E., ed. 1988. *The American Woman 1988-89: A Status Report.* Women's Research and Education Institute. New York: W.W. Norton & Co.

Roberts, A.R., ed. 1984. *Battered Women and Their Families: Intervention Strategies and Treatment Programs.* New York: Springer Publishing.

Rosaldo, Renato, Gustav L. Seligmann, and Robert A. Calvert. 1974. *Chicano: The Beginnings of Bronze Power.* New York: Morrow.

Roudiez, Leon S., ed. 1980. *Desire in Language.* Trans. Thomas Gora, Alice Jardine, and Leon S. Roudiez. New York: Columbia University Press.

Rowbotham, Shelia. 1973. *Woman's Consciousness, Men's World.* New York: Penguin.

Ruiz, Vicki L. 1984. "Working for Wages: Mexican Women in the Southwest, 1930-1980." Working paper no. 19, Southwest Institute for Research on Women. Tucson: University of Arizona.

———. 1987. *Cannery Women, Cannery Lives.* Albuquerque: University of New Mexico Press.

Sacks, Karen. 1974. "Engels Revisited: Women, the Organization of Production and Private Property." In *Women, Culture and Society*, eds. Michelle Rosaldo and Louise Lamphere, 207-222. Stanford: Stanford University Press.

Sacks, Karen Brodkin, and Dorothy Remy, eds. 1984. *My Troubles Are Going To Have Trouble With Me: Everyday Trials and Triumphs of Women Workers.* New Brunswick: Rutgers University Press.

Sadlier, Darlene. 1986. "Form in Novas Cartas Portugesas." *Novel* 19, (3): 246-63.

Salinas, Judy. 1977. "The Role of Women in Chicano Literature." In *The Identification and Analysis of Chicano Literature*, ed. Francisco Jiménez, 191-240. Binghamton, N.Y.: The Bilingual Press.

Sánchez, Rosaura. 1990. "The History of Chicanas: Proposal for a Materialist Perspective." In *Between Borders: Essays on Mexicana/Chicana History*, ed. Adelaida Del Castillo, 1-29. Encino, Calif: Floricanto Press.

Sanday, Peggy. 1974. "Female Status in the Public Domain." In *Women, Culture and Society*, eds. Michelle Rosaldo and Louise Lamphere, 189-206. Stanford: Stanford University Press.

Sandoval, Chela. [1982] 1990. "Feminism and Racism: A Report on the 1981 National Women's Studies Association Conference." In *Making Face, Making Soul: Haciendo Caras*, ed. Gloria Anzaldúa, 55-71. San Francisco: Aunt Lute Foundation.

Schlesinger, Mark, and K. Kronebusch. 1990. "The Failure of Prenatal Care Policy for the Poor." *Health Affairs* (Winter): 91-113.

Schlissel, Lillian. 1982. *Women's Diaries of the Westward Journey.*

New York: Schoken Books.

Scott, Joan Wallach. 1988. *Gender and the Politics of History*. New York: Columbia University Press.

Segura, Denise. 1984. "Labor Market Stratification: The Chicana Experience." *Berkeley Journal of Sociology* 29: 57-91.

――――. 1986. "Chicanas and Triple Oppression in the Labor Force." In *Chicana Voices: Intersections of Class, Race, and Gender*, ed. Teresa Cordova, et al., 47-65. Austin: Center for Mexican American Studies.

Serra, Junipero. 1955. *Writings*. Ed. Antoine Tibesar. 4 vols. Washington, D.C.: Academy of American Franciscan History.

Shengold, Leonard. 1989. *Soul Murder: The Effects of Childhood Abuse and Deprivation*. New Haven: Yale University Press.

Sluzki, C.E. 1979. "Migration and Family Conflict." *Family Process* 18 (4): 379-390.

Solís, Julia M., Gary Marks, Melinda García, and David Shelton. 1990. "Acculturation, Access to Care, and Use of Preventative Services by Hispanics: Findings from HHANES 1982-84." *American Journal of Public Health* 80 (December): 11-19.

Sosa-Riddell, Ada. 1974. "Chicanas and El Movimiento." *Aztlán: Chicano Journal of the Social Sciences and the Arts* 5 (Spring/Fall): 155-65.

Spallone, Patricia, and Deborah Lynn Steinberg. 1987. *Made to Order: The Myth of Reproductive and Genetic Progress*. New York: Pergamon Press.

Strauss, M., and E. Gelles, eds. 1989. *Violence in American Families: Risk Factors and Adaptation to Violence in 8145 Families*. New Brunswick, N.J.: Transaction Publishers.

Sutherland, E. 1970. "Colonized Women: The Chicana, An Introduction." In *Sisterhood is Powerful, An Anthology of Writings from the Women's Liberation Movement*, ed. Robin Morgan, 376-79. New York: Vintage.

Swerdlow, Amy, and Hanna Lessinger, eds. 1983. *Class, Race, and Sex: The Dynamics of Control*. Boston: G.K. Hall.

Takaki, R. T. 1979. *Iron Cages: Race and Culture in Nineteenth Century America*. New York: Alfred Knopf.

Tanner, L. B. 1970. "Congress to Unite Women—What Women Want." In *Voices From Women's Liberation*, ed. L. B. Tanner, 124-26. New York: New American Library.

Taylor, Ronald B. 1975. *Chávez and the Farm Workers*. Boston: Beacon Press.

Thiebaux, Marcelle. 1982. "Foucault's Fantasia for Feminists: Woman Reading." In *Theory and Practice of Feminist Literary Criticism*, eds. Gabriela Mora and Karen Van Hooft, 45-61. Ypsilanti, Mich: The Bilingual Press.

Thomas, Alfred Barnaby. 1941. *Teodoro de Croix and the Northern Frontier of New Spain, 1776-1783*. Norman: University of Oklahoma Press.

Thomas, Robert J., and William J. Friedland. 1982. "The United Farm Workers Union: From Mobilization to Mechanization?" Working Paper no. 269, Center for Research on Social Organization. Ann Arbor: University of Michigan.

Tienda, Marta, and Patricia Guhleman. 1985. "The Occupational Position of Employed Hispanic Women." In *Hispanics in the U.S. Economy*, ed. George J. Borjas and Marta Tienda, 243-73. New York: Academic Press.

Todorov, Tzetvan. 1982. *The Conquest of America*. Trans. Richard Howard. New York: Harper and Row.

Tolleson Rinehart, S. 1988. The Consequences of Gender Consciousness for Public Policy and Participation. Paper presented at the annual meeting of the Midwest Political Science Association, Chicago.

Torres, Rodolfo D., and Adela de la Torre. 1991. "Latinos in the U.S. Political Economy: Income Inequality and Policy Alternatives." In *Hispanics in the Labor Force*, ed. E. Meléndez. New York: Plenum Press.

U.S. Dept. of Labor. 1978. *Layoff Time Training: A Key to Upgrading Workforce Utilization and EEOC Affirmative Action, A Case Study in the Northern California Canning Industry*. R & D Monograph no. 61. Washington, D.C.: U.S. Government Printing Office.

Valdéz, Dorotea. 1874. Reminiscences of Dorotea Valdéz, Monterey, California, 27 June 1874. Manuscript collection, Bancroft Library, University of California, Berkeley.

Vélez-Ibañez, Carlos G. 1980. "'Se me acabó la canción: An Ethnography of Non-Consenting Sterilizations Among Mexican Women in Los Angeles." In *Mexican Women in the United States: Struggles Past and Present*, eds. Magdalena Mora and Adelaida del Castillo, 71-93. Occasional Paper no. 2. Los Angeles: University of California Chicano Studies Research Center Publications.

Vidal, M. 1971. "New Voices of La Raza: Chicanas Speak Out." *International Socialist Review* 32 (October): 7-9, 31-33.

Villarreal, José Antonio. [1959] 1970. *Pocho*. Reprint. New York: Anchor Books.

Walker, L. 1979. *Battered Women*. New York: Harper & Row.

_____. 1984. *The Battered Woman Syndrome*. New York: Springer Publishing.

_____. 1985. "Feminist Forensic Psychology." In *Handbook of Feminist Therapy: Women's Issues in Psychotherapy*, eds. L.B. Rosewater, and L.E. Walker, 274-283. New York: Springer Publishing.

Weber, Francis J. 1975. "People in God." In *California Catholicism*. Los Angeles: Chancery Archives.

Weeks, Jeffrey. 1981. *Sex, Politics and Society: The Regulation of Sexuality Since 1800*. London: Longman Group Ltd.

Wigel, Sigrid. 1986. "Double Focus: On the History of Women's Writing." In *Feminist Aesthetics*, ed. Gisela Ecker, trans. Harriet Anderson, 59-80. Boston: Beacon Press.

Wilcox, C., L. Sigelman, and E. Cook. 1989. "Some Like It Hot: Individual Differences in Responses to Group Feeling Thermometers." *Public Opinion Quarterly* 53: 246-57.

Wilson, Michael, and Deborah Silverton Rosenfelt. 1978. *Salt of the Earth*. Old Westbury, N.Y.: Feminist Press.

Ynstancia de Doña Eulalia Callis. 1785. Ynstancia de Doña Eulalia, Muger de Don Pedro Fages, governador de Californias, sobre que se le oyga en justica, y redima de la opresión que padece, 23 augosto 1785. Archivo General de la Nación, Provincias Internas. Microfilm. Bancroft Library, University of California, Berkeley.

Zavella, Patricia. 1984. "The Impact of 'Sun Belt Industrialization' on Chicanas." *Frontiers* 8 (Fall): 21-27.

_____. 1985. "'Abnormal Intimacy': The Varying Work Networks of Chicana Cannery Workers." *Feminist Studies* 11 (3): 541-558.

_____. 1987. *Women's Work and Chicano Families: Cannery Workers of the Santa Clara Valley*. Ithaca: Cornell University Press.

Contributors

Norma Alarcón is Associate Professor of Chicano/Ethnic and Women's Studies at the University of California, Berkeley. She is the author of a book on the feminist Mexican writer Rosario Castellanos, *Ninfomanía: The Feminist Poetics of Difference in the Work of Rosario Castellanos*, and numerous articles and essays on Chicana writers.

Judith Baca is a Professor of Art at the University of California, Irvine whose muralist activism in Los Angeles has redefined the concept. Her work has been exhibited all over the world.

Cordelia Chávez Candelaria is Professor of English and Chicano Studies at Arizona State University, Tempe. She is the author of a collection of poetry, *Ojo de la cueva/Cave Springs*, and a book of critical essays, *Chicano Poetry: An Introduction*.

Antonia I. Castañeda, Assistant Professor of Chicano and Women's Studies at the University of California, Santa Barbara, is the author of several essays on the colonial history of California.

Lillian Castillo-Speed, Head Librarian of Ethnic and Chicano Studies at the University of California, Berkeley, has published numerous books and articles indexing Chicano scholarship.

Adela de la Torre is a member of the faculty in the Department of Health Administration, California State University, Long Beach, and Chairperson of the Chicano Studies Department. She has conducted research on maternal health issues, the status of Chicano Studies programs, and Chicana policy concerns. Her work on reproductive technologies includes information on health care policy and health care delivery for Chicanas/Latinas.

Yvette Flores-Ortiz is assistant professor in Chicano Studies, at the University of California at Davis. She is a licensed clinical psychologist, specializing in the treatment of family violence, physical child abuse and incest recovery. Her current research focuses on Latina/Chicana health status, in particular high risk sexual and behavioral practices which increase the likelihood of HIV infection. She is an international consultant in the areas of alcoholism, drug abuse, HIV infection prevention and in the treatment of violence.

Erlinda Gonzáles-Berry is Professor of Chicano Culture and Literature in the Department of Spanish and Portuguese at the University of New Mexico. Her publications include numerous articles on Chicano literature, two edited books, *Pasó por aquí: Critical Essays on the New Mexican Literary Tradition, 1542-1988*, and *Las Mujeres Hablan* (with Diana Rebolledo and Teresa Márquez), and a novel, *Paletitas de guayaba*.

Juana Alicia is a Chicana artist living in San Francisco. She is a muralist, illustrator, painter, and lithographer. She states that her "work reflects her historical and cultural matrix and consciously addresses the inherent conflicts in being a minority woman within this society." Her work has appeared in the book *The Sexuality of Latinas* also published by Third Woman Press.

Emma Pérez is Assistant Professor of History at the University of Texas at El Paso, where she teaches Chicana/o history. Her publications include "A la Mujer: A Critique of the Partido Liberal Mexicano's Gender Ideology" in *Between Borders*, excerpts from her novel "Gulf Dreams" in *Chicana Lesbians: The Girls Our Mothers Warned Us About*. "She has served others in more intimate ways: The Domestic Service Reform in Yucatan," in *Aztlan*, forthcoming.

Beatriz M. Pesquera is Associate Professor and Chair of Chicano Studies at the University of California, Davis. She is the co-editor of *Building With Our Own Hands* and author of numerous essays on Chicanas.

Elba Sánchez is a Chicana who was born in México and grew up in San Francisco. She is a teacher and coordinator for the Spanish for Spanish Speakers Program at the University of California,

Santa Cruz. She is founding co-editor of *Revista Mujeres*, a biannual, bilingual journal for Chicanas and Latinas, published at the University of California, Santa Cruz.

Denise M. Segura is Assistant Professor of Sociology at the University of California, Santa Barbara. She has published numerous articles on Chicanas and Mexican immigrant women in the labor force, Chicana feminism, and Chicana political consciousness. Currently she is working on a book-length manuscript on Chicana feminism, co-authored with Beatriz M. Pesquera of the University of California, Davis.

Adaljiza Sosa Riddell has taught in the Chicano Studies Program at the University of California, Davis for the past twenty-one years, eleven of them as director of the Program. She describes herself as a Chicana feminist and contributed to the establishment of the Chicana/Latina academic support organization, Mujeres Activas en Letras y Cambio Social (MALCS). She is currently Coordinator for the Chicana/Latina Research Project, an organized research program focusing on Chicana/Latina scholars and issues.

Carla Trujillo received a Ph.D in educational psychology from the University of Wisconsin, Madison. Her dissertation concerned professor-student interaction in the classroom. Her current research concerns the psychology of Chicanas. She is an administrator at the University of California, Berkeley. In addition to her administrative responsibilities, she teaches a course on women of color through the Ethnic Studies department at UC Berkeley, and another through the Women's Studies department at San Francisco State University. She has co-authored a chapter in a book on adolescents and her articles have appeared in the *American Education Research Journal* and the *International Journal of Sports Psychology*. She edited *Chicana Lesbians: The Girls Our Mothers Warned Us About*, which won the 1992 Lambda Literary Award for Best Lesbian Anthology.

Patricia Zavella is Associate Professor in the Community Studies Board at the University of California, Santa Cruz. She is the author of *Women's Work and Chicano Families: Cannery Workers of the Santa*

Clara Valley, and *Everyday Contradictions of Working Mothers: Mexican Americans and Anglos in the Sunbelt* (forthcoming).

Books available from Third Woman Press

CHICANA LESBIANS: THE GIRLS OUR MOTHERS WARNED US ABOUT edited by Carla Trujillo. Winner of numerous awards, including the Lambda Literary Award for Best Lesbian Anthology. ISBN 0-943219-06-X, $10.95

THE SEXUALITY OF LATINAS edited by Norma Alarcón, Ana Castillo and Cherríe Moraga. An anthology of short stories, poetry, essays, art, drama and more by thirty-seven Latina contributors. ISBN 0-943219-00-0, $10.95

NEIGHBORS by Joan Woodruff. A magical and compelling novel set in New Mexico, by the author of *Traditional Stories and Foods: An American Indian Remembers*. ISBN 0-943219-08-6, $11.95

CHILIAGONY by Iris Zavala, translated by Susan Pensak. This Puertorriqueña's famous short novel is a work of "fabulous inventions and mental witchcraft." ISBN 0-943219-02-3, $5.95

MY WICKED WICKED WAYS by Sandra Cisneros. Now in its third printing, this book by the author of *The House on Mango Street* and *Women Hollering Creek* is the most famous, and infamous, collection of Chicana poetry. ISBN 0-943219-01-9, $8.95

VARIACIONES SOBRE UNA TEMPESTAD by Lucha Corpi, translated by Catherine Rodríguez-Nieto. Poetry from the acclaimed and prize-winning poet (*Palabras de mediodía*) and novelist (*Eulogy For a Brown Angel*). Bilingual, Spanish and English. ISBN 0-943219-05-1, $8.95

THE MARGARITA POEMS by Luz María Umpierre-Herrera. Intensely personal and moving poetry from the author of *Y Otras Desgracias/And Other Misfortunes*. Puerto Rico's most outstanding poet and essayist. ISBN 0-943219-02-7, $5.95

SPEAK TO ME FROM DREAMS by Barbara Brinson Curiel. Rich, evocative poetry from the author of *Nocturno* and *Vocabulary of the Dead* that captures the essence of growing up Chicana. ISBN 0-943219-03-5, $8.95

Back issues of THIRD WOMAN journal still available at $8.95 each: TW3 *Texas and More*; TW2:2 *International Perspectives*; TW2:1 *Southwest/Midwest*

Also available through Third Woman Press:
ESTA PUENTE, MI ESPALDA: VOCES DE MUJERES TERCERMUNDISTAS EN LOS ESTADOS UNIDOS edited by Cherríe Moraga and Ana Castillo, the Spanish adaptation and translation of the best-selling *This Bridge Called My Back: Writings by Radical Women of Color*. ISBN 0-910383-19-7. $10.00

Send for a free catalog. For all orders please add $1.50 for the first book and $.50 for each additional book. California residents add state and local sales tax. Make checks payable to Third Woman Press. Send to: Third Woman Press, Ethnic Studies, Dwinelle Hall 3412, University of California, Berkeley, CA 94720.